IN MEMORIAM
FOR
KATHY

THE TRIAL
OF
INEZ GARCIA

BY
KENNETH W. SALTER

A JUSTA PUBLICATIONS BOOK
1976

EDITORIAL JUSTA PUBLICATIONS, INC.
P.O. Box 9128
Berkeley, California 94709

First Printing: January 1976

Library of Congress Catalog Card Number: 75-42992
ISBN Paperback: 0-915808-02-1
ISBN Hardcover: 0-915808-03-X

About the Author

Kenneth W. Salter received his J.D. degree from Boalt Hall, the School of Law, University of California at Berkeley in 1967. From 1967–1971 he coordinated pre-law studies and directed the interdisciplinary freshman composition program in the Department of Speech, University of California, Berkeley. Since 1971 professor Salter has taught pre-law courses and directed field studies in the Department of Speech-Communication, San Jose State University, San Jose, California.

Professor Salter is an Associate Editor of the Barristers *Bailiwick,* a publication of the San Francisco Bar Association. He has written numerous articles on a wide range of subjects related to law and jurisprudence. He is the author of *The Pentagon Papers Trial,* a casebook on the trial of Daniel Ellsberg and Anthony Russo published by Justa Publications.

CONTENTS

INTRODUCTION

Background to the Trial

Inez Garcia, a 30 year old Latina woman who grew up in Spanish Harlem had moved to Soledad, California in 1971 with her eleven year old son in order to be near her husband, Juan Cardenas. He was in prison for participation in a political bombing while involved with Anti-Castro Cuban Nationalist organizations.

During Ms. Garcia's two years in Soledad she had worked as a farm laborer in the nearby lettuce fields, had drawn welfare, and had a reputation in the dusty, farm-labor town best known for its nearby prison as a chaste, devout Catholic wife. She proudly claimed that for the two years she had lived in Soledad, "no one got in my pants."

On the evening of March 19, 1974 she was visiting with some women friends at the apartment which she was in the process of moving into. Inez was sharing the apartment with Fred Medrano, who was planning to return to his native Texas within the month. At approximately 8:45 p.m. two friends of Medrano's arrived at the apartment while Medrano was smoking marijuana with an acquaintance, Cris Solis. Louie Castillo and Miguel Jimenez had been drinking heavily when they arrived. They continued drinking and started to get fresh and abusive with Inez Garcia and the other women present. The other women left at this point.

A fight erupted between Medrano and Castillo over whether Medrano and Inez Garcia were "hometown." Jimenez joined the fight and Medrano was beaten up. After the fight Jimenez threatened Medrano with a knife. According to Inez Garcia, Jimenez and Castillo forced her to go outside with them where the wiry, seventeen year old Castillo raped her in the alley behind the apartment building while the 300 pound Jimenez looked on. According to Inez Garcia's testimony in the trial, "(T)hey told me that I thought I was too good for the mens in Soledad and that they were going to show me what a hometown boy was." This happened between approximately 9:10 and 9:20 p.m. Jimenez and Castillo then left.

At approximately 9:30 p.m. Inez Garcia received a phone call allegedly from a friend of Jimenez and Castillo. The caller laughed at and taunted Inez Garcia and threatened to kill her if she didn't get out of town. Inez Garcia called her family in Florida; then loaded her son's .22 rifle and set out to look for the men who had phoned her. She encountered Castillo and Jimenez on the street six blocks from her apartment at approximately 9:37 p.m. Medrano was there with his car. Inez Garcia claimed that Jimenez had his knife out and she started shooting with the .22 rifle. Jimenez was killed by one of several bullets and Castillo ran into a nearby park and escaped injury when Inez Garcia's rifle jammed.

Inez Garcia and Medrano left the scene of the shooting in Medrano's car. They went to the house of the women who had been with Inez earlier in the evening. A short while later the police arrived and Inez Garcia surrendered to the police peacefully.

Inez Garcia told the arresting officers that Castillo and Jimenez had tried to rape her. After she was booked she was examined by a jail doctor for drugs and alcohol but not for rape. She was charged with first degree murder.

The case had all the markings of a routine murder case involving a group of hot blooded Latinos in this predominantly Chicano farm labor town of approximately 5,000 people. The case was routine enough to assign to a prosecutor who would be trying his first murder case in his third year out of law school. The prosecution would contend that the fight and shooting had been over drugs and not over rape.

Inez Garcia's husband upon learning of the incident suggested retaining the famous criminal lawyer, Charles Garry. Mr. Garry was well known and respected by the inmates at Soledad for his defense of Huey Newton, Bobby Seale and other members of the radical Black Panther Party. Mr. Garry agreed to defend Inez Garcia and at the same time the case was attracting the attention of feminists in the San Francisco Bay Area.

Inez Garcia was released on $5,000.00 bail in July, 1974 and began to speak to women's groups in the Bay Area. The Inez Garcia Defense Committee was launched to publicize the up-coming trial, raise money for the defense, and encourage large numbers of women to attend the trial in Monterey, California. A house was rented by members of the Defense Committee in Monterey and Inez Garcia lived there with several women members while awaiting trial. It was here that Inez Garcia started to change and to become politicized.

The devout Catholic woman had been unable to fully state to the police that she had actually been raped because of the shame and humiliation which she felt. In the months that followed, however, she was to learn to talk of the rape though her shame, humiliation and anger did not subside. By the time of the trial in September, 1974, Inez had found a new voice. She was no longer able to present herself to the jury as she had been—the passive and submissive woman who was too shy to discuss the rape with anyone except her priest in the privacy of the confessional. In the presence of the jury that new voice of Inez Garcia was openly to accuse the trial judge of being prejudiced against her and being a sexist. Her outburst was met with the active support of many militant feminists and critics in the gallery who hissed and shouted their support for her. The judge, a 68 year old Republican, was in his last year on the bench and was known to pack a pistol underneath his judicial robes.

THE ISSUES

Shortly after the formation of the Inez Garcia Defense Committee, the *New York Times,* the television news, and the wire services picked up the story of Inez Garcia. With the national news coverage, the issues posed by the case were catapulted into the national limelight. Inez became a symbol of the rape victim who fought back. The trial became a focal point for raising fundamental emotional and legal issues about rape. Is rape such a violent act against a woman that it gives the woman victim the right to return the violence—even to the point of homicide?

The case squarely forces us to re-examine many of the prevalent, stereotypical attitudes and assumptions held by various sectors of society about rape. The case puts in issue the *macho* myth that rape victims "were asking for it" or that they "should relax and enjoy it."

All across the country, men and women alike have responded to Inez Garcia's act of retaliation just as they did on August 27, 1974 when Clarence Alligood, the 62-year-old night jailer at the Beauford, North Carolina Jail was foundslain with an icepick. Joan Little said she had stabbed the white jailer as he was trying to rape her in her cell. She was acquitted.

Inez Garcia's case was not as clear cut as that of Joan Little on many points. Whereas Joan Little testified she killed her attacker during the attempted rape, there was a twenty minute interval between the alleged rape and the shooting by Inez Garcia of one of her two attackers. The alleged rapist, Louie Castillo, a self-confessed heroin addict and junkie, was to live to face Inez Garcia in court and deny the rape. Did Inez Garcia kill more in vengeance than self-defense? Did she have time to cool off and premeditate a killing? Much of the testimony on the crucial questions of fact is disputed and contradictory as to what happened in the interval between the alleged rape and the shooting. There are no clear cut and easy answers to the tough questions posed by the trial. For that reason alone the record of the trial provides a fascinating and controversial vehicle for exploring these issues in the classroom.

THE DEFENSE

Defense Attorney Charles Garry stated after the trial that "(m)y aim in the trial was to establish for the court the effect of rape upon a woman—not the right of vigilantism."

The strategy of the defense was to premise Inez Garcia's actions on a defense of diminished capacity; to argue to the jury through the use of expert psychiatric testimony that after the rape, Inez was hysterical and didn't know what she was doing. She was so emotionally upset, that this woman with a prior history of mental instability, was so affected by the rape that it thrust her into such a state of mental impairment that her hysteria and terror made her seek to kill in self-defense.

Such a legalistic defense was bound to create differences of opinion among those who championed Inez Garcia's cause. To some, the act of Inez Garcia in killing her attacker was perceived as a sign of strength, while the defense of impaired capacity was seen as a sign of weakness that was calculated to evoke sympathy for the defendant and excuse her actions. Instead, many women are interested in attacking the double standard of justice which they associate with the male dominated police and courts in which the acts of a man who killed after seeing his wife raped or upon finding her in the arms of another man would not have to argue "diminished capacity" but would be accorded leniency.

To others, Inez was an illiterate and highly impressionable Latina woman who, with no previous political involvement was set-up by radical feminists. They had hoped to promote their cause through the medium of the trial forum to prove that rape is the ultimate act of political oppression against women.

The controversy still rages.

THE TEXT

While the book was designed primarily as a textbook to facilitate the study of a complex murder-rape trial in college classrooms, it was also intended to be a book that would be of interest to the general reader concerned with the resolution of the controversial issues posed by the trial. The text includes the indictment, the prosecution and defense opening statements, the closing statements, the Judge's jury instructions, and the testimony presented by both sides including the dramatic testimony of Inez Garcia. At the end of each section there are a series of questions for classroom discussion or independent study that relate to the issues and strategies of the trial. The questions are also designed for use as guides for jury simulation.

Due to space limitations, the testimony and evidence presented in the trial related to the charges against Inez Garcia's co-defendant, Fred Medrano, has been omitted except where it bears on the charge of murder against Inez Garcia.

The author has attempted to present in this volume the issues of alleged murder and rape in the actual context of the trial process itself. The student and general reader is given the requisite framework and evidence from which to make his or her own judgment on the guilt or innocence of Inez Garcia on the charge of murder, and to assess the complex underlying issues and attitudes about rape and aggression that are raised by the trial, the trial process and the law itself.

The portions of the transcript used in the test are selected and edited from the 14 volumes of actual trial transcript and the many additional volumes of supporting briefs, documents and other trial related materials. The author wishes to express his appreciation to the law firm of Garry, Dreyfus, McTernan, Brotsky, Herndon & Pesonen, Inc., for making available to him its copy of the trial transcript and supporting materials and especially to attorney Charles Garry for his kind assistance without which this writing project would not have been possible. The author wishes as well to thank his research assistant, Marty Toole, for her many devoted hours of toil that made this text possible.

JURY DELIBERATION

The questions for discussion and analysis throughout the text are designed to provide a framework for class discussion of the case as well as the framework for mock jury deliberations. The format for mock jury deliberations is to discuss the text for the initial class meetings to identify the issues and familiarize the class with the charges in the indictment and testimony by witnesses for the opposing sides.

Upon the completion of class discussion, the class is randomly divided into two groups of six, eight, or twelve jurors. Each student jury is instructed to elect a foreperson to review the charges in the indictment and the judge's jury instructions. The juries then deliberate their verdict using the questions for discussion and analysis and jury instructions as their guidelines. Each jury is instructed to apply the definitions of homicide, diminished capacity, self-defense, and justifiable homicide to the charge in the indictment and to assess the evidence pro and con. The foreperson should attempt to identify the issues of fact that the jury must decide in order to arrive at a verdict.

When each jury has arrived at a unanimous verdict of guilty or not guilty, the written note is delivered to the instructor who serves as the judge. If the jury cannot agree on a verdict at the end of the period assigned for jury deliberations, a mistrial is declared by the instructor.

After all juries have reported their verdicts, the results are posted on the blackboard and the class is invited to assess its jury deliberation experience.

THE INDICTMENT

September 4, 1974

1:30 o'clock P.M.

THE COURT: Let the record show the defendants are in court with their counsel and twelve potential jurors and two alternates also in their proper places.

Now, the first thing we will do in the case of People vs. Alfred Medrano and Inez Garcia is swear in the jury and the alternates will stand and be sworn as part of the jury.

(Jury sworn.)

THE COURT: Be seated, please. Now, we will have the Clerk read the information and state the pleas—let's see, an information on indictment.

THE CLERK: An indictment, Your Honor.

THE COURT: Read the indictment and state the pleas.

THE CLERK: Superior Court of the State of California for the County of Monterey.

The People of the State of California, plaintiff, versus Alfred Medrano and Inez Garcia, defendants.

Number CR 4259.

Indictment:

The Grand Jury of the County of Monterey hereby accuses Alfred Medrano and Inez Garcia, of a felony, to wit: murder in violation of Section 187 of the Penal Code of the State of California, committed as follows:

That on or about the 19th day of March, 1974, in the County of Monterey, State of California, said Alfred Medrano and Inez Garcia, did then and there murder Miguel Jimenez, a human being.*

The names of the witnesses are listed on there and it is endorsed by the foreman of the Grand Jury, Mr. Howard Allen, dated the 8th day of

* Freddie Medrano was additionally charged with aiding and abetting the commission of a felony.

April, 1974, signed by the Clerk of the Court, Ernest A. Maggini, by Deputy Clerk Harriet Tavernetti.

I will further state to you, ladies and gentlemen, at the time the defendants were arraigned, Mr. Medrano stated his true name as Alfred Medrano, and Mrs. Garcia stated her true name as Inez Garcia, and each entered a plea of not guilty.

(RTA 1-2)

THE PEOPLE'S OPENING STATEMENT
THE CHARGE OF MURDER
THE DISTRICT ATTORNEY'S VIEW

MR. BRAUDRICK: Ladies and gentlemen: It is my opportunity to give you what is called an opening statement. An opening statement is not argument, it is merely a statement of the facts which we will be presenting from the witness stand in order to—we give you an opening statement so you will have some acquaintance with those facts before you here and the witnesses. Now, we will have quite a few witnesses in this case. First of all, I would like to introduce Sergeant Perez from the Soledad Police Department. He is the investigating officer from the Soledad Police Department that is aiding me in the prosecution of this case. Our first witness will be Officer Armstrong who was on March 19 a policeman with the City of Soledad, and he will testify that he received a call shortly before ten o'clock in the evening and that call was referring to a shooting. He responded to Monterey Street in the City of Soledad across the street from the park and found a man lying sort of in an alley on a sidewalk area and he was bleeding. He immediately summoned an ambulance. He will testify that when he got there, there were a few other people there. He secured the scene. There was a knife laying next to the body of Miguel Jimenez, the man he knew as Miguel Jimenez. He will also identify some diagrams and photographs of the area.

Our next witness will be a man by the name of Lipsky and he will testify that he worked in a pharmacy in the City of Soledad and also is a volunteer ambulance driver and that he responded to a shooting and picked up Miguel Jimenez and gave him first aid and took him to the hospital. He will tell you what sort of wounds Mr. Jimenez had at the time he picked him up and he will also tell you about a slug that fell out of the clothing of Mr. Jimenez.

Our next witness is going to be Louie Castillo. Louie Castillo will testify he is seventeen years old and has lived in the City of Soledad most of his life. He dropped out of high school and that he presently lives with his aunt. He did live with his aunt at that time back in March.

He will testify that he knew the defendants, Mr. Medrano and Inez Garcia, and that he had known them for some time and that he had lived next door to them for about a month, during the month that they had lived in this duplex. He will testify that he went to their house frequently and that on occasion he bought heroin from Freddie Medrano. He will also testify that he purchased heroin from another friend of his by the name of Joe Mendoza. He went on the evening of the 19th to the residence of Inez Garcia and Freddie Medrano and they were drinking, and Louie went there with his friend, Miguel Jimenez, who is sort of a Mutt-and-Jeff combination. Louie Castillo weighs about a hundred and thirty-five or a hundred and forty pounds, quite thin, and Miguel Jimenez, the man who was later that evening killed, weighed in excess of three hundred pounds, a huge man. They went to their house and were just engaging in conversation and Louie and Freddie started to get into an argument. Louie was saying to Freddie that Freddie thought he was such a big man because now he was a big guy selling all the heroin in the City of Soledad and that he was an outsider and he, Louie, was a hometown boy who lived and was raised in Soledad and he was telling Freddie that he was getting—basically he was getting too big for his pants, and this led, this conversation or this argument led into a—to Freddie calling Louie outside and Louie going outside and there is a fight outside. Louie comes back in the house and at that point, a few minutes later, Freddie comes into the house and another fight starts and this time, Freddie and Louie are scruffling and they fall down to the ground and it would appear as though Louie was getting beaten up by Freddie, and at that point, Miguel Jimenez picked up Freddie off of Louie and beat up Freddie and hit him numerous times in the face and caused him to bleed, leaving blood drops which we will show you photographs of on the floor. There was some further conversation. Louie will testify that Inez Garcia, who was present got involved in the fight, not in the fight but she was yelling as Miguel Jimenez was beating up Freddie. There was another party there present, a man by the name of Chofero Solis.

Now, Louie will testify that they stayed at the house for a little longer and Freddie went into the bedroom or the bathroom or into another room anyway and they went outside with Inez Garcia and that Miguel was talking to Inez, and they went back—Louie will be able to testify that he doesn't know what they were talking about because he wasn't close enough to hear them but they went back into the house and later they left. They walked a couple of blocks down Monterey Street toward what would be the downtown area of Soledad and at that point, they went a couple of blocks and they stopped by Joe Mendoza's house, and Joe Mendoza was home and they went into the house. Louie will testify that they stayed there for about forty minutes. He will testify that Louie, or rather that Joe Mendoza phoned up Freddie and

Inez' house and talked to them on the phone and that Miguel Jimenez also talked to them on the phone, but he did not talk to them on the telephone. They were there for about forty minutes and they started then to walk down Monterey Street and had gone about a half a block when Louie looked around and saw Freddie's car pull right behind him. He will testify that Miguel was standing on the street side as they are walking down side by side and the car pulled up, and that he saw Freddie driving the car, that he saw Inez Garcia get out of the car with the rifle and start shooting, and at that point, he ran across the street into the park and kept going. He will testify Freddie was driving the car and that Inez used the rifle and shot Miguel Jimenez.

Our next witness will be Crisofono Solis and he will testify that he was at—he went to Freddie's, Freddie Medrano's house and that he wanted to get some marijuana so he and Freddie got into a car and went to Gonzales to try to buy some marijuana. He will testify that actually before they left that they smoked one or two marijuana cigarettes, sharing the cigarettes, in other words, two in total and went to Gonzales to find some marijuana and they were unable to find any and they went back to his house. They had another marijuana cigarette and Solis was basically sitting there as a passive observer as Freddie and Louie Castillo got involved in the fight. Mr. Solis will testify that the argument was over the fact that the defendant Freddie Medrano was an outsider who was selling heroin and that Louie Castillo and he were fighting over this, and this is what the verbal argument was which later erupted into a fist fight, a wrestling match, and then with Miguel Jimenez beating up Freddie. Mr. Solis will further testify that after Louie Castillo and Miguel Jimenez left the house that Freddie and Inez talked about killing Miguel Jimenez. They first—he will testify that Freddie stated he wanted to go get them with a gun and that Inez said, no, let me do it because my family has got money and they can get me out of jail. They then started to clean up the house and they talked on the telephone to Joe Mendoza and they then—then Freddie went into the bedroom, his bedroom and got a shotgun and got a .22 rifle and that Freddie asked Inez if she had any shotgun shells and she said yes, and she went and got some shotgun shells. Inez loaded the .22 rifle and Freddie loaded the shotgun. He said they then left the apartment or the duplex and Solis stayed in the house. He said he heard the door slam and they drove away. At that point, he got into his car and as he drove down Monterey Street, he saw Freddie's car heading back toward Freddie's house with the lights off and then make a left turn.

The next witness will be David Ferrel and Dima Gallardo and they will testify that they are both around fifteen or sixteen; that they were standing on the porch just one house down, one house up from where the shooting took place and that they saw Louie Castillo and Miguel

Jimenez walking down the street and said hello to them and they walked past them and they saw Freddie's car drive up and park and they saw Inez Garcia shooting. At that point, they told people to call an ambulance and they said or they will testify that the car left.

Elmer Moran will testify that he lives one house—well, actually the shooting took place almost in his front yard; that he heard the shots, saw the car drive away with its lights turned off and before the car drove away, he heard a woman's laughter.

Our next witness will be Rosa Bracamonte and possibly William Bracamonte, I don't know if he will testify yet or not, and Alicia Alcaraz. Alicia will testify that she is Rosa's sister and that she lives on the other side of town and that that night she went down to her sister's house because they were having a domestic quarrel and she went down there to try to make peace. She got down there and one thing led to another and the police were called. The police came and were trying to settle the disturbance and then all of a sudden the police left and the officer including Sergeant Perez will testify that they left that house to go to the killing of Mr. Jimenez. They were there for a few minutes afterwards and Freddie Medrano and Inez Garcia came into the house, and Inez said that she had killed Miguel or that she had shot Miguel. There was a conversation between Inez and a young man by the name of Juan Carbajal. Inez asked Juan to hit her in the side of the head with his fist to give her some bruises. She also asked him to rip her blouse. Alicia then engaged in conversation with Inez and Freddie Medrano and they decided that they would go to Alicia's house. Alicia lives on the other end of town across from the school, but it is on the outskirts of the city. They went there because they could park the car behind the house and it couldn't be seen. They went there and they were there for a little while and the police came and arrested Inez.

There will be further testimony by Alicia that when she first gave her statement, she didn't mention anything about the fact that she had seen Inez Garcia before she came to her house. There will also be testimony by both Mr. Solis and Louie Castillo that when they gave the statements to the police, they did not mention anything about their involvement in heroin traffic because they were afraid to talk about heroin to the police.

There will be a couple of other witnesses, there will be a man from the Department of Justice who tested some shells that were found at the scene of the shooting and looked at some slugs that were recovered from the body and clothing of Miguel Jimenez. He will testify that as far as the slugs are concerned, he can't tell what gun they came from because of their condition but that the shells found in the street near where the shooting occurred were fired from this rifle.

Our last witness will be Dr. Titus. Dr. Titus will testify he performed the autopsy on Miguel Jimenez and that the cause of death was death by a gunshot wound.

Now, this opening statement is just an outline of the evidence. There may be additional witnesses. There may be some witnesses that won't be called. I tell you now that Joe Mendoza will not be called as a witness. There will be testimony during the trial that Joe Mendoza is–I believe–well, he is in the hospital and possibly now he is at Stanford Hospital with a brain tumor. Thank you.

(RTA 3-10)

QUESTIONS FOR DISCUSSION AND ANALYSIS

The Indictment (pgs. 1-2)

Note that Section 187 of the California Penal Code makes reference only to the crime of murder and doesn't distinguish between murder in the first or second degree or manslaughter. What advantage, if any, does this give the prosecution in the presentation and proof of their case? See the Judge's instructions to the jury for the definitions of homicide and manslaughter.

1. Why does the indictment charge both Inez Garcia and Freddie Medrano with murder when Inez admits she shot Miguel Jimenez?

DEFENDANT INEZ GARCIA'S OPENING STATEMENT

THE DEFENSE'S VIEW OF THE MURDER CHARGE FROM DEFENDANT GARCIA'S OPENING STATEMENT

THE COURT: Mr. Garry, do you have an opening statement?

MR. GARRY: I sure do, thank you, Your Honor.

If the Court please, counsel, ladies and gentlemen of the jury: It is my responsibility to tell you what we expect the evidence to show. I am not going into detail of what all the evidence is to be because I prefer to have you hear the evidence from the mouths of the witnesses who are under oath. I want to say at the outset that the only thing that is important in this trial and in any other trial is the ascertainment of the truth. Whatever I say to you here in my opening statement, I want you to hold me responsible for the things I say to you as the truth. I don't intend to deviate and I will not permit any of our witnesses to deviate from the truth because the ascertainment of the truth is the only important thing and it is the only victorious thing you can ever have in a court of law.

I want to say at the outset that you have already been apprised of the presumption of innocence and you also know that statements of counsel, neither Mr. Braudrick nor myself nor Mr. Worthington are evidence. The evidence comes from the mouths of these witnesses.

I represent Inez Garcia. Inez Garcia is aged thirty. You have already been told on voir dire* that she does not read or write in any language. You have already been told that she cannot tell time. She can't look at a clock or a watch and be able to tell what time it is. You have been told that in the last years, she has had mental breakdowns and emotional breakdowns where she has been confined in hospitals in New York City and in Miami, Florida. You have been told that in voir dire, so I asked you these questions to see if it would make any difference in your attitude toward her.

You have been told that she was in Soledad for the sole and express

---

* Preliminary examination of witnesses or jurors.

purpose of or for the purposes of visiting her husband whose name is Juan Cardenas. He has been confined under the name of Juan Cardenas. He has not been confined under the name of Garcia and the evidence will show that when he was arrested, he said his name was Juan Cardenas and by the time he got to Garcia, all they got was Cardenas. So this is his mother's family name.

Juan Cardenas as the evidence will show is a refugee from Cuba. He is what they call an anti-Castro Freedom Fighter and he has been in prison involving some of his activities in that area. I hope that Juan Cardenas' political views one way or the other will not make any difference. It has not made any in my taking this case and when I say his case, his wife's case.

I want to say briefly to you that Inez Garcia, aged thirty, will present herself to you as a very genuine human being. You will be able to see her and hear her state what happened on that evening that you did not hear from the opening statement of the prosecution that the first thing that Inez Garcia said was that she was raped and attempted to be raped and none of that was presented to you. One of the things that you are going to be able to see and we intend to bring forward in this trial is the fact that the person who actually did the raping and the attempted raping has never been charged. The police chief of Soledad Prison—or Soledad township—knew as late as 11:30 on the 19th of March that this lady in her emotional state, a very emotional state, the evidence will show, said that she had been raped or attempted raped.

You will be able to hear this tape, if it is available. I have not heard the tape but I have seen the transcription of that tape and hopefully you will be able to hear from her own language in her own emotional broken down English and what she said at the time, and yet not one thing has been done. The evidence will show to see——

MR. BRAUDRICK: Your Honor, I believe that he is now engaging in argument.

MR. GARRY: I am talking about what the evidence will show.

THE COURT: There is no materiality shown at this point. The police do not have to charge everybody as you know, and that is immaterial as far as the guilt or innocence of these defendants are concerned.

MR. GARRY: The evidence will show that she was raped. The evidence will show that she was threatened. The evidence will show that after she was raped, this man Mendoza—Miguel Jimenez and Louie Castillo came over or went there and threatened Mrs. Garcia to leave Soledad and leave the country; that she was not to be around there and that they were going to see that she was exterminated. It was in this state of hysteria and state of animation that the evidence will show that this rifle was picked up by Mrs. Garcia and she walked about five blocks and she killed Miguel Jimenez and she tried to kill Louie Castillo who got away.

The evidence will show that Miguel held her while Louie Castillo raped her behind the house. The evidence will clearly show that.

The evidence will clearly show that Mrs. Garcia in a state of frantic fear and humiliation and disgust and anger killed this man within fifteen or twenty minutes after the event took place.

The evidence will show that the police never bothered checking her inner garments or panties to see whether in fact there had been semen.

The evidence will show that nothing was donc to pay any attention to the fact that this lady was raped.

The evidence will further show and we will put on evidence that the attitude of the police and the law enforcement agencies toward women who get raped is such as ignoring it.

The evidence will further show and we will present evidence that it became so alarming over women who get raped——

THE COURT: Counsel, I cannot permit this. We are trying a woman for murder. There is no man on trial for rape and the attitude of the police for rape or murder as far as I am concerned has nothing to do with the guilt or innocence of this woman.

THE DEFENDANT GARCIA: But, Your Honor, that is the reason I killed the man.

THE COURT: We are not trying a cause, we are trying a woman, Mrs. Garcia, and a man, Mr. Medrano, and I am not going to make this courtroom a forum for a cause. We are trying simply a criminal case and nothing else, and please be guided thereby.

MR. GARRY: The evidence will show, ladies and gentlemen of the jury, that Mrs. Garcia did the only thing that was humanly possible in order to be able to safeguard her dignity, her mentality, and her own loss, and the evidence will abundantly show that.

The evidence will show that Miguel Jimenez was drunk, and his autopsy and medical exmaination will show that he had .16 blood alcohol.

The evidence will show that Miguel Jimenez and Louie Castillo, the men who raped Inez Garcia, from four o'clock in the afternoon on had been drinking and using pot or dope or whatever else they were using throughout that entire afternoon up until the time of the incident that took place.

The evidence will show that there is not one scintilla of evidence connecting Mr. Medrano, Freddie Medrano, with this charge of murder. The entire activities that was done by Mrs. Garcia herself and Mr. Medrano had nothing whatever to do with the killing of Miguel Jimenez.

Did Your Honor say something?

THE COURT: Was that intended to be funny?

MR. GARRY: No.

THE COURT: There was a noise in the back of the room.

MR. GARRY: I heard something.

THE COURT: It was one of those young people back there.

MR. GARRY: I'm sorry, I thought––

THE COURT: Certainly I said nothing. I wouldn't say it in that tone of voice.

MR. GARRY: The evidence will show as I have outlined it and you can hold me responsible for whatever the evidence is.

Thank you very much.

THE COURT: Mr. Worthington:

MR. WORTHINGTON: Your Honor, on behalf of defendant Medrano, we will reserve our opening statement.*

(RTA 11-16)

* Upon the conclusion of District Attorney Braudrick's opening statement, each defense attorney has the opportunity to present his opening statement to the jury with his overview of the case. Mr. Worthington, Mr. Medrano's attorney, chose to reserve his opening statement until presentation of witnesses for the defense. This allows the defense an opportunity to reassert its view of the case upon the conclusion of the prosecution's case.

OPENING STATEMENTS

The function of the opening statement in criminal cases is to give the prosecution and defense lawyers an opportunity to present their overview of the case to the jury so that the jury understands how the testimony of each witness relates to the charges in the indictment and what each side must prove as a part of their case. The opening statement is also used to familiarize the jury with the evidence and testimony it will see and hear. The burden of proof is on the prosecution to prove beyond a reasonable doubt that the defendants committed the crime as charged in the indictment.

QUESTIONS FOR STUDY AND ANALYSIS

1. What are the differences in theory about the charge of murder to be found in each side's opening statement on the following points:
   (a) the motive for the shooting of Miguel Jimenez.
   (b) Freddie Medrano's involvement in the shooting incident.
   (c) the issue of rape and Inez Garcia's state of mind.
   (d) the truthfulness of witnesses.
2. Why does Mr. Braudrick characterize Louie Castillo and Miguel Jimenez as a "Mutt and Jeff" combination?
3. What is the significance of Mr. Garry's explanation that Inez Garcia's husband is known by his mother's family name—Cardenas—and not Garcia to the jury? Why does Garry mention the reason for Juan Cardena's incarceration?
4. Are Mr. Garry's statements "argumentative" as Mr. Braudrick claims? Attorneys are not allowed to engage in argument in their opening statements.
5. What is the significance of the Judge's interruption of Mr. Garry's statement about the attitude of police toward women that get raped?
6. Has Mr. Garry hinted that he is going to use the courtroom as a forum for a cause as claimed by the Judge?
7. Are the Judge's comments fair or prejudicial to the defense in the light of the disruption by a spectator?
8. Does Inez Garcia's statement to Judge Lawson help or hurt her case?

THE CASE FOR THE PEOPLE

The People's first witness was Robert L. Armstrong. The prosecution sought through his testimony to establish that a homicide occurred and to describe the scene of the crime as he found it.

ROBERT LANE ARMSTRONG, SWORN

DIRECT EXAMINATION

BY MR. BRAUDRICK:

Q Mr. Armstrong, on March 19, 1974, what was your occupation?
A Police Officer for the City of Soledad.
Q And how long had you been a police officer?
A Approximately two and a half years.
Q Now, bringing your attention shortly before ten o'clock on the evening of March 19, did you have occasion to respond to a call on Monterey Street?
A Yes, sir.
Q Whereabouts did you go?
A It was on Monterey Street between First Street and Pine Street.
Q What did you find when you got there?
A I observed five to six individuals standing on the east side of Monterey Street adjacent to an alley entrance around what appeared to be an individual lying in a prone position.

(RT 1)

The remainder of Armstrong's direct testimony involved identifying various photographs taken of the scene of the crime and to identify a photo of Miguel Jimenez lying at the scene of the crime with a black and silver hunting knife by his left leg.

CROSS-EXAMINATION

BY MR. GARRY:

Q. Mr. Armstrong, are you a police officer at Soledad at the present time?

A No, sir.

Q And were you discharged or did you resign?

A I resigned, sir.

Q Was that over——

MR. BRAUDRICK: Your Honor, I object going into anything like this. . . .

(RT 7)

The defense sought to relate Mr. Armstrong's resignation to the failure of the Soledad Police Department to enforce narcotics laws. The court sustained the prosecution's objections to this line of inquiry.

BY MR. GARRY:

Q Mr. Armstrong, do you know the defendant Inez Garcia?

A Yes, sir.

Q And over what period of time have you known her?

A One and a half years.

Q And did you purchase a shotgun from her at one time?

A Yes, sir.

MR. BRAUDRICK: Objection, Your Honor, that is beyond the scope of direct.

(RT 8)

The Court sustained the prosecution's objection but ruled that Mr. Armstrong could be called as a defense witness if the defense wanted to pursue this line of questioning.

The prosecution's second witness was Fred Lipsky.

FRED LIPSKY, SWORN
DIRECT EXAMINATION

BY MR. BRAUDRICK:

Q Mr. Lipsky, what is your occupation?

A I am a stock control at the Soledad Pharmacy and also volunteer with the City of Soledad Ambulance Service.

Q Now, bringing your attention to March 19, at about 10:00 o'clock in the evening, did you have occasion to go in the ambulance to a reported shooting on Monterey Street in the City of Soledad?

A Yes, I did.
Q What did you do when you got there?
A We brought out the gurney and we went over to where the subject was lying. We did notice that he was alive and we picked him up immediately and put him in the ambulance and started off for the hospital.
Q I show you People's Number Two, this photograph of a man with quite a large amount of blood. Can you recognize—
MR. WORTHINGTON: I object to counsel characterizing photographs, Your Honor, that the jury hasn't even seen.

(RT 11)

The remainder of Lipsky's direct testimony involved his identification of a bullet that fell out of Miguel Jimenez' T-shirt and rolled on the ambulance floor. Lipsky testified that he gave the spent slug to the Soledad Police Department.

The prosecution's next witness is Louie Castillo who testifies concerning his activities involving Miguel Jimenez and the two defendants on March 19, 1974. Castillo denies raping Inez Garcia and identifies Ms. Garcia as the person who shot Jimenez and attempted to shoot him.

LOUIE CASTILLO, SWORN
DIRECT EXAMINATION

BY MR. BRAUDRICK:
Q Mr. Castillo, how old are you?
A Seventeen.
Q Where do you live?
A Soledad
Q How long have you lived there?
A All my life.
Q Do you know Freddie Medrano?
A Yeah.
Q Do you know Inez Garcia?
A Yeah.
Q How long have yow known Freddie Medrano?
A About a year or two.
Q Do you see him very often?
A Yeah, I used to live next door to him.
Q Did you see him very often before March 19, 1974?
A Yes.
Q Why did you see him?
MR. WORTHINGTON: Objection, this is irrelevant.

MR. BRAUDRICK: Your Honor, it goes to the motive, I think we can go into the heroin traffic——

MR. WORTHINGTON: I object to that. Now, I object to that, Your Honor, and I move that it be stricken. We are getting in evidence that should be on an offer of proof and I will have to move for a mistrial on that ground.*

THE COURT: Denied. It is for motive. . . .

BY MR. BRAUDRICK:

Q Could you read back the last question?

(Reporter reading question.)

THE WITNESS: You mean Fred?

BY MR. BRAUDRICK:

Q Yes.

A I used to go see him a lot because I used to get dope from him.

Q Okay. What kind of dope did you get from him?

MR. WORTHINGTON: I object, that is irrelevant. . . .

(RT 16-17)
[September 5, 1974]

THE COURT: Mr. Castillo, you are under oath. Proceed.

BY MR. BRAUDRICK:

Q Mr. Castillo, what kind of dope did you get from or purchase from the defendant Freddie Medrano?

MR. WORTHINGTON: Objection, irrelevant.

THE COURT: I understand it is for motive.

MR. BRAUDRICK: Yes, Your Honor.

THE COURT: Limited to that purpose.

MR. WORTHINGTON: What difference does it make what kind, Your Honor?

THE COURT: It is limited to that purpose. You may proceed.

THE WITNESS: Heroin. . . .

BY MR. BRAUDRICK:

Q Now, how often did you go over to his house or see him before March 19, 1974?

A About every day. I use to live next door to him.

Q How long did you live next door to him?

A How long ago?

Q How long did you live next door to him?

A About three months, around there. . . .

BY MR. BRAUDRICK:

Q Okay. Now, bringing your attention to March 19, 1974, did you have occasion to see the defendant, Freddie Medrano?

---

* An offer of proof is made before the judge without the jury present. The judge determines whether the proof may be submitted to the jury.

A That day?
Q Yes.
A Yes.
Q About what time was it when you first saw him?
A About when I went to his house or what–about 8:30.
Q In the evening?
A Yes. . . .
Q Who went with you?
A Mike* and some friend of mine, Manuel Olivas.
Q Why did you go to the house?
THE WITNESS: To visit. . . .
MR. BRAUDRICK: Who was at the house when you got there?
A Freddie and Inez and some guy named Crisofono Solis.
THE COURT: Now, by Freddie, whom do you mean?
THE WITNESS: Freddie Medrano. . . .
Q How many apartments are there in the building? †
A. Two.
Q What did you do when you got in the house?
A Started drinking and started talking.
Q Had you been drinking before?
A Yes.
Q What had you been drinking before?
A Beer.
Q Had you used any narcotics of any kind that day?
A No.
Q That includes heroin and marijuana. You used none of that?
Q Yes, was just drinking.
Q Who were you drinking with at Medrano's house?
A At whose house?
Q Medrano's house.
A With Mike and Manuel, that's Chofero and Cris. We are all drinking in there and Inez. We're drinking Apricot Brandy.
Q Did you have any conversations while you were in the house?
A Yes.
Q Who did you talk to?
A I talked to both Freddie and Inez. We just talking. . . .

BY MR. BRAUDRICK:

Q Now, did you have an argument with anybody?
A Yes, it was Freddie.
Q Okay, what started the argument?
A Well, he started bragging about himself. He's the type of guy that always brags on what he has and what he does, and he started, you

---

* Miguel Jimenez.

† Castillo is referring to the duplex in which Freddie Medrano and Inez Garcia live in one unit and the witness lives in the other.

know, he was dealing dope and he was——

MR. WORTHINGTON: Objection. That's nonresponsive. I move the part about dealing dope be stricken. He answered the question when he said the argument started when Freddie was bragging.

THE COURT: After the word brag, the rest is stricken as nonresponsive. . . .

MR. WORTHINGTON: I think at this time the jury ought to be admonished.

THE COURT: Disregard everything after the word bragging. . . .

BY MR. BRAUDRICK:

Q What did Freddie say as he was bragging?

A Well, he said that—that, you know, he was bragging, you know, he was saying to us that, you know, he was—he wanted to be top man, you know, of, you know, of the town, I guess—you know, of the town.

THE COURT: All right.

BY MR. BRAUDRICK:

Q Okay what did you say to that?

A That's what the argument started. He told me he was never going to make it because he wasn't a home town guy. . . .

BY MR. BRAUDRICK:

Q Okay. What happened during the argument?

A Well, when the argument was going on, Freddie Medrano, he called me on the outside, you know, and we went outside to the front outside his house, and we went outside, you know, and he started telling me, he said I was a punk, you know. He is older than I am, you know.

Q What did you say to him?

A I didn't say nothing, just kind of—he just kind of grabbed me and I hit him in the face.

Q Okay. Then what happened after you hit him in the face?

A He just took off walking toward town, you know, and I went back inside the house.

Q What did you do when you got back inside the house?

A I went inside the house and I told Mike what had happened, you know. Mike thought it was funny, and then about four minutes later, Freddie comes in charging at me again.

Q Okay. What happened when he charged at you?

A We started fighting and wrestling and we were wrestling on the ground, and Mike, you know, picked him up and started hitting him.

Q Okay. Where was Inez Garcia during the fight that took place inside the house?

A She was in the kitchen when the fight was going on, you know, they were trying to stop it, her and Cris Solis.

Q Did you—when you were fighting inside the house, did you punch him at all?

A Who?

Q Freddie Medrano.

A Yes, when we were on the ground.

Q What exactly did Miguel Jimenez do, or Mike?

A He picked him up and he threw him against the couch and started hitting him, you know.

Q Okay. What did you do after that?

A Well, I went out toward Mike. I told him, "All right, let's go and forget it," you know, "and stop the fight."

Q What did Freddie do?

A Well, after that, Mike had told Freddie he better stop his dealing or else get out of town, and Freddie answered, "Yeah, un-huh, I will."

MR. WORTHINGTON: Your Honor, excuse me.

MR. BRAUDRICK: Dealing refers to what?

THE WITNESS: Dope.

MR. WORTHINGTON: I move that the last answer and question be stricken and the jury admonished referring to Freddie's dealings. It cannot be used as evidence of the truth of the content of that statement.

MR. BRAUDRICK: Your Honor, it goes to the motive.

We have the person killed here telling Freddie Medrano shortly before the killing that he better get out of town and he better stop dealing dope.

THE COURT: It is limited to motive and that is all. It will be received for that limited purpose.

MR. WORTHINGTON: Could the jury be admonished that that doesn't mean that he was dealing in dope and it cannot be used as evidence of that?

THE COURT: He is not on trial for dealing in dope.

MR. WORTHINGTON: That is what I want the jury to know.

THE COURT: I will tell them that.

MR. WORTHINGTON: Could you tell them now, please. I think it is an important matter.

THE COURT: Well, all matters and questions and answers dealing with dope goes to the question of motive for the commission of the crime and no other purpose and that includes the question and answer just now heard. Proceed.

BY MR. BRAUDRICK:

Q Okay. Where did the conversation that Mike had with Freddie take place?

A In the living room.

Q Okay. Where was Inez Garcia?

A Everybody was in the living room.

Q Okay. What did you do after Mike told Freddie to get out of town?

A We took off and we started walking out the door toward Joe Mendoza's and Inez comes running out toward Mike and started telling Mike to forget about everything.

Q And whereabouts did this conversation take place?

A Right in front of the house.

Q Right by the front door?

A A couple of steps away. . . .

Q How long did the conversation take?

A Just a couple of minutes, a minute or two minutes, I guess.

Q And did you talk to her at all?

A No, I was a couple of steps away, waiting for Mike.

Q Were you able to overhear any of the conversation?

A No, just that part where she told Mike to forget about everything.

Q Okay. Now, going back to when you were in the house, did Mike have a weapon at any time?

A Yes, he did.

Q Where did he get it from?

A I didn't see it with him. I just saw that he had one. I don't know.

Q I show you People's number four. Can you recognize this knife?

A He had this one.

Q Okay. What did he do with the knife?

A He didn't do much with it. When he was telling Mike, I mean, when he was telling Freddie to get out of town, he was showing it to him.

Q How was he showing it to him?

A He had it in his hand.

Q Could you demonstrate how he was showing the knife to Freddie?

A Yeah, he had it like this. He was telling Freddie to get out of town and he had it in his hand.

Q Okay. What did he do with the knife after that, do you know?

A He put it in his pocket.

Q Okay. Now, where did you go after the conversation with Inez outside the house?

A To Joe Mendoza's house.

Q How did you get to Joe Mendoza's house?

A We walked.

Q Did you stop anyplace on the way to Joe Mendoza's house?

A No. . . .

Q All right. Why did you go to the house?

A We were waiting—we went to his house to tell him what happened.

Q Why did you want to tell him what happened?

A Because Joe and Freddie had this disagreement, you know, and we went to his house to let him know.

Q What kind of disagreement? . . .

THE WITNESS: Well, Joe Mendoza had burned Freddie for, I think it was about a hundred dollars.

BY MR. BRAUDRICK:

Q What do you mean burned?

A Well, Freddie left some dope with Joe, and Joe had burned him for it. . . .

BY MR. BRAUDRICK:

Q Did Freddie ever have any conversations with you about Joe Mendoza burning him?

A Yes.

Q When was that?

A I think right after it happened.

Q What did Freddie say about the burn?

A He didn't say much, just told me that Freddie had–Joe had burned him and he was a little pissed off about it. . . .

BY MR. BRAUDRICK:

Q What did you do when you got to Joe Mendoza's house?

A Well, we had–I had let him know what happened, you know, and we sat down and he called then–Joe Mendoza called to Freddie's house and used the name as Tiger and we started arguing on the phone. . . .

Q What did Mike do?

A He was just sitting there, you know, talking to Joe, telling him what had happened, you know, and I think he got on the phone. I can't remember. I think he was arguing with somebody on the phone too.

Q Was it the same time Joe Mendoza was on the phone?

A Yes.

Q How long did Mike talk on the phone?

A A couple of minutes–about a minute, I guess. He didn't talk long.

Q Okay. What did you do after–what did Mike do after he finished talking on the phone?

A When Joe got the phone and he just argued then he just hung up and just–we, you know, after that–after that phone call happened and everything we just told him, "We'll see you man," and then Joe Mendoza tells, "You guys better be careful." That's what he told us. "You guys be careful."

MR. GARRY: I'm going to ask that go out if Your Honor please. It's purely hearsay. Not in the presence of any defendant. . . .

MR. BRAUDRICK: I have no objection to the part of his answer which Joe Mendoza said, "Be careful," being stricken.

THE COURT: All right. That will go out. The jury is admonished to disregard it.

BY MR. BRAUDRICK:

Q After your conversation with Mendoza, what did you guys do then?

A Well, then we were going to the Youth Center and we just walked across the street towards the Youth Center. We got to—we didn't get too far. We got to the alley and when we were getting there, we turned around and saw Freddie Medrano's car coming behind us real slow.

Q And how long were you at Joe Mendoza's house?

A I guess about forty minutes, I guess. . . .

Q Okay. Now, did you see anybody you knew as you walked on Monterey Street?

A Yes, I did.

Q Who was that?

A David Ferrel and Dima Gallardo.

BY MR. BRAUDRICK:

Q And what did you do when you saw them?

A They were outside in front of the house, and we just—when we passed by, we just said hi to each other and kept walking. . . . Well, we kept walking and were getting towards the alley and turned around and told Mike, "Here comes Freddie's car." . . .

THE WITNESS: Then as we turned around, Mike was toward my left, Freddie's car parked behind us a couple of steps, and his passenger opened and Inez Garcia just opened the door and got out and started shooting. No questions asked. . . .

Q Who was driving the car?

A Freddie Medrano.

Q Inez Garcia say anything before she started shooting?

A No.

Q What kind of a firearm did she use to shoot at you?

A A rifle—a .22.

THE BAILIFF: The weapon is clear, Your Honor.

THE COURT: All right.

MR. BRAUDRICK: Your Honor, we would like this .22 rifle——

MR. GARRY: We will stipulate that that is Inez Garcia's .22 and she had it with her and she did shoot.

THE COURT: That night she did shoot?

MR. GARRY: Yes, we will so stipulate.

THE COURT: And she did shoot the now deceased, Miguel Jimenez?

MR. GARRY: Yes, but not as described by the witness, but the fact that she did shoot and also attempted to shoot the witness.

THE COURT: All right. The rifle will be received in evidence. Marked eleven. . . .

Q Had you seen this rifle before she got out of the car to shoot it?

A What do you mean, that day?
Q Yes.
A No, no, I didn't that day.
Q Had you seen it at any time before?
A Yes.
Q Okay. When had you seen it previously?
Q Inside the house.
Q Whose house?
A Freddie's house.
Q Who had the rifle?
A They had it in the closet.
Q Whose closet?
A Freddie's.
Q Okay. Now, what happened as she started shooting at you?
A I took off running toward the park.
Q What happened to Mike?
A Well, when I came back, he was there laying dead. . . .

BY MR. BRAUDRICK:

Q Mr. Castillo, I think my last question to you had you ever seen any other weapons besides the .22 rifle at the house?*
A Yes.
Q What kind of weapon?
A Shotgun.
Q And how was the shotgun stored?
A In that case you got right there. . . .
Q Okay. And what was it used for at Freddie Medrano's house?
A He stored a shotgun in it.
Q What?
A Used to hold a shotgun in it.
Q What kind of shotgun?
A A one-barrel pump.
Q When did you see the shotgun?
A About a week before.
Q A week before the shooting?
A Yes.
Q Okay. Whereabouts in the house did you see it?
A In Freddie's room.
Q Did you talk to Freddie about it?
A He showed it to me.
Q How did Freddie show it to you?
A Pulled it out—just showed it to me.
Q Pulled the shotgun out of that case?
A That case.
Q What did he tell you about the shotgun?

---

* Mr. Braudrick is referring to Fred Medrano's apartment.

THE WITNESS: He told me he had bought it for some money—$30.00.

(RT 15-69)

CROSS-EXAMINATION

Q When was the last time that you had had a shot of heroin before that time?
A I think it was the day before.
Q On the 18th?*
A Yes.
Q Where did you have this shot of heroin?
A At Freddie's house.
Q At Freddie's house?
A Yes.
Q Who was present?
A Just me and Freddie.
Q Just you and Freddie?
A Yes.
Q You say you had a shot there?
A Yes.
Q You have a key to Freddie's house, don't you?
A Yep.
Q So, you can go there any time you want to?
A Yeah, if I wanted to.
Q And you did, too, didn't you?
A No.
Q Over what period of time have you been using heroin?
A About going on two years, I guess, two years.
Q How old are you now?
A Seventeen.
Q Then you started when you were fifteen. Is that right?
A Yeah.
Q Would you tell the jury how far you have gone in school?
A Eighth grade.
Q And then you quit school. Is that right?
A That's right.
Q And is it safe to say that ever since you quit school, you have been living off the streets in Soledad?
A Once in a while, and I work once in a while, too.
Q Not very often?
A No, not very often.

* Mr. Garry is referring to March 18, 1974, the day before Jimenez was shot.

Q And you have also been trafficking in selling heroin, have you not?

A Yeah.

Q And as a matter of fact, at one time you sold some heroin or what you alleged to be heroin to an undercover agent, isn't that right?

A That's right.

Q So you gave him some bogus substance and told him that it was heroin, is that right?

A That's right.

Q What did you have in that bogus substance?

A Baking soda and sugar.

Q And you sold that for how much?

A $250.00.

Q And the person that you sold it to had no sense of humor and had you arrested, isn't that right?

A That's right.

BY MR. GARRY:

Q How long had you known Mr. Medrano?

A For about a year or two years.

Q Well, is it two years or a year?

A I can't recall.

Q Is it correct to say that up until the 19th of March, 1974, you considered yourself a good friend of Mr. Medrano?

A Yes.

Q How long had you known Inez Garcia?

A About two years I guess.

BY MR. GARRY:

Q Had you ever had any altercations or any arguments with Mrs. Inez Garcia?

A Arguments, you mean?

Q Yes.

A No.

Q And as a matter of fact, you always considered her good people?

A Yes.

Q And so that the jury will understand what you mean by good people, will you tell them what you mean by that?

A She was friendly and helpful, and when somebody needed help, she was willing to help anybody.

Q And she was very helpful to the people in the community in Soledad, isn't that right?

A That's right.

Q That is the reputation she had?

A That's right.

Q Now, sir, getting back to the 19th of March, 1974, would you tell us when you first started drinking on that day?

A About 4:30.

Q And you have told us about being with Vincent, your friend?
A Uh huh.
Q You left him, didn't you?
A Right.
Q About 4:00?
A Uh huh.
Q Who did you meet up with after that?
A With Mike Jimenez.
Q Mike Jimenez. Is that right?
A That's right.
Q And how long had you known Mike Jimenez?
A Since I lived in that town, all my life, I guess.
Q In other words, you had been friends with him for many years?
A Yes.
Q How many years had you been living in that town?
A Now, it is about nine years.
Q Nine years?
A Yes.
Q Now, sir, how big a man was Mike Jimenez?
A He wasn't too tall, but he was a heavy-set man, weighed about 300 pounds, I guess.
Q And he would be using heroin, too, wouldn't he?
A On occasion.
Q And the two of you would have a fix together, isn't that right?
A Once in a while.
Q I see. Now, how old a man was Mike Jimenez?
A He had turned twenty-one.
Q And he weighed over 300 pounds, did he not?
A Yes, he did.
Q Can you tell us what you did that afternoon beginning at 4:00 o'clock?
A I met him on the corner, I think, where Manuel Olivas lives, right there on the corner of the empty lot where he lives, and we went—I met Mike and asked him what he was doing and he was going down to Manuel's house and we went down to his house and Manuel was putting a fender and a door on his car, and then we went there and got two six-packs and we drank about two six-packs when we were helping him put the door on.
Q When you talk about two six-packs, what do you mean by that?
A Of beer.
Q And that is twelve cans?
A Twelve cans.
Q When did you finally finish drinking the twelve cans of beer?
A About 6:30 or 6:00 o'clock.
Q Six or 6:30, then? And what did you do after that?
A We still finished what we were doing, fixing the fender and put-

ting the door on and then we took off riding around and then we went and bought another six-pack and it was about—it was me, Mike, Manuel and that is about all.

Q Now, that is eighteen cans of beer. Is that right?

A That's right.

Q When you went to Freddie Medrano's house, what time did you get there?

A At about 8:30, around there.

Q What did you do between 6:30 and 8:30?

A Well, when we finished—by the time we finished fixing the car, it was around 7:30 or 8:00 around there, and we went and got another six-pack and rode around.

Q You rode around?

A Yeah, until from about 7:30.

Q I see. Now, sir, who was there when you arrived at 1760-A?

A Inez and Freddie, and some guy named Cris Solis.

Q Anyone else?

A A guy named Bobby Urquidez, but he left about five minutes later.

Q Anyone else?

A No.

Q How about Alicia?

A Well, they had come in and they left right away after we got there.

Q And how about Rosa?

A Yes, she was there, too, and they left.

BY MR. GARRY:

Q They left when you got there?

A When everybody got there.

Q But when you arrived there, they were there. Isn't that right?

A I recall, I think so.

Q Were there four to six children there at the same time?

A Yes, they had kids.

Q And they were all in the house, isn't that right?

A That's right.

Q When you arrived there?

A I think so, yes—— No, I don't remember. I can't recall.

Q All right. Were you invited to be there?

A Well, we just, like, friendly—we just going in and out of that house all the time.

Q You were friends?

A Yes.

---

* This refers to the apartment occupied by Fred Medrano and Inez Garcia. Louie Castillo testified that he had been staying at 1760-B, the other apartment in the duplex, with his aunt and uncle for the last two months.

Q Who is "we"?

A Me and Mike used to get along with Freddie and know Inez pretty good and go down there all the time.

Q Beg your pardon?

A Used to know them pretty good and used to go down there all the time.

Q Inez had only been there less than a week; isn't that right?

A No, about a couple of weeks.

Q She hadn't even unpacked had she?

A She had been out in the room.

Q I know, but her things were not unpacked; isn't that right?

A I don't—I didn't know.

Q Is that 'cause you had never been in her room?

A Well, I never been in her room.

Q That's what we want to find out. You had never been in the room; isn't that right?

A Yes.

Q And have you ever been in Freddie's room?

A Yes.

Q And there are two bedrooms there in that house; isn't there?

A Yes.

Q Now, when you got there, what was Inez Garcia doing?

A She was standing by the stove, I think.

Q She was cooking, wasn't she?

A Yes, I think so.

Q And how was she dressed?

A She had some blue jeans on and a black blouse, I think. Can't recall.

Q Black blouse?

A Yes, it was flowers on it—or green one, a green blouse with blue jeans. I remember.

Q And where was Freddie when you arrived there?

A In the room, in his room.

Q In other words, he was not in the living room when you arrived there?

A Not when we arrived. He came out right after.

Q And you say this is around 8:30?

A Around 8:30.

Q What did you do? What did you and Mike do when you arrived there?

A We went and sat on the table and went into the refrigerator and got a beer.

Q You went in the refrigerator and got a beer?

A Yes.

Q Did anyone invite you to have a beer?

A No, but I had to ask Inez if there was any beer, and she said, "Yeah, it's in the refrigerator."

Q What else did you do?

A We sat down and started drinking the beer.

Q Now did you have any hard stuff?

A Yes, we had a bottle of Apricot Brandy.

Q Where did you get that?

A Mike had got it from the store. He bought it.

Q When did he buy that?

A Before we got to Fred's house, we stopped and he got it.

Q In other words, before you got to Freddie's house?

A Yes, he had it. Had it with him.

Q And was this a fifth?

A No, it was—no, it wasn't a fifth. It was just a small bottle.

Q All right. And what else did he have to drink?

A That's all. Just that.

Q Wasn't there a bottle of whiskey too?

A Yes, but Inez was drinking that straight.

Q Was that a fifth?

A No, it was a pint, I think.

Q Pint. And how long did you remain there before Freddie arrived on the scene?

A About ten minutes—fifteen.

Q Isn't it a fact, and if it isn't a fact you will tell me, isn't it a fact Inez Garcia said that they were going to have dinner and for you people to leave?

A No, she didn't tell us that.

Q I see. Did she appear—did she welcome you to be there?

A Yes.

Q She did?

A Yes, she didn't say nothing or anything.

Q You remember when Mike stole a knife from the kitchen, from the cupboard?

A No, I didn't see him.

Q You didn't see him take it?

A No.

Q Did you see Mike with a knife?

A After the fight, yes, when I saw the knife at the fight.

Q Well, you didn't see him take the knife?

A No, I didn't.

Q Had you seen the knife before?

A I don't remember.

Q I see. Would you say Mike was pretty drunk?

A No, he could handle his liquor pretty good.

Q Well, had you drunk as much as he had?

A Yes.

Q In other words, whatever amount of alcohol that was consumed by him, you had consumed an equal amount; isn't that right?

A Yes, probably.

Q Maybe more; isn't that right?

A I guess, I don't know.

Q I see. Now, was anybody eating when you arrived there?

A I don't remember.

Q Did anyone start to eat after you arrived there?

A Yes.

Q Who?

A Freddie. I think he was—he sat down and eat, I think.

BY MR. GARRY:

Q How long were you there before an argument took place between you and Freddie?

A About 45 minutes or around there, I guess.

Q Twenty-five minutes?

A Forty-five minutes, I guess.

Q In other words, you were there for 45 minutes before the argument started?

A Yes.

Q And in the 45 minutes, what were you and Mike and Freddie doing?

A We was just drinking and talking like we always do, you know.

Q Was Freddie drinking?

A No, he wasn't.

Q Now, what were you talking about in that 45 minutes?

A I don't remember, arguing.

Q And had you ever had any arguments with Freddie on any other occasions?

A No.

Q In other words, your relationship was friendly on other occasions?

A Yes.

Q And it was always friendly with Inez Garcia on other occasions?

A Uh-huh.

Q That's a correct statement; isn't that right?

A Yes.

Q Okay. Now, sir, isn't it true that you don't even remember what the argument was about right now?

A No, the argument was about him bragging about, you know,——

Q About bragging?

A Yes.

Q Had he bragged on any other occasions?

A Yes, once in awhile.

Q Once in awhile. Was there any reason why you called him a T.B. person?
A A T.B. person?
Q Yes.
A What do you mean, because he had T.B. or anything?
Q Yes.
A I don't remember calling him that.
Q You don't?
A No, I don't.
Q Did you call him that?
A I don't remember calling him that.
Q You knew he had tuberculosis?
A Yes, I did.
Q And you knew he was on complete disability with the United States Armed Services?
A Yes.

BY MR. GARRY:

Q And you knew that he was not a well person, did you not?
A Yes, I did.
Q And sir, isn't it true that you testified before the Grand Jury?
A Yes, I did.
Q Were you telling the truth to the Grand Jury?
A Yes.
Q You swore to tell the truth; isn't that right?
A Yes, I didn't tell them about the dope, 'cause I knew dope was illegal.

BY MR. GARRY:

Q And your mind was clearer then than it is now; is that right?
A Not about what facts took place on the 19th of March.
Q And you told those ladies and gentlemen of the Grand Jury that the argument was over home town boy?
A Yes, he was bragging. He wasn't a home town guy.
Q I beg your pardon?
A Yes, I told them that.
Q You told them that? Was that the truth?
A Yes, part of it.
Q And you were asked to tell the entire truth, were you not?
A Yes.
Q And you didn't?
A No, 'cause——

BY MR. GARRY:

Q And you kept things from that Grand Jury; isn't that right?
A Yes.

BY MR. GARRY:

Q Now, you didn't say one word in there about the fact that anything was said about selling of dope, did you?

A No.

Q And by the way, when is the first time that you ever told the District Attorney that the involvement involved discussion of dope?

A About a month ago, I guess, I can't really recall. I spoke to a lot of people.

Q When you say you spoke to a lot of people, let's start out with whom you spoke to?

A All right. Investigators, District Attorney people, and people like that.

Q Now, do you remember talking to Mr. Worthington and Mrs. Richards* and myself yesterday afternoon in the District Attorney's office?†

A Yes.

Q And do you remember telling me that you talked to the District Attorney's office two months ago?

A Yeah, and I told you—like I told you, I couldn't recall the exact time it was.

Q But, you did say that it was at least two months ago, isn't that right?

A Yeah, at least I thought.

Q Well, sir, so there is no question about what you told me, you did tell me that it was over two months ago that you talked to someone from the District Attorney's office and told them about dope, isn't that right?

A Yeah, I told you it was about a month or two, maybe.

Q Well, now, you want to make it a month or two?

A Like I told you yesterday, it might have been a month or two, and you said two, and I said, yeah, maybe.

Q As a matter of fact, you said it was about four months and when I pinned you right down to it, you said it was two months, isn't that right, sir?

A Yeah, that's right.

Q I am not misstating anything, am I?

A No.

Q Is that right?

A That's right.

---

* Mrs. Richards is Pat Richards who works as Mr. Garry's para-legal assistant.

† Pursuant to defense request, the defense was allowed to examine Mr. Castillo about the alleged drug connection to the argument between Castillo and Medrano on the night of March 19, 1974.

THE COURT: Oh, well, a stipulation is conclusive evidence of the facts stipulated to. I suppose that's sufficient.*

MR. GARRY: That's very good, Your Honor. I couldn't have done any better myself if I had tried to.

THE COURT: Thank you, Mr. Garry.

BY MR. GARRY:

Q Mr. Castillo, isn't it a fact that you began to change your story regarding narcotics to divert the attention in this case against yourself, because you had been accused by Inez Garcia of raping her; isn't that right?

A It's not right.

Q It's not right?

A No.

Q That isn't the reason you diverted and tried to change the story regarding narcotics in this case?

A No, it's not.

Q Isn't it a fact, Mr. Castillo, that when you arrived at the house, whatever time you arrived—8:30 or so on the 19th of March—you put your arms around Inez Garcia and said that she was your girl?

A No, I didn't.

Q And you did the same thing to Alicia, did you not?

A Did not.

Q So, that if either one of them were to testify that you did do that, that would not be correct?

A I did not.

Q You did not?

A No.

Q Could you have done so without knowing that you did because of your alcoholic condition?

A Nope.

BY MR. GARRY:

Q No, isn't it also true that you told Mr. Medrano about the T.B., and that he was nothing but a T.B.er, but you also told him, did you not, that you would treat him the same way as you treated a man by the name of Conutro Gonzales whom you said you had knifed?

A I did not tell him that.

Q It's a fact, is it not, that you did knife Conutro Gonzales?

A Yes, it's a fact. It happened.

Q And you did it?

A Yes, I did it.

Q But you did not tell that to Mr. ——

---

* Mr. Braudrick stipulated to the Court that Louie Castillo first told an investigator for the District Attorney on August 22nd or 23rd that the argument between Castillo and Medrano on 3-19-74 was about narcotics. This was during jury selection for the trial approximately two weeks before.

A Did not tell him that.

Q Did you ever tell him that?

A No.

BY MR. GARRY:

Q Sir, isn't it true that during the entire conversation and during this entire period of time in the evening of March 19, 1974, not one word was said about heroin?

A No, it's not—it's—well, the arguing was about it. About——

Q Was there one single word said mentioning the word heroin?

A Yes, there was.

Q Tell us what was said about heroin?

A Well, Mike had told him that he was for—he thought he was bad because he was dealing, in that, you know, he was dealing heroin, and he was always bragging about himself, and that's what the argument was, you know, mainly about his bragging and about his dealing dope.

BY MR. GARRY:

Q Is it your testimony, sir, that Mike Jimenez said that to Mr. Medrano?

A Yes.

Q Because Mike Jimenez did not like people to sell heroin?

A No, it's just the way that Freddie was—always bragging about himself. That's all.

Q Mike had no opposition to you selling—dealing with heroin, did he?

A No.

Q And he had no opposition with using heroin himself?

A No.

Q Then, how did the conversation come in about the question of heroin? How did that fit into the context of the argument that took place over home town and not home town?

A The main—like I told everybody, the main argument was he—he's the type of dude that brags all the time about himself, what he has, and what he could do, he says, and then Mike didn't like that idea with him bragging.

Q I see. Now, was there anything said by you about heroin? Did you mention the word heroin that entire evening?

A Yes, I told him that that—'cause he was dealing, he thought he was bad coming from me. I told him the same thing. I told him, "you are not going to make it, because you're dealing in dope. You think you are Mr. Big Man around town."

Q You were dealing dope, too? Did you consider him competition?

A He wasn't around then. He was in the Army or something like that.

Q He was in the Army?

A Yep.

Q He told you he was in the Army, right?

A Right.

Q Sir, you told us before lunch that you told many people about the conversation that evening. Who else did you tell that about dope being a part of the argument that evening?

A Just Mendoza.

Q You told Mendoza?

A I told him what happened with the argument, because he was bragging about himself and everything.

Q Any one else?

A No, not that I recall.

Q So, when you said you told many people, you didn't mean that?

A Many people–about what? The argument about dope?

Q I asked you this just before lunch? A Yes.

Q Who did you tell in the law enforcement bodies about the fact that the argument involved dope?

A I didn't tell nobody until a couple of weeks, now that you–that the exact date came out about the dope, you know, what the reason was, because of the dope.

Q Who did you tell it to besides the District Attorney's office?

A Nobody.

Q So, when you said before lunch that you told many people that, that was not true, was it?

A You meant many people by–I must–didn't understand your question or something.

MR. GARRY: Sir, you said you told Mendoza about the conversation that you have had with Mr. Medrano?

A Yes, I told him about that–about the conversation was the argument about.

Q You knew, did you not, that Mr. Mendoza–Joseph Mendoza–had a contract out on Mr. Medrano?

A No, not until after the killing–after the, you know,––.

Q You found out about it after the killing?

A After that, yes.

Q Didn't he tell you––

MR. BRAUDRICK: Objection, Your Honor, hearsay.

MR. GARRY: Well, he opened up the conversation. I'm entitled to go into it.

THE COURT: Well––

MR. BRAUDRICK: I would ask––

MR. GARRY: This goes to the motive and the entire subject matter. It discusses hate.

MR. BRAUDRICK: If there's going to be a discussion, let's have it outside of the presence of the jury.

THE COURT: We are not going to take time out from the jury all the time. Go ahead, objection overruled.

BY MR. GARRY:

Q Isn't it a fact that Mr. Mendoza told you after you left the Medrano place, when you told him about the fight that you had with Mr. Mendoza, and how you and Mr. Jimenez had beaten him up, that he told you that he had a contract on this man at that time?

MR. BRAUDRICK: Objection.

THE WITNESS: I heard that after what had happened, after—that's when I found out about that contract.

MR. GARRY:

Q You found out about the contract when Mr. Mendoza told you; isn't that right?

A Not that night.

Q When did he tell you?

MR. BRAUDRICK: Objection.

THE WITNESS: After the killing.

MR. BRAUDRICK: That's hearsay, all of Joe Mendoza.

THE COURT: For the impeachment of this man though.

MR. BRAUDRICK: How does that go to the impeachment?

THE COURT: Proceed.

BY MR. GARRY:

Q Isn't that a fact, sir, that he told you about the fact that he had a contract meant that he wanted Mr. Medrano killed?

A That night, no.

Q When did he tell you?

A After what had happened.

Q That same night?

A No.

Q The next day?

A Yes, I think it was—the day later, I think.

Q Didn't he also tell you, sir, that he and Mike told Inez Garcia that if he didn't—if she didn't leave the County immediately that they would wipe her out?

A No, he did not tell me that.

Q He didn't tell you that?

A No, he did not tell me that.

Q He didn't tell you that?

A No, he didn't.

Q Didn't he also say that's exactly what he wanted Medrano to do?

A He wanted Medrano out of the town, but he did not tell me about Inez.

Q Didn't he tell you that he wanted Medrano killed?

A Did not.

Q What do you understand when a person like Joe Mendoza says,

"I have a contract out on Medrano." What does that mean?

A That's after—that's after the murder, I mean, that means to kill him.

Q My question is, what does it mean?

A It means to kill somebody.

Q So that Mr. Medrano had a contract against him by Mr. Mendoza, isn't that right?

A Yes, that's what he told me after.

Q And the man that you spent some forty-five minutes to an hour with after you had beaten up Mr. Medrano, isn't that right?

A That's right.

Q And then on top of that, you and Mike and Mendoza telephoned the home of Mr. Medrano and talked to Inez Garcia; isn't that right?

A No, they—Joe Mendoza talked on the phone.

Q And you heard the conversation and threats, did you not, sir?

A No, I didn't. I—well, I wasn't paying any attention to them. They were arguing.

Q Is that because you were eating oranges at the time?

A The TV was on. I wasn't paying any attention to it.

Q You were not paying any attention, and yet you are the one that told Mr. Mendoza about——

A About the fight.

Q The beating and fight as working over that you gave Mr. Medrano?

A Yes, I did.

Q And he immediately picked up the telephone; isn't that right?

A That's right.

Q And he used the name Tiger; isn't that right?

A That's right.

Q And why did he use the name Tiger?

A Because he didn't want to use his own name or something?

Q Well, it's because if he had used his own name, Mr. Medrano would not talk to him; isn't that right?

A I don't know. When you get to know somebody, you get to recognize his voice, I guess.

BY MR. GARRY:

Q Sir, let's go back to the apartment now after you had beaten up—you and Mr. Jimenez had beaten up Mr. Medrano. Okay? How long did you remain on the premises after that?

A A couple of minutes, I guess, about three or four—three minutes, not too long.

Q Could it have been fifteen minutes?

A No, I don't think so.

Q Could it have been ten minutes?

A It could have been ten minutes.

Q All right. Isn't it a fact that Mr. Medrano went to his room and cleaned up?

A Yes, he went to his room, but he came right back out.

Q Well, wasn't he bleeding before he went into his room?

A Yes, he was.

Q Wasn't he bleeding from his mouth and his nose?

A From his nose—I didn't bother to look.

Q But, he was bleeding?

A Yes, he was.

Q And there was blood all over the floor; isn't that right?

A Yes, sir.

Q And he came out—came back out after he had cleaned his face up; isn't that right?

A Yes, he came back out.

Q Did he, when he came back out, did he make any kind of threats to you or to Mike Jimenez?

A No, he didn't.

Q Did anyone, while you were still there, make any threats to you and to Mike Jimenez.

A Nope.

Q You are positive about that?

A Positive about that.

Q And it was after the beating that Mr. Medrano received, that Mr. Jimenez took this knife out of his pocket; isn't that right?

A That's right.

Q And did he say anything when he took this knife out of his pocket?

A No, he was just telling Freddie after that fight happened—was just telling Freddie to stop his dealing or get out of town, and Freddie had a rag on his nose and was telling him, "All right, I will."

BY MR. GARRY:

Q Now, you have never made that statement before, have you?

A No.

Q And you just now made that up while you have been sitting there; isn't that right?

A No, I have said before—you had asked me about—about the knife and I told you.

Q You told me about the knife, but you never said that Freddie said that Mike Jimenez said that, "You get out of town." . . .

BY MR. GARRY:

Q But you had never said until just now—until just now that Mike Jimenez said to Freddie, "I want you to get out of town," and Freddie said, "I will."

A Earlier I had told you before noon—you had asked me—somebody had asked me what Mike had told Freddie, and I told you.

Q That was over the telephone, wasn't it?
A No, that was—that was inside the house.
Q That's true, isn't it?
A That's true.
Q He did say this?
A Yes.
Q He threatened him; isn't that right? He had the knife in his hand at the time?
A He had a knife and was telling him to get out of town or stop his dealing, and Freddie said, "All right. I will."
Q He said stop his dealing? Until today, when did you ever say that statement to anybody?
A I don't recall.
Q As a matter of fact, you never have said that to the District Attorney's office before, have you?
A Don't remember.
Q Well, you know you never said that, did you, sir?
A I think I have. I'm not too sure, but I think I did—no——
Q My question is, before today, before you got on this witness stand today, had you said that to anybody in the District Attorney's office?
A I think I—I think I did tell somebody. I don't remember.
Q Who did you tell that to?
A I don't remember telling somebody—I mean, I can't remember, you know, who.
Q Did you tell that to Mr. Perez here, Sergeant Perez?
A I don't recall.
Q Did you tell it to Mr. Braudrick?
A I don't remember. I don't—told you I don't recall. I can't remember who I told it to.

BY MR. GARRY:

Q Let's talk about Inez Garcia for a minute. Isn't it a fact that when you and Mike Jimenez left the house, Inez Garcia said, "Don't worry about things. Things will be fine."
A She told Mike that outside, yes, she did.
Q And you heard that?
A Yes, when she had told Mike to forget about everything.
Q In other words, Inez Garcia after that time had no animosity against either you or Mr. Jimenez?
A No.
Q That's true, isn't it?
A Yes, that's true.
Q Now, isn't it a fact that you and Mr. Jimenez outside in the back of the house started browbeating and pushing Inez Garcia around?
A No, we didn't.

Q Isn't it also a fact that you raped her?
A No, I didn't.
Q Do you think it's something to laugh about?
A No, it's not true.
Q If it was true, you wouldn't admit it, would you, sir?
MR. BRAUDRICK: Object. Argumentative.
THE COURT: Sustained.

BY MR. GARRY:

Q It's also true, is it not, that Mr. Jimenez showed that knife to Inez?
A Don't recall.
Q On page 30, if Your Honor please, of the Grand Jury transcript—I wonder if Your Honor would inform this jury about what a Grand Jury is, and what the Grand Jury is not? The defendants are not represented there by counsel, the District Attorney is the only one that's there, plus the witness, so that they will get the full flavor of this.

THE COURT: Well, the Grand Jury is selected from the citizens of the County to serve for a period of time, normally one year, although to cover a period of actually serving a year and a half. That is covered as a change in the law, and there are two ways whereby a case can be brought to the point of trial in California.

One is by proceeding before a Magistrate resulting in binding of, and then on the basis of that, the District Attorney's file and information, and the other way and the one way used in this case is for the Grand Jury to be convened by the District Attorney, and evidence is produced and then if there is in the minds of the Grand Jury a prima facie case, a true bill is found and an indictment is laid before the court, and upon the basis of that, the trial jury is convened as you have been, and that's what was done here by way of information, and as counsel has indicated, it is true that the defendant is not represented in the proceedings before the Grand Jury.

Proceed.

MR. GARRY: Thank you, Your Honor. On page 39, beginning with line 2 and ending with line 7, Your Honor.

"What kind of a knife was it?" —this is Mr. Castillo before the Grand Jury testifying, Your Honor.

"Q What kind of a knife was it?
"A I really don't know. I think it was one of those kitchen knives.
"Q Did you see where he got that?
"A No, he had it with him.
"Q Did he show it to anybody that evening?
"A Yes, he showed it to Inez."

BY MR. GARRY:

Q You gave those answers to those questions, did you not, sir?
A Yes, I did.

. . .

Q Isn't it a fact that the shooting took place out in the street?
A No, in the alley.
Q It was in the alley?
A Yes, right there when—we were at the alley.
Q Isn't it also a fact that you were beating up on Mr. Medrano again for a third time?
A No.
Q That's not true?
A That's not true.
Q Isn't it a fact that Mr. Jimenez had a knife—beginning to throw it at the time that the shooting took place?
A Now, I didn't see that.
Q Did you ever see a knife?
A Inside the house, yes, I did.
Q And you never saw the knife again after that?
A No.

. . .

Q And is it also true that the police gave you no blood test to see how much alcohol you had been drinking that night?
A That's true.
MR. GARRY: I have no further questions, Your Honor.
THE COURT: Mr. Worthington?
MR. WORTHINGTON: Thank you, Your Honor.

CROSS-EXAMINATION

BY MR. WORTHINGTON:
Q Mr. Castillo, the last time you can remember shooting up any dope was—well, did you say about a week ago?
A Yes.
Q You didn't shoot yesterday?
A Nope.
Q And you didn't shoot this morning before you came here?
A No.
Q And you didn't shoot during any of the breaks?
A Nope.
Q Is your habit such at this time that you feel the withdrawal symptoms when you don't shoot dope?
A No.
Q So, you are feeling all right, now?
A Yep.

Q Now, on the 19th of March, 1974, did you see any dope at Freddie's and Inez's apartment?

A Nope.

Q In fact, you have never seen any stash of dope in Freddie's apartment, have you?

A No.

. . .

BY MR. WORTHINGTON:

Q Mr. Castillo, did you start the argument with Freddie?

A I think I did. I'm not too sure. Yes, I think I did.

Q You did, didn't you?

A Yes.

. . .

Q Now, do you recall talking to a man who identified himself as my investigator, a man by the name of Jack Johns? . . .

A Yes.

Q Okay. That was about a month ago, wasn't it?

A Yes.

Q And he asked you what started the fight, didn't he?

A Yes.

Q What did you tell him?

A Told him 'cause about Freddie's bragging. I think I told him.

Q You didn't say a word about the dope, did you?

A No. He didn't really ask me very many questions, either.

Q Did he ask you about the cause of the argument?

A Yes, he had asked me what happened, you know, what had happened. I told him—I told him the main reason was about Freddie's, you know, bragging, and all that, and he just had told me, "Well, my name is so and so, and I want to get to know you. I'm going to make an appointment to see you again." And that's about it. He didn't really stay too long.

Q Did you intentionally mislead him?

A What do you mean mislead?

Q Told him the best you remembered at the time, didn't you?

A Yes.

Q You didn't say anything about dope being involved in that argument at all?

A No.

Q In fact, you told him the argument was over who was top home town boy?

A Yes, I told him.

Q Just like you told the grand jury, and that was about a month ago?

A I guess it was.

Q About two weeks before this trial started?

A I guess. . . .

Q Two weeks before trial up to that point, you hadn't changed your story yet, had you?

A No.

Q You hadn't. Not with the district attorney's office, not with us, not with my investigator, not with your friends?

A No, I had——

Q Is there anybody that you told a different story to before August 23rd, 1974?

A I don't remember. I don't recall.

. . .

(RT 125-145)

The prosecution's next witness is Chrisofono Solis, 22, known to the defendants as "Chofero." Solis testifies that he was with defendant Medrano from 6 p.m. on during the evening of March 19, 1974, and was present during the fight and relates the circumstances surrounding the defendants leaving the apartment "to get" Mike Jimenez and Louie Castillo. Solis' testimony is offered to attempt to corroborate Castillo's testimony that the fight was about drugs and that Inez Garcia was not molested or raped.

CHRISOFONO SOLIS, SWORN
DIRECT EXAMINATION

BY MR. BRAUDRICK:

Q Mr. Solis, what is your occupation?

A I'm a laborer.

Q Where do you work right now?

A I'm working at Murphy's.

Q What is Murphy's?

A A tomato shack, tomato packing company.

Q Is that down in Soledad?

A Yes.

Q Do you live in Soledad?

A Yes.

Q And do you know the defendants, Freddie Medrano?

A Yes, I know him.

Q And do you know Inez Garcia, also seated here?

A Yes.

Q How long have you known Inez Garcia?

A About—I only met her about six times.

Q Can you recall when you first met her?

A Yes, there at the camp.
Q At Jimenez Camp?
A Yes.
Q And when did you first meet Freddie Medrano?
A When we were—there in Soledad.
Q And how long before this shooting was that?
A About two weeks.
Q Okay. Now, bringing your attention to March 19, 1974, did you have occasion to go see Freddie Medrano?
A Yes.
Q Whereabouts did you first see him?

. . .

A Yes, I saw him about six—six o'clock that afternoon.
Q Okay. Where did you first see him?
A I went to his house.
Q Why did you go to his house.
A I went to see if he knew where I could find a lid.
Q A what?
A A lid.
Q What's a lid?
A Marijuana.
Q Have you ever used heroin?
A No.
Q Have you ever bought heroin?
A No.
Q Okay. What happened when you got to his house?
A He was making a—he was calling down to Texas.

. . .

BY MR. BRAUDRICK:
Q Who was at the house?
A There were—there were three other girls there besides Freddie and Inez.

. . .

Q Okay. What did Freddie do after he finished his phone call to Texas?
A I think he stayed there about an hour talking; and as he was talking, he got out a pouch he had of grass; and we started smoking some there.

. . .

BY MR. BRAUDRICK:
Q How many cigarettes did he make?

A We smoked two.
Q Two apiece or did you share?
A We shared.
Q Okay. Whereabouts did this take place in the house?
A Inez's room.
Q How long of the time did you spend smoking the marijuana?
A We stayed there about two hours.
Q Okay. What did you do then?
A Then we went to Gonzales.
Q Why did you go to Gonzales? . . .
THE WITNESS: We went to look for a lid.

. . .

BY MR. BRAUDRICK:
Q When you say "we" who do you mean?
A I wanted some, and he said he knew some guys there.

. . .

BY MR. BRAUDRICK:
Q Okay, what happened when you got to Gonzales?
A We stopped there at a house there and Freddie got off.
Q Did you get out of the car?
A No.
Q Then what did you do?
A We went back to Soledad.
Q Where did you go?
A We stopped at a liquor store.
Q What did you do at the liquor store?
A Freddie got out. He bought—I don't know what he bought.
Q Did he buy some liquor?
A I don't know.
Q Where did you go from the liquor store?
A We went to his house.

. . .

BY MR. BRAUDRICK:
Q Okay. About what time did you get to his house?
A About eight—between 8:30.
Q What did you do when you got to his house?
A We went to Inez's room when we got there.
Q What?
A When we got there.
Q What did you do in Inez's room?
A We smoked another one.
Q Did you and Freddie share one cigarette?

A Yes.
Q Marijuana cigarette?
A Yes.
Q Who was at the house when you got back?
A Inez and a few girls were there. There was—there was still a few girls there, same girls.
Q Do you know Louie Castillo?
A Yes.
Q And do you know—and did you know Miguel Jimenez?
A Yes.
Q Okay. What did you do after you smoked the joint in Inez's bedroom?
A We stayed there and Inez came and said that Mike and Louie were there.

. . .

BY MR. BRAUDRICK:
Q What did you do after Inez told you that?
A We went to the living room and sat down on the dining table.
Q Okay. Now, who was at the house at that point?
A Only Freddie and Inez and Louie and Mike.
Q And yourself?
A Yes.
Q Okay. What happened then?
A Then we started talking there.
Q Did you have anything to drink?
A No.
Q Did anybody else have anything to drink?
A They had a beer there, and Inez was drinking from about—from a glass.
Q Do you know what she was drinking?
A I think it was whiskey.

. . .

BY MR. BRAUDRICK:
Q Okay. Was there an argument at Mr. Medrano's house that night?
A There was.
Q When did the argument start?
A About 8:30.
Q Okay. Were you there when the argument was going on?
A Yes.
Q Who else was there when the argument was going on?
A Inez and Louie and Mike and myself and Freddie.
Q Who was arguing?
A Louie and Freddie.

. . .

BY MR. BRAUDRICK:

Q What were they arguing about?

A They were arguing about town boy.

Q What exactly were they arguing about? What were they saying back and forth?

A He said that Freddie thought that he was big shit there in town.

Q And what did Freddie say?

A Freddie said that he didn't—he didn't thought he was big there.

. . .

Q What was Louie saying during the argument?

A He kept on picking on Freddie, and Freddie talking back to Louie.

Q What were the words that he was saying?

A He was saying that Freddie wasn't nothing there in town, and he wasn't as big as he thought he was.

Q Okay. When he said that, he told Freddie that he wasn't as big as he thought he was, what was he referring to?

A About drugs.

Q What kind of drugs?

A Hard drugs.

Q What do you mean by hard drugs?

MR. GARRY: Well, just a minute now. If Your Honor please, is this what the witness said or is this what he thought he said? Now, it's important to know that.

THE COURT: I don't know. Wait a minute. What was the question?

(Question read by the reporter.)

MR. GARRY: I move to strike that upon the grounds that that's his interpretation, not what was said. We want to know what was said.

THE COURT: Yes, I agree with that. That's stricken. The jury is admonished to disregard it.

BY MR. BRAUDRICK:

Q Was there any mention of drugs?

THE WITNESS: No, he didn't actually say it, but——

BY MR. BRAUDRICK:

Q But what?

A That's what they were talking about?

. . .

BY MR. BRAUDRICK:

Q Okay. Were you there when the fight started?

A Yes.

Q Whereabouts did the fight first start?
A They were outside.
Q What was said before they went outside?
A Freddie told Louie to go outside with him.
Q What exactly did Freddie say? Can you remember?
A He said, "Let's go outside—me and you alone."
Q How long were they outside?
A About three minutes. Then Louie came back alone.
Q Did Freddie come back in later?
A He came about five minutes after Louie had come in.
Q What happened when Freddie came back in?
A They started fighting again.

. . .

Q What did Mike Jimenez do?
A He went to fight with Freddie.

BY MR. BRAUDRICK:

Q Did you get involved in the fight at all?
A I tried to hold Mike as he was going towards Freddie.
Q And what happened then?
A And Mike told me to back off.
Q To what?
A Back off.
Q Okay. What did Mike do then?
A He started toward Freddie.
Q What did he do to Freddie?
A He didn't do nothing at that moment. Then, when Inez got in between them, Freddie went—tried to get away, and Mike went after him, and he got him at the sofa.
Q Okay. What did Mike do then?
A He punched him about three times.
Q Whereabouts did he hit him?
A Face.

. . .

Q What happened after Mike punched Freddie?
A Freddie got a bloody nose and Mike stopped.
Q What did Freddie do after Mike stopped?
A He went to his room.

. . .

Q Okay. Now, what happened after Freddie left the room?
A He went to his room and then he came back with a towel trying to stop the bleeding.

Q What did Mike and Louie do then?
A They stayed there and then Freddie went to the bathroom to wash up.
Q What were they doing?
A They were standing there like they owned the place.
Q As if they owned the house?
A Yes.
Q What was Inez doing then?
A She was saying to them, why did they do that, beat up Freddie.

BY MR. BRAUDRICK:

Q What did they say to Inez?
A And they didn't listen to her, they kept on talking about themselves.
Q I show you People's Number Four which appears to be a kitchen knife. Have you seen a knife similar to that before?
A Yeah.
Q Okay. When did you first see it?
A When Mike got it from the kitchen table there.
Q And was that before the fight?
A Yes.
Q Was it before the argument?
A Yeah.
Q What did Mike do with the knife after he got it from the kitchen table?
A He put it underneath the coat pocket.
Q Did you see him take it out of his pocket after he put it in his pocket?
A Yes.
Q When did he do that?
A After the fight.
Q What did he do with the knife?
A He got it out and pointed it at me and Freddie.

. . .

Q And what did he say as he pointed it?
A I can't remember what he said.
Q Were you scared?
A Yeah, a little bit.
Q Where was Inez when he was pointing the knife?
A She was making some coffee, I think.
Q And where was Louie?
A There behind Mike.
Q All right. Now, what happened after Freddie went to the bathroom?

A We waited for Freddie to come out.
Q Did he come out?
A Yeah.
Q When he came out, were Louie and Mike still there?
A Yeah.
Q How much longer did they stay?
A They stayed about five minutes later.
Q Did they leave together?
A Yes.
Q Did Inez stay in the house?
A She did.
Q Did you see her go outside the house?
A She probably went to the doorway.
Q How long was she at the doorway?
A A little while, about a minute.
Q Was she talking to anybody?
A Yeah, to Mike and Louie.
Q Could you hear any of the conversation?
A No.
Q Okay. What did she do?
A She came back.
Q Did you see Mike and Louie again that night?
A No.

. . .

BY MR. BRAUDRICK:
Q Who was left at the house after Mike and Louie left the house?
A We three, me, Freddie and Inez.
Q What did you do?
A Freddie told me to get out.
Q What?
A Freddie told me to get out.
BY MR. BRAUDRICK:
Q What did you do when Freddie told you to get out?
A Inez told him I wasn't part of them.
Q You weren't part of the fight?
A Yeah, that I wasn't helping them beat him up.
Q What did Freddie do after he told you to get out?
A Then he forgot about what he told me to get out, and then he started talking that he wanted to get Mike and Louie.
Q What was he saying?
A He said I want to see him die. I want to be there when he dies.
Q Was Inez in the house then?
A Yeah, she was.

. . .

BY MR. BRAUDRICK:

Q This was after Mike and Louie had left. Is that right?
A Yes.
Q How much longer after?
A About five minutes.
Q Did Inez leave the house after that?
A No.
Q Did she leave the house later that night?
A No, I left two days later.
Q No, did Inez leave the house?
A No.
Q Later that night?
A They left later.
Q Was Inez' blouse ripped?
A No.
Q Did she have any bruises?
A Nothing, I didn't notice any.
Q How was she acting?
A Upset.

. . .

BY MR. BRAUDRICK:

Q What did Inez say when Freddie said that he wanted to kill Mike, that he wanted to see him die?

A She said that he couldn't do it because if he did it, he wouldn't be able to get out.

. . .

THE WITNESS: Then she said that if he wanted, she could do it.

BY MR. BRAUDRICK:

Q What did Freddie say?
A He didn't want to take Inez.
Q What?
A He didn't want to take Inez. He asked me if I could take him to look for Mike.

BY MR. BRAUDRICK:

Q Did he tell you why he wanted to look for Mike?
A Yeah, he said he wanted to kill Mike.
Q Okay. What did Inez say after she told Freddie that he shouldn't do it because he couldn't get out?
A She said she could do it because she had money, or her family had money to bail her out the next day.
Q What did Freddie say after that?

A He just heard what she was saying.

. . .

BY MR. BRAUDRICK:

Q Did you see any weapons?

A Yeah.

Q When did you first see the weapons that night?

A After they got a phone call from Soledad.

BY MR. BRAUDRICK:

Q Okay. How much longer after Mike and Louie had gone did they get the phone call?

A About ten minutes later.

Q During that ten minutes, were they talking all the time?

A Yeah.

Q And what were they talking about?

A Mainly about going to look for Mike.

Q What were the exact words they were using?

. . .

THE WITNESS: Inez said that she–they shouldn't have come and beat him up in their own house and they were talking mainly about that, and about Freddie wanted to get Mike.

BY MR. BRAUDRICK:

Q Did he say anything about how he was going to get Mike?

A He said he wanted to kill him.

Q Was there any discussion about guns before the phone call?

A No.

. . .

Q How long did they talk on the phone on the call from Soledad?

A For about five minutes?

Q Who was talking on the phone?

A Inez picked up the phone and Freddie told her to hang it up and Inez kept on talking.

Q What was she saying?

A I don't remember what they were saying.

Q Okay. Did Freddie talk on the phone at all?

A Yeah, he went to Inez' room and talked on the other phone there.

Q Can you remember what he said?

A No.

Q Okay. What happened after the phone call?

A Then, Freddie started–went to the room and got the .22 and then he went and got the shotgun and Inez started to make a call, a long distance call.

Q Where did she make the call to?
A I don't know, it was a long distance call.

. . .

BY MR. BRAUDRICK:

Q Did you overhear her conversation on the phone, the phone call she made?
A I did.
Q What did she say?
A She said that someone had come and beat her up in her apartment.
Q And what else? . . .
A And that if she got into trouble, that was to let them know so they could get her out.

. . .

Q Now, this phone call that she made that you just related, was this after Freddie went into the bedroom and got the .22 rifle and the shotgun?
A Yeah, that was when Freddie was going to get the rifle.
Q That is when she was making the call?
A Yeah.
Q I show you People's Number Eleven, the .22 rifle, does this appear to be similar to the rifle that Freddie brought out of the bedroom?
A It is.
Q Did he bring this rifle out of his bedroom or her bedroom?
A His bedroom.
Q What kind of a shotgun was it he brought out?
A Air pump.

BY MR. BRAUDRICK:

Q When did you first see the shotgun?
A After he brought the .22 out.
Q He brought the .22 out and then went back and got the shotgun?
A Yeah.
Q Was the shotgun in a case?
A Yes.
Q Okay. When did you first actually see the gun itself?
A When he brought it and unzippered it.
Q Where did he unzipper it?
A There in the living room.

BY MR. BRAUDRICK:

Q Have you ever seen this* before?

---

* Referring to the shotgun case.

A Only that night.

. . .

Q Okay. What did Freddie do after he brought the shotgun out and the rifle out?

A He brought the rifle out and he brought the .22 bullets, too, and then he asked Inez if she had some shotgun shells.

Q What did Inez say?

A She said that she had some twelve gauge shotgun shells in her room.

Q Okay. Was this after she got off the phone call she was making?

A Yes.

Q Okay. What did she do?

A Then she went toward where the rifle was and she started to load the .22.

. . .

BY MR. BRAUDRICK:

Q Did Freddie load any of the guns?

A He loaded the shotgun.

Q Now, when they were loading the guns, did they talk at all and by that, I mean, did Freddie and Inez talk at all?

A They were talking there, but I didn't listen to what they were saying.

Q Why not?

A I didn't hear them. I was near there, but I wasn't paying any attention to them.

Q How were you feeling at that time?

A Scared.

Q Is that why you stayed at the house?

A Yes.

. . .

BY MR. BRAUDRICK:

Q Okay. After they loaded the guns, what did they do?

A They started to clean up the place there.

Q Clean up the house?

A Yeah.

Q What do you mean, they started to clean it up, what were they doing?

A They emptied some ash trays and the bottles of whiskey that was in the kitchen.

Q Where did they throw out the whiskey in the kitchen?

A Freddie took them out and throwed them at the trash can.

Q Did he take the garbage out?

A Yes, he did.
Q Where were you when he was taking the garbage out?
A I was there sitting down.
Q Where was Inez?
A She was there in the kitchen.
Q How much time did they spend cleaning up the house?
A About three minutes.

(RT 158-186)

. . .

September 11, 1974

SOLIS DIRECT EXAMINATION (Cont.)

Q Okay. What did they do after they cleaned the house?
A They got the guns and went outside.
Q Where were the guns just before they went outside?
A There was a big chair and the guns were on top of that.
A And who took the guns out of the house?
A Freddie and Inez.
Q And what gun did Freddie take?
A Twenty-two.
Q And what gun did Inez take?
A Shotgun.
Q How did Freddie carry the gun out?
A He wrapped it in a white sheet and put it inside his coat.
Q How did Inez carry the shotgun out?
A In the case.
Q I beg your pardon?
A It had a case.
Q Are you sure whether or not she had it in the case or out of the case when she took it out of the house?
A I think they took it out of the house in the case.

. . .

BY MR. BRAUDRICK:

Q Did they go out of the house at the same time?
A Yes, they did.
Q About what time was it when she left the house?
A About almost ten.
Q Okay. What did you do after they went outside the house?
A I went and waited there about two minutes and Freddie had told me to turn out the lights.
Q Did you see them get in the car?
A No.

BY MR. BRAUDRICK:

Q Did you hear the car start up?
A Yeah, I heard the door slam.
Q Okay. How long after they went outside the house did you hear the door slam?
A Just as they went out.
Q Did you hear one door or two doors slam?
A Two doors.
Q Did the car start up then?
A Yeah.
Q Okay, what happened then?
A Then I waited there and then I took off.
Q Did you hear the car drive away?
A Yeah.

. . .

BY MR. BRAUDRICK:

Q I show you People's Number Fourteen for identification. It appears to be a woman's blouse. Can you recognize this blouse?
A Yes.
Q Who was wearing this blouse the last time you saw it?
A Inez.
Q Was the blouse ripped when she walked out with the shotgun that night?
A No.
Q Did she have a coat or anything on top of it?
A I don't think so.
Q Was the blouse ripped while she was in the house cleaning up?
A No.
Q After you got in your car, what route did you take home?
Q Could you see—well, what did you see as you drove down Monterey Street?
A What was the question?
Q What did you see as you drove down Monterey Street?
A I saw Freddie's car with his lights off.
Q Whereabouts did you see Freddie's car?
A I saw it turn. It was about a block away.

(TR 188-199)

CROSS-EXAMINATION

BY MR. GARRY:

Q Mr. Solis, I am going to ask you some questions and if you don't understand my questions, say so and I will repeat it. Is that okay?
A Okay.
Q I talked to you last week, did I not?

A You did.
Q In the District Attorney's office?
A You did.
Q Do you remember my telling you that all I was interested in was the truth?
A Yes.

. . .

Q Now, how long had you known Inez?
A I met her down at the camp about–since February–yeah, about February or March.
Q February or March?
A Yeah.
Q In other words, all you had known her was less than a month?
A Yeah.
Q Is that right?
A Yes.
Q How did you happen to meet her?
A I met her down at Minga's house.
Q Whose house?
A Minga.
Q Minga?
A Yeah.
Q You live with Minga, don't you?
A I do.
Q And now so we will understand where Minga was living, she is living at the Jimenez Camp.* Is that right?
A She is.
Q And you are living at Jimenez Camp?
A Yes.

. . .

Q And that is how you met Inez?
A No.
Q Did you know Inez before you moved in with Minga?
A That is where I met her.
Q That is what I asked, that is how you met Inez?
A Yes.
Q Isn't that correct?
A Yes.
Q Was she living with Minga at the time?
A She was.
Q Then she moved out?

* The Jimenez camp is a farm labor camp managed by a relative of Mike Jimenez.

A Yes.
Q And moved in with––
A Freddie.
Q At Freddie's place. Is that correct?
A Yes.
Q And Freddie was going to move out the first of April, isn't that right, and she was going to take over the apartment?
A I don't know.
Q You don't know that?
A No.
Q Was that discussed in your presence?
A Maybe it was.
Q Maybe it was?
A Yeah.

. . .

Q Now, sir, you came there at six o'clock in the evening before* you had even had dinner. That's what you have told me; isn't that right?
A Yes.
Q And you came there to, as you told the Court and jury Thursday afternoon, you came there to get a lid; is that right?
A Yes.

BY MR. GARRY:

Q How many smokes would that make? How many joints could you put together with a lid of marijuana?
A About thirty.
Q Thirty?
A Yes.

. . .

Q And tell us the conversation you had when you got there with Mr. Medrano?
A When I got there, Inez said that Freddie was–was talking on the phone. So, I went, and I went inside.
Q Now, that doesn't mean anything to me. I'm sure that it's clear in your mind, but let me ask a couple of questions. You went inside where?
A His–where Freddie was calling from.
Q Where was he calling from?
A Inez's room.
Q What?
A Inez's room.

* Referring to the evening of March 19, 1974.

Q Inez's room?
A Yes.
Q Now, the telephone is in Inez's room; is that right?
A Yes.
Q There is no telephone in Freddie's room?
A No.
Q There is a telephone also in the living room; isn't that right?
A Yes.
Q And by the way, did Mr. Medrano know you were going to—was he expecting you on this?
A No.
Q In other words, you just dropped in?
A Yes.
Q You didn't telephone him and tell him you were going to come over, did you?
A No.
Q And you went into his room, and he was telephoning; is that right?
A Yes.
Q How long was he on the telephone?
A About an hour.
Q And what were you doing in that whole hour?
A I was sitting down there.
Q You were sitting on the bed in Inez's room?
A Yes.
Q For a whole hour?
A Yes.
Q While the man was talking to Texas?
A Yes.
Q Was he speaking in English or Spanish?
A Both.
Q Both?
A Yes.
Q And you were listening in on a man talking to—who was he talking to?
A He said his girlfriend or a girl he knew there.
Q And here is a man that you had never seen before except three times before and you walk into his room where he is talking to his girlfriend for an hour and you sit there and listen to the conversation. Is that right?
A Yeah.
Q Is that what you want to tell us?
A Yes.
Q And were you doing anything else in this whole hour?
A We were.
Q What were you doing?

A He rolled up a joint.
Q A joint, that is what you said, isn't it?
A Yes.
Q And you were in a room with him for two hours, isn't that right?
A Yeah.
Q And in the two hours' time, one hour of it you were smoking a joint with him while he was talking on the telephone. Is that right?
A Yes.
Q And the other hour, he was not on the telephone and the two of you were still in the room still smoking a joint. Is that right?
A Yes.

. . .

Q And Mr. Solis, how long did it take to smoke a joint?
A About ten minutes.
Q About ten minutes and in this two hour time you were smoking the joint?
A We smoked two.
Q Two?
A Yes.
Q And as a matter of fact, you smoked several joints, isn't that right, sir?
A Several?
Q Several, more than two?
A No.
Q How do you know it was only two?
A I know.
Q Well, these joints only took twenty minutes and you still have a hundred minutes left, isn't that right?
A Yes.
Q Now, where did these two joints spring from, where did they come from?
A He brought them out.
Q He brought them out?
A Yeah.
Q While he was on the telephone?
A Yes.
Q Where did he get it?
A I don't know. He had it beside the bed.
Q Beside of whose bed?
A Inez' bed.
Q Was it in a can?
A Yeah.
Q It was on the top of the bed?
A He was on one side of the bed and there was a small table there.

BY MR. GARRY:

Q How does marijuana affect you, sir?
A It makes you happy.
Q Anything else?
A No.
Q Does it make you kind of a zombie?
A What is that?
Q It makes you stupid? Does it make you stupid?
A No.
Q You know what I mean by stupid?
A I know.
Q What type of marijuana were you smoking on this particular day?
A I don't know.
Q Weren't you told that you were smoking Colombian weed?
A He said it was Colombian.
Q Who said it was Colombian?
A Yes.
Q Why did you tell me that you didn't know?
A I didn't know.
Q Had you ever smoked Colombian weed before?
A No.
Q It is much more powerful and much stronger than any other type of marijuana, isn't it?
A I don't think so.
Q You don't think so?
A No.

BY MR. GARRY:

Q Sir, after two hours, did you leave the premises?
A Yes.
Q So that—and how did you leave the place?
A We went in my car.
Q You were driving?
A Yes.
Q And were you happy?
A I was.
Q How many cigarettes did you have to smoke, how many joints did you have to smoke before you started feeling the effects of it?
A One.
Q One?
A Yes.
Q And on this particular day, you had three. Isn't that right?
A On that night, yeah.
Q All right. Now, how do you know it is not more than three?
A I know.
Q How do you know?
A I remember.

Q And did you have any alcohol to drink?
A No.
Q You do drink, though, don't you?
A I do.
Q What do you drink when you drink?
A Budweiser.
Q That is beer, isn't it?
A Yes.
Q Do you know Mr. Castillo, don't you?
A A little bit.
Q He testified here that you had something to drink that night. Is that true?
A No.
Q And he is not telling the truth?
A I don't know. I wasn't drinking that night.
Q I know, but he says you were and that is not true what he said. Is that right?
A I didn't hear him.

. . .

Q And where did you go?
A To Gonzales.
Q Where?
A Gonzales.
Q Where did you go in Gonzales?
A We cruised around.
Q And how long did you cruise around?
A About five minutes.
Q In Gonzales?
A Yes.
Q How far is Gonzales from where Mr. Medrano was living on Monterey Street in Soledad?
A About eight miles or six.
Q And did you stop at any place?
A When we were going over there?
Q Yes.
A No.
Q Well, after you cruised around, what did you do?
A We came back to Soledad.
Q You never stopped any place all during that time, was that your testimony?
A We stopped at a liquor store.
Q Aside from the liquor store and while you were cruising around in Gonzales, did you stop any place at all?
A No.

(RT 199-222)

. . .

BY MR. GARRY:

Q Mr. Solis, when we broke for noon recess, you testified that when you went to Gonzales, you didn't stop any place at all until you came to the liquor store where Mr. Medrano bought some things at the liquor store, isn't that right?

A Yes.

Q That is not true, is it?

A It is.

Q Page 165 of his testimony, Your Honor, last Thursday on lines 16 to 21, question by Mr. Braudrick. "Okay. What happened when you got to Gonzales? A We stopped there at a house there and Freddie got off. Q Did you get out of the car? A No. Q Then, what did you do? A We went back to Soledad." Line 22: "Where did you go? We stopped at the liquor store."

Which statement of yours is true, the one that you stopped at Gonzales or the one that you testified here this forenoon and what you testified to right here after lunch?

A What I told you before lunch.

Q I beg your pardon?

A We didn't stop, I thought we did.

Q Then, what you said to the jury on your oath last Thursday was not the truth. Is that right?

A What do you mean?

Q Last Thursday, you said you stopped at Gonzales.

A I told you?

Q I beg your pardon?

A I told you. I told you that we did, but we didn't. We didn't stop anywhere there in Gonzales.

Q Then, what you said Thursday was not true. Is that right?

A Yes.

Q Now, when you stopped at the liquor store, what did Mr. Medrano buy?

A I don't know.

Q Well, isn't it a fact that you told the police and you told the Grand Jury when you testified before them that he bought groceries there, isn't that what you said?

A He came back with a bag from the liquor store.

Q My question is, didn't you tell the police——

A Yes.

Q And didn't you tell the Grand Jury that Mr. Medrano bought some groceries at the liquor store?

A I did.

Q And why do you tell us today that you don't know what he bought?

A Because I don't. I knew it was groceries, but I didn't know what else it was.

Q You didn't have any difficulty telling the Grand Jury that it was groceries, did you?
A No.
Q And yet today you tell me that you don't know what it was? Now, which is the truth?
A He bought something from there.
Q Was it groceries?
A I think so.
Q Now, when you parked your automobile on the right side of his automobile, did anyone call you at that time?
A Yes.
Q Who called you?
A Mike.
Q And where was Mike—when you talk about Mike, you are talking about Mike Jimenez?
A Yes.
Q Where was Mike Jimenez when he called you?
A On the other side of the street.
Q In other words, across the street?
A Yes.
Q Is that correct? Was he in an automobile?
A Yes.
Q And what did he say to you?
A That—"Chofero, I want to talk to you."
Q Who is Chofero?
A I am.
Q Is that a nickname?
A Yes.
Q And you didn't go over to see what he wanted. Is that right?
A No.
Q Why not?
A I didn't thought it was important.
Q Isn't Mike a very close friend of yours?
A He is a friend.
Q Is he a close friend?
A No.
Q How about his brother, Frank?
A He is.
Q He is a close friend, isn't he?
A Yes.
Q And he is still a close friend of yours?
A He is.
Q Is that correct?
A Yes.
Q And how long has he been a close friend of yours?
A Since I met him.

Q That doesn't help me.
A Since 1970.
Q 1970?
A Yes.
Q And how long have you been a friend of Mike Jimenez?
A We used—since that time, too.
Q Since 1970?
A Yeah.
Q Is that right?
A Yeah.

. . .

Q When did you see Frank last?
A About a week ago.
Q And you had a talk with him?
A We talked.
Q Now, sir, you didn't think what Mike had to say was important and that is why you didn't go to see what he wanted. Is that right?
A Yes.
Q And was Mr. Medrano with you at the time?
A He was.
Q And what did you do at that point?
A Freddie went inside and I got out of the car and went inside, too.
Q When you say you went inside, what do you mean by that?
A At Freddie's apartment.
Q Where did you go in Freddie's apartment?
A To Inez' room.

. . .

Q Okay. Now, sir, what terminated or what stopped your smoking pot in the bedroom with the door closed at a quarter to nine?
A Inez came in.
Q Inez came in?
A Yeah. She knocked first and then she came in.
Q What did she say?
A She said that Mike and Louie were there.
Q Was she irritated when she said that?
A She didn't seem happy about it.
Q Now, when you say she didn't seem happy about it, what do you mean by that?
A She wasn't glad that they were there.

. . .

Q What did Freddie do when he came out of the living room?
A He started talking.
Q Didn't he start eating, sir?

A No.

Q Is it your testimony that Mr. Medrano did not eat at that time?

A He had a sandwich when we got there.

Q I beg your pardon?

A He had a sandwich.

Q When?

A When we got there at 8:30.

Q When you arrived there at 8:30, you say he had a sandwich?

A Yes, sir, he did.

Q Where did he eat the sandwich?

A There in the kitchen.

Q In the kitchen. How long did that take?

A About two minutes—three minutes.

Q You mean he just gulped it down?

A Yes.

Q Did you have anything to eat?

A No.

Q So, as I understand it, you have not had anything to eat all afternoon and all evening up to this time, have you?

A I had in the afternoon.

Q When did you have something to eat in the afternoon?

A When I got home.

Q I asked you earlier, this forenoon, if when you finished work did you have anything to eat. You said no; isn't that right?

A Yes.

Q And after you finished—you finished work at five o'clock and at six o'clock you got to Freddie's place; isn't that right?

A Yes.

Q And you told me up to that time you hadn't had anything to eat?

A Yes.

Q When did you eat?

A After I got home.

Q When?

A About 5:15.

Q Well, you want to tell us that you ate after you got home after work; is that right?

A Yes.

Q You know that before noon you told me you had not eaten. You know that, don't you?

A Yes, but I remember I did eat.

Q Isn't it true that you just say anything that comes along without thinking what the facts are?

MR. BRAUDRICK: Objection. That is not a fair question.

THE COURT: No, I think it's a fair question. Objection overruled.

. . .

Q As a matter of fact, he did not eat a sandwich; isn't that right? He sat at the table and ate what Mrs. Garcia had prepared in the kitchen; isn't that right?
A No.
Q That's not right?
A She hadn't—she hadn't done supper yet.
Q At 8:30 at night she hadn't fixed supper yet?
A She said that she had cooked some, but she had it in the refrigerator.
Q Sir—excuse me, Your Honor.
THE COURT: Mr. Solis, do you understand the questions by counsel—anyone or all of counsel have been asking you?
THE WITNESS: I think I do.
THE COURT: Do you have trouble understanding English?
THE WITNESS: No.
THE COURT: I think you said you finished high school.
THE WITNESS: Yes, I did.

. . .

Q At any time that evening not one word was said about drugs; isn't that right, sir?
A We talked about it.
Q Was there one single word said that evening between Mike, Medrano and Castillo about drugs in that argument?
A They did.
Q Tell me what was said?
A He said that they did not want to—him to get into there.
Q Mr. Solis, remember the other afternoon in the District Attorney's office?
A Yes.
Q I asked you the same question, remember that?
A Yes.
Q And you said not one word was said about drugs, isn't that right?
A Yes.
Q Were you lying to me at that time?
A I didn't remember at that time.
Q My question is—I asked you very clearly, do you remember that?
A Yes.
Q I said I want you to tell us the truth, remember that?
A Yes.
Q I said we are not interested in anything but the truth, remember that?
A Yes.
Q And I asked you the question, in that entire evening, was there

one word said about drugs, and you said to me, no. Isn't that right?

A Yes.

. . .

BY MR. GARRY:

Q Mr. Solis, on Monday, April 8, 1974, you were called as a witness by the State of California to be a witness before the Grand Jury at that time, remember that?

A April when?

Q April 8, 1974.

A I think I do.

Q And you testified under oath, isn't that right?

A Yes.

Q You swore, you put up your hand and swore to tell the truth, and nothing but the truth, is that right?

A I did.

Q And they explained what rules of perjury would be, isn't that right?

A I don't think so.

BY MR. GARRY:

Q My question is, you knew since you had sworn to tell the truth that you had to tell the truth, isn't that right?

A I did.

Q And you knew you could be punished for not telling the truth, didn't you?

A I did.

BY MR. GARRY:

Q And they asked you to tell us exactly what the argument was about, isn't that right?

A Yes.

Q Did you at any time tell them that the argument was over drugs?

A I don't think so.

Q Well, you did not, did you?

A I don't think so.

Q Well, you know you did not, isn't that right?

A No.

Q You don't know that you did or didn't?

A I don't know if I did or not.

Q Page 9 of the Grand Jury testimony, if Your Honor please, first and the preceding page, it said, "Do you know what time this was," and you testified it was around nine or eight-thirty or somewhere in there, nine fifteen. Question by Mr. Barnes of the District Attorney's Office. "Q What was the argument about? A About town boys."

Q By that, you mean the people who were native to the town and people who were not native to the town.

A Yes.

Q And then the foreman wants him to speak up, and then he repeats the question. About the town boys and Mr. Barnes asking the question again, who was arguing about this home-town non-home-town town boys?

A Louie and Freddie.

BY MR. GARRY:

Q Now, that night on March 19, after this event happened, did you talk to the police that night?

A No.

Q When did you first talk to the police?

A The next day.

Q That would be on March 20?

A Yes.

Q What did you tell the police the fight was about?

A I didn't mention anything about drugs.

Q You told them exactly what the conversation was about, though, didn't you?

A Yes.

Q And you didn't mention one single time anything about drugs, isn't that right?

A No.

Q And when you talked to Mr. Worthington and Mrs. Richards and myself in the District Attorney's Office, you emphatically said there wasn't one single word about drugs. Is that right?

A Yes.

Q And this afternoon, you say that they were talking about drugs. Is that right?

A Yes.

. . .

Q What time did the fight start?

A About nine.

Q How do you know it was nine?

A About.

Q How do you know it was about nine?

A Because I think it was about nine.

Q Was there a clock in the living room?

A No.

Q So, you are just guessing at the time. Is that right?

A Yes.

Q Who hit first?

A Freddie did.

Q I beg your pardon?

A Freddie.

Q Freddie hit first.

A When they came back, when Freddie came back from outside.
Q Freddie hit him first?
A Freddie threw the first punch.
Q Are you sure?
A Yes.
Q When did you say that for the first time?
A Right now.

MR. GARRY:

Q Did it look good to you?
A No, I wanted to help Freddie, but I couldn't help Freddie at that moment.
Q You couldn't help Freddie because you didn't want to offend Mike who has been your friend since 1970; isn't that right?
A Yes.
Q And his brother was your very close friend since 1970; isn't that right?
A Yes.
Q That's why you didn't want to get into the act at all?
A Yes.
Q And that's why Freddie, after they left, and after he had the heck kicked out of him, he said, "You are a no good S.O.B.," isn't that right? Isn't that right?
A He said something like that.
Q And he ordered you out of the house. He said you weren't worth it to have around or even consider as an acquaintance much less than a friend. That's what he said to you; isn't that right?
A Yes.
Q And he said you are no good. You stand there and allow a 300-pound man to almost kill him and you would do nothing; isn't that right?
A Yes. . . .

I told him I couldn't fight against Mike. He said that Louie lived next door to him because I told him Mike was there and if I got in Mike's way, he will be after me.

BY MR. GARRY:

Q You were scared of Mike, weren't you?
A I was.
Q And you are still scared of the Jimenez family, aren't you?
A No.
Q You are not?
A No.
Q Isn't that why you are changing your story in this case?
A No. The rest of the family are very friendly.
Q You are not scared of the rest of the family?
A No.

Q They are—you are only scared of Mike Jimenez. Is that right?
A A little bit. I was a little bit scared of him.
Q What?
A I was a little bit scared of him.
Q Why, had he ever threatened you?
A No, his size.
Q What?
A His size.
Q You were scared of his size?
A Yes.
Q Now, let's get back to the knife situation. He took that knife before there was ever an argument, isn't that right?
A He did.

. . .

Q Did you ever tell Freddie that Mike Jimenez had taken a knife?
A No.

. . .

Q You just kept that to yourself?
A Yes.
Q Was Inez upset over the fact that he took the knife?
A A little bit.
Q When you say little bit, how did she show the fact that she was upset?
A She didn't like the idea of it.
Q And the knife that we are talking about that was taken from the cabinet is People's Number Four, isn't that right, that I am holding up in the air?
A It is.
Q You had seen Mike Jimenez on other occasions throwing knives, have you not?
A No.
Q Never?
A No.
Q Have you ever seen Mike Jimenez in the possession of a knife on any other occasion?
A No, I knew he had a knife there, one of those he used to throw.

. . .

Q Did you leave at that time when he ordered you out of the house?
A No.
Q Why didn't you?
A Inez told him that I didn't have any part of it.

Q What?

A Inez told him that I didn't have any part in it—his being beaten up.

Q Inez told him that you had not helped Mike and Louie?

A Yes.

Q Is that what you are saying?

A Yes.

Q Isn't it a fact, Mr. Solis, that when Mike and Louie left, Inez Garcia went outside with them?

A She probably went to the doorway.

Q When you say she probably did, she went outside. She closed the door and was not in the room after this; isn't that right?

A I don't think so.

Q What do you mean you don't think so? You are not sure? Isn't that right?

A She probably went to the door to——

Q Probably. We're not interested in probably. We are not interested in guess work. You don't remember whether she went outside or not; is that your testimony?

A She went to the doorway.

Q She went only to the door?

A Yes.

Q Did she talk to Mike and Louie?

A I think she did.

Q What did she say to them?

A She was too far away.

BY MR. GARRY:

Q Was Inez friendly with Mike and Louie when they left?

A I don't know.

Q What do you mean, don't know.

A I didn't hear.

Q You didn't hear her yelling and screaming, did you?

A No, she seemed friendly.

Q So that when Mike and Louie left, Inez was friendly with them?

A She seemed.

Q Outside of telling them earlier that they shouldn't have done what they did to Freddie?

A Yes.

Q And she did that in a nice way, didn't she?

A She probably was glad——

Q What?

A She probably was glad for them to leave.

Q I didn't ask you what you thought. Whether she was glad or not. When she told them that they shouldn't have done this to Freddie, she did it in a nice way, didn't she?

A No.
Q How did she do it? How did she say it?
A I didn't hear her.
Q You didn't hear her?
A Yes.
Q Well, then how do you know she said, "You shouldn't have done this to Freddie," if you didn't hear it?
A When she said that she was in the living room.
Q What?
A When she said that, she was in the living room inside.
THE COURT: Read it back, please.
(Answer read by the reporter.)

MR. GARRY:

Q Well, I'm asking you did she say that in a nice way?
A She was still outside.
Q The question was did she say it in a nice way? . . .
THE WITNESS: In a nice way? No.

MR. GARRY:

Q How did she say it? Tell us how she said it?
A A little bit mad.
Q What?
A A little bit mad.
Q A little bit mad?
A Upset.
Q She said, "You shouldn't have done that to Freddie."
A To Freddie? No.
Q That's the way she said it, didn't she?
A No.
Q Tell us how she said it. You were there. I wasn't there.
A She said that, "You shouldn't have done it—beat him up."
Q That's all she said?
A Yes.
Q Nothing more?
A No.
Q And about five minutes later they left; is that right?
A Yes.
Q And you don't know what was said during that five-minute period?
A No.
Q And you don't know whether she went outside with—when they left or not, do you?
A She went to the doorway.
Q What?
A She went to the doorway.

Q How do you know that? How do you know she only went to the door?

A I think that's where I saw her.

Q What?

A I think that's where I saw her.

Q You think that's where you saw her?

A Yes.

Q But you don't know, do you?

A No.

THE COURT: All right. We'll take the afternoon recess. Fifteen minutes, ladies and gentlemen.

(Short recess.)

. . .

Q Do you remember when Freddie Medrano here, who is sitting here, looking at you, do you remember him asking you where is Inez?

A No.

Q Don't you remember that?

A No.

Q And you said, Inez is outside with Louie and Mike?

A No.

Q Are you positive of that?

A I am.

. . .

BY MR. GARRY:

Q Did you ever make the statement to the police that I am not sure about the shotgun that I saw Inez load the .22 rifle with the bullets and then Freddie took the rifle outside the apartment. Did you ever make that statement to the police?

A I probably did.

Q What?

A I did.

Q Did you—you did make that statement, didn't you?

A Yes.

Q You did?

A Yes.

Q All right. You told this district attorney this morning that there was no tear on the blouse?

A That day.

Q That is what you testified to; is that correct?

A That is.

Q It is a fact, is it not, that you did not look to see if there was any tear?

A I would have known it if there was a tear.

Q My question is you did not look to see whether there was a tear, isn't that correct?

A I did.

Q You did look?

A Yes.

Q It is true, is it not, that you never noticed any tear?

A I didn't notice.

Q And you didn't notice because you didn't look to see if there was any tear, isn't that correct?

A I did look.

Q I beg your pardon?

A I did look.

Q Page 13 of the Grand Jury testimony, Your Honor.

THE COURT: Very well.

BY MR. GARRY:

Lines 5 to 8 where the district attorney, Mr. Barnes, is asking this question. Question. Did you notice whether her clothes were torn or not? Answer. No. Question. You didn't see them or didn't notice? Answer. I didn't notice.

Q You gave that answer to that question, didn't you?

A I did.

Q Was that the truth?

A Yes.

Q Mr. Solis, no gun or guns were brought out by Inez or Freddie until there was a telephone call that came in from Soledad, isn't that right?

A Yes.

Q Did she say she was just threatened? Her life was just threatened again?

A No.

Q Nothing like that was mentioned, is that your testimony?

A Yes.

Q Didn't you tell me in the District Attorney's office last week that after the telephone call and during the telephone call, Inez said that, "My life has been threatened, and I was ordered to leave the area."

A No.

Q You deny making that statement to me?

A I do.

Q Do you recall Inez making a telephone call immediately after the call from Soledad?

A She did.

Q Do you know who she called?

A Her family, I think.

Q How do you know it was her family?
A She said that she had talked to her family.
Q You told the police she called her lawyer?
A Yes, I did. First, I——
Q Which is it now, the lawyer or her family?
A I don't know who she talked to.
Q Then why did you say that it was her family then?
A I thought it was her family.
Q But originally she said she had called her lawyer; isn't that right?
A Yes.
Q Now, which is it?
A She wanted to talk to her lawyer.
Q As a matter of fact, she called and said, "My life is threatened." Didn't she?
A No.
Q Did you hear the conversation?
A She talked——
Q My question is, did you hear the conversation?
A Yes.
Q Do you know what she said?
A I do.
Q What did she say?
A She said someone had come and beat her up in her house, and if she'd got into trouble, to let them know that she had.

. . .

THE WITNESS: She said she was calling them to let them know that someone had come and beat her up in her house, and if she did something–got into trouble that to let them know to bail her out.

. . .

Q Do you remember what the police said to you, what else happened, and you stated Inez called the lawyer in Los Angeles?
A I think she was saying that to Freddie. She called because "I want someone to find out in case something happens," and then later a telephone call came and I thought it was a tip. Did you give that answer to the police officer?
Q Did you give that answer to the police officer?
A I gave him something like that.
Q So, what you told the police officer is not what you heard on the telephone, you said to the police that that is what Inez said to Freddie, isn't that right?
A That is what I told to the police is what I remembered that night.
Q My question is, isn't that what you told the police that first time

that you talked to them about this that what you heard is Inez telling Freddie?

A I think that was.

Q So, it wasn't what you heard on the telephone at all because you didn't hear anything on the telephone?

A She told us what she told.

Q But, a few minutes ago you told me that is what you heard on the telephone?

A I did.

Q You weren't telling the truth, were you?

A I was.

. . .

(TR 223-297)

CROSS-EXAMINATION

BY MR. WORTHINGTON:

Q I'm asking you what you told us in the district attorney's office last Wednesday. Is it not a fact, Mr. Solis, that you told us specifically that the argument was over whether home boys were better than outsiders and that Mike and Louie were laughing at Freddie because he was a tuberculosis victim?

A No.

Q You don't remember telling us that?

A I've told you that.

Q You did tell us that?

A But the first part of that I told you before.

Q And you told us that nothing else was involved, didn't you?

A I told you something about drugs.

Q You are sure about that?

A Yes.

Q When was the first time you ever told anybody about that?

A The second time I talked to the policeman.

Q You didn't tell the police the first time, did you?

A No.

Q You didn't tell the grand jury?

A I think I did.

Q The fact of the matter is that you didn't hear anything about drugs in the argument, isn't that true?

A No.

Q As a matter of fact you just made that up and that was your conclusion that drugs had something to do with why they were arguing, isn't that true?

A I knew something about it.

Q Isn't—as a matter of fact after this incident occurred you have been talking to Louis Castillo, haven't you?
A No.
Q You haven't?
A I talked to him.
Q You did talk to him?
A Yes.
Q When was the last time you talked to him?
A Sunday.
Q Sunday?
A Yes.
Q Before you testified?
A No.
Q After you started testifying?
A Yes.
Q All right. When was the time before that that you talked to him?
A Before that?
Q Yes.
A Only when we were waiting in the jury room.
Q While you were waiting in the jury room before you testified?
A Yes.
Q Is that right?
A Yes.
Q But, after you testified to the grand jury?
A Yes.
Q All right. And while you were in the jury room talking to Castillo he told you his story was going to be the whole thing was over drugs, didn't he?
A No.
Q That is when you made this up about drugs, isn't it?
A No.
Q You didn't hear a word about drugs but you took his word for it and you followed his story, isn't that true?
A No.
Q Did you talk to Castillo before you talked to the police for the second time?
A No.
Q You had not talked to them—him?
A No.
Q Do you know Frank Jimenez, don't you?
A Yes.
Q He lives at the Jimenez camp where you do?
A Yes.
Q You have talked to him several times since March 19th, haven't you?

A Yes.

(TR 307-309)

SEPTEMBER 12, 1974

BY MR. WORTHINGTON:

Q In the conversation or argument that Louie and Freddie had, in your presence, you didn't hear them say any words about drugs, did you?

A No.

Q None at all?

A No.

Q Your statements to the effect that they were talking about drugs or about dealing are only your conclusions, aren't they?

A No.

Q You didn't hear anything about drugs?

A I heard before.

Q You had heard some other time?

A Yes.

Q You told us on Wednesday last week—you told me and Mr. Garry and Mrs. Richards, did you not, that you did not know anything about any alleged drug dealing by Freddie Medrano.

A I told you he was dealing.

Q Isn't it a fact that you asked him if he could find you one small lid of marijuana?

A I did.

Q And he couldn't find you even one lid of marijuana, could he?

A He tried.

Q He tried, and he couldn't do it, could he?

A Yes.

Q This is the man you call a big drug dealer?

A Not big, small.

(TR 319-320)

RE-CROSS EXAMINATION

BY MR. GARRY:

Q Now, I asked you the question when did he mention he—when did he* discuss with you as to whether you were scared in the Grand Jury when you gave the testimony on April the 8th, 1974, and you said yesterday, didn't you?

A Yeah.

---

* Mr. Garry is referring to Mr. Braudrick, the prosecutor, and is examining Mr. Solis on his discussions with the prosecutor regarding his testimony.

Q That's not true, is it?
A It is.
Q He asked you yesterday?
A Yeah.
Q If you were scared before the Grand Jury?
A I was nervous.
Q Before the Grand Jury?
A Yes.
Q He mentioned the Grand Jury?
A No.
Q But you just got through telling me when I asked you the question when was the last time he asked you the questions or discussed with you whether you were scared before the Grand Jury——
A He didn't actually say scared.
Q He didn't mention Grand Jury either, then, did he?
A No.
Q And you lied to this jury already, haven't you, in the last five minutes?
A Yes.
Q Sir, you also lied to me too, didn't you, when you told me that there was not one word of any drug mentioned at any time in the conversation between Louie, Freddie, and Mike?
A I did.
Q And you think that's funny, don't you?
A Yeah.

(TR 356)

. . .

BY MR. GARRY:
Q Mr. Solis, so we would be perfectly clear, you made one statement to the police the next day, did you not?
A Yes.
Q And that was March 20th, the day after; is that correct?
A Yes.
Q You did not mention anything about smoking marijuana at that time?
A They didn't ask me.
Q Well, anyway, not one word was mentioned.
A Yes.
Q You say they didn't ask you?
A Yeah.
Q Right?
A Yes.
Q Okay. Now, the next time that you answered questions, you saw the police again on the 25th of March, did you not?

A Yes.

Q At that time, you said that you smoked a joint?

A Yes.

Q Is that correct?

A Yes.

Q And it's at that point that you say Mr. Braudrick was asking you these questions?

A Yes, I think it was.

Q And it was at that time that he told you you did not have to worry about saying that you smoked marijuana, or words to that effect; is that correct?

A Something like that, yes.

MR. GARRY: At this time, Your Honor, if you please, I would like to stipulate from the District Attorney's office that he was not present, and that he never asked this man one single question on that day. That is on the 25th of March at Soledad.

MR. BRAUDRICK: That's correct. The stipulation is, Your Honor, that Sergeant Perez, Mr. Santos and Investigator Rodriguez from the District Attorney's office was present on the 25th at Soledad.

THE COURT: All right.

MR. WORTHINGTON: And that Mr. Braudrick was not. . . .

THE COURT: Mr. Braudrick was not there.

MR. WORTHINGTON: I entered into the stipulation also.

THE COURT: All right.

MR. GARRY:

Q Now sir, it's a fact, is it not, that the reason that you are nervous and you say you are scared at times is because you have lied to the police from the very inception as to the fact that you have denied seeing the shooting and being present at the scene of the shooting?

A No.

Q As a matter of fact, sir, when you testified that you left in your car at ten minutes—at eight minutes to—ten minutes to ten on your car clock and you were at—within one block of where that car that you claim is the Medrano car making a left hand turn from Monterey Boulevard into First Street at that time, you had already seen what had taken place on the street, on Monterey Boulevard, and you have been lying about it all this time, haven't you, sir?

A No.

MR. GARRY: I have no further questions.

. . .

(RT 364-65)

The Prosecution's next witness was Elmer Moran who lived in an upstairs apartment across the street from the scene of the shooting.

ELMER MORAN, SWORN

DIRECT EXAMINATION

BY MR. BRAUDRICK:

Q Mr. Moran, where do you live?

A 1201 Monterey Street.

Q And that's in the City of Soledad?

A That's right.

Q And how long have you lived there?

A About twelve years.

Q And you were living there on March 19, 1974?

A Yes.

Q What's your occupation?

A Farm laborer.

Q Okay. Bringing your attention to about ten o'clock or shortly before ten o'clock on the night of March 19, 1974, what were you doing at about that time?

A I had come back from a meeting in Greenfield.

Q Were you at home?

A Yes.

Q Now, did anything attract your attention shortly before ten o'clock?

A Yes.

Q Okay. What was that?

A I heard shots.

Q Do you know how many shots you heard?

A About six or seven.

Q Okay. What did you do after you heard the shots?

A I went to the window, opened the curtains. I didn't see anything and then I walked to the front window and opened the curtains.

Q Okay. What did you see?

A An old model car parked across the street.

Q Do you know what kind of a car it was?

A Chevrolet.

Q Did you hear anything?

A I heard a woman's laughter.

. . .

Q What did you see the car do?

A Pulled back, then take off with the lights off—turned off on First Street.

Q Okay. What did you do after you saw the car pull away?

A Closed the curtains and went back inside to where the wife was laying in bed.

Q Okay. What direction did the car go in?
A South.

CROSS-EXAMINATION

BY MR. GARRY:

Q And where were you when you heard the six or seven shots?
A I was in the bedroom with the wife.
Q And were you talking to her?
A About the meeting, yes.
Q And it was about 9:40 when you heard the shots?
A Yes.
Q All right. Now, tell us what you did after you heard the six or seven shots?
A Well, I asked her where the kids were. She said they were all supposed to be inside the house. So, I went to check the rest of the rooms and they were all there. That's when I went and opened the front living room windows.
Q And what did you see?
A The car.
Q And was the car standing still or was it moving?
A It was standing still at the time.
Q I see. And what else did you observe besides the automobile?
A I saw a person standing by the car—the lefthand side, and go around to the passenger's side and get in.
Q And did you see what that person looked like?
A No.
Q Could you tell us whether that person that went into the passenger's side was a woman or a man?
A I couldn't tell.
Q And that's because it was dark?
A Yes.

. . .

Q All right. Now, were the lights* off or on?
A They were off.
Q There were no lights at all? Is that correct?
A No.
Q Did you recognize the automobile? Had you ever seen it before?
A No.
Q Now, you said you heard the laughter of a woman, is that right?
A Yes.

---

* The lights referred to are those of Medrano's automobile.

Q And when did you hear the laughter of a woman? At what point?

A When this person was standing by the car.

Q Now, was this a woman's laughter you heard or a girl's laughter you heard?

A I don't—it was just a feminine voice.

Q Three or four days, well, later, the police came and talked to you, and you told them that, you told them what you had observed?

A Yes.

Q And did you remember telling them at that time, that it was a girl's laughter that you heard?

A No, I don't remember.

. . .

Q Do you recall, now that you have read and refreshed your memory with the police report that you used the word, it was a girl's laughter that you heard; isn't that right? That's what you told the police at that time?

A I guess, yes.

Q That's what you did tell them, isn't that right? And at that time, your recollection was that it was a girl's laughter, was it not?

A (No response.)

Q Please answer audibly, so the report can——

A Yes.

. . .

MR. GARRY:

Q Now, did you go to the—to the scene where the—where the shooting had taken place?

A After I called the police, yes.

Q You went out there, and who was there—strike that. Did you go to the body where Mr.—where the body was laying?

A About three feet from it.

Q And who was there with you, if you know?

A I went there alone.

Q David Farrell didn't go with you, did he?

A He was already there.

Q Did you, sir, see a knife in and around the body?

A No.

Q When you were within three feet of there?

A No.

Q Did anybody while you were there touch the body?

A No.

Q No one went near the body to see whether he was—whether the body was still alive or dead?

A I don't remember.

Q You say you don't remember. Why? Is that because of the excitement that you——

A Right.

Q That you might have not been able to recollect? Is that right?

A Right.

. . .

Q How soon after you arrived, did the ambulance arrive?

A It must have been fifteen–sixteen minutes.

Q In other words, did the police and the ambulance get there about the same time?

A Well, the police got there first.

Q Then the ambulance came after that?

A Yes.

Q How soon after that?

A Oh, I don't know. About seven or eight minutes.

(TR 375-388)

The prosecution's next witness, Juan Carbajal, testified to the arrival of Inez Garcia and Freddie Medrano at the house of his aunt, Rosa Bracamonte, shortly after the time of the shooting. The prosecution sought to establish by Carbajal's testimony and others present in the Bracamonte residence that Inez Garcia received her bruises and became disheveled after the shooting.

JUAN CARBAJAL, SWORN

DIRECT EXAMINATION

BY MR. BRAUDRICK:

Mr. Carbajal, where do you live?

A Hereford, Texas, or that's where I have my residence home.

Q What's your occupation?

A Truck driver, tractor driver, field worker, everything.

Q Okay. Were you living and staying in the City of Soledad when Mike Jimenez was killed?

A Yes.

Q Why were you in the City of Soledad?

A Well, my grandmother was in the hospital and we were waiting to see what was going to turn up. We came on vacation from Hereford.

Q Do you have relatives besides your grandmother in Soledad?

A Yes, sir.

Q Who is that?
A My aunt, my uncles.
Q Now, do you know William and Rosa Bracamonte?
A Yes, my aunt and my uncle.
Q And Alicia Alcaraz?
A What?
Q Alicia Alcaraz?
A Yes, my aunt.
Q Now, the night that Mike was shot—Mike Jimenez was shot—were you at your aunt and uncle's or William and Rosa's house?
A Yes, sir.
Q Okay. Where is that house located?
A It's Monterey Street, I think, some place.
Q In the City of Soledad?
A Yes, sir.
Q What—did you have an argument with your uncle that night?
A Yes.

MR. BRAUDRICK:

Q About what time did the argument take place?
A I don't know about what time, but there was a police officer there in a couple of minutes, after that.
Q Okay. Who else was there before the police got there?
A Before? It was me, my Uncle Willie, Rosa, and Alicia, and the small ones.
Q What do you mean by the small ones?
A Well, Rosa's babies. They were asleep. . . .
Q Who called the police?
A Rosa.
Q Did you get—did you fight with anybody?
A Willie.
Q Before the police came?
A Willie.
Q Did you actually get engaged in fighting one another?
A Well, I didn't get a chance to hit him, but I grabbed hold of him, bounced him a couple of times against the wall. That's about it.
Q You say you were angry at that point?
A Yes, sir.
THE COURT: This is your uncle you are talking about?
THE WITNESS: Yes, sir.

. . .

Q Okay. How long—how long were the police there?
A Not very long. They asked him to get out, then they had a little talk and he had to leave on an emergency, I think.
Q Why did the police have to leave?

A Well, I think they said there was a shooting somewhere. . . .

. . .

Q Okay. What did you do then?

A Well, we kept on arguing, because we were going to start it all over again, and—well, and Alicia told me to settle down and then Inez and Freddie came—well, they stopped at the door and knocked. Can't say they stopped, but they knocked anyway.

Q How long after the police left did Inez and Freddie come to your house?

A Oh, it couldn't have been more than five minutes, at the least, I think.

Q Had you met Freddie or Inez before that?

A No.

Q What did Freddie look like when he came in the house?

A Well, first place, I thought it was a husband and wife fight. . . .

THE WITNESS: He had a little scratch, I think it was, on the right side, or left side—somewhere around here (indicating) a little scratch. Just a fingernail scratch.

BY MR. BRAUDRICK:

Q What did Mr. Medrano say when he came in your house?

A Well, the way I recollect it, it was—he didn't say nothing at first, and then—well, Inez said, "I shot a—Mike." Whoever Mike was, I didn't know, and she said, "I shot him five times in the heart and once in the forehead," and then, if I might be mistaken on this, I don't know. It's been quite a few months ago. I recollect that I thought Freddie had said—turned to Willie and said, "Hey, there, Willie, hit her, Willie." But I might be wrong. But then, I might be wrong on that.

. . .

BY MR. BRAUDRICK:

Q Did Inez and Freddie come in together?

A Yes, sir.

Q Okay. Did Freddie say anything after you think he said to Willie to hit her, Willie?

A No, I don't think so. Not at that point.

Q Did Inez say anything then?

A We were talking, and Inez—I think Inez turned to him—to Freddie, and asked him to hit her, and Freddie wouldn't do it, and then she turned to me and asked me to hit her, but I couldn't do it, 'cause I didn't even know the girl. And my aunt, —well, I turned to look out the window, and my aunt told me to hit her. So, I said, "Hold her," and turned around and struck her.

Q What did you hit her with?

A My hand——fist.

Q Your fist?
A Yes.

. . .

BY MR. BRAUDRICK:

Q Okay. What did Inez do after you hit her?
A She almost hit the ground after I hit her.
Q Okay. What kept her from hitting the ground?
A I think it was Alicia. I don't know how she got back there or anything. Alicia or—and Freddie were back there and stopped her from hitting the ground.
Q What happened then?
A Well, I got back to get ready to hit another punch.
Q You got ready to hit another punch?
A Yes, sir.
Q Okay. Then what happened to Inez?
A Well, Inez got up and they asked her—let's see—I think she said, "I have a little slight headache," and they took her into the kitchen and give her an aspirin.

. . .

BY MR. BRAUDRICK:

Q I show you a blouse, People's Number Fourteen. Can you recognize this blouse at all?
A Yes, sir.
Q Where did you first see this blouse?
A On Inez.
Q And when you first saw it, was it ripped like this?
A Yes, sir.
Q Was her body exposed at all?
A Well, not that I could see, sir, but like I say, I wasn't examining her—not after she came in like that. Umm, she could have been—well, her hair was all damaged up. I couldn't say she was hurt in any way.

. . .

BY MR. BRAUDRICK:

Q Did you say anything to Inez Garcia before you hit her?
A Well, first place, I throw my coat on top of her. I usually wear a sport coat or a suit or another, and I put my coat on her. I threw it at her. Told her to cover up.
Q Why did you do that?
A Asked her to cover up.
Q What did you want her to cover up?
A Her breasts.
Q Were they showing through the ripped blouse?
A One side of it.
Q Was she doing anything to cover herself up?
A No, sir.

Q Did she say anything at that point?

A I think she said they tried to rape her, as I recall.

Q Who said that? Did she say that, or did Freddie say that?

A Inez.

Q Did Freddie say anything then?

A Well, not at that time, but later on, he said that–that–going back for the rifle, and we were driving around too. They went back and got the rifle, and then he said they parked, and she just swang the door open and shot him.

. . .

Q How long was Inez in the kitchen?

A Not very long, and then–yeah–Freddie yelled up to Alicia, my aunt, to see if they could stay with her–spend the night. In other words, at her place, and then–well, I don't think Alicia heard, 'cause she did not answer, and I went into the kitchen, and asked her. Alicia just yelled back, "Yes."

Q Was this when Inez was in the kitchen?

A Yes.

Q Okay. What did Freddie do after that?

A Well, I don't know, 'cause soon as we came out, me, Alicia, and Inez got out of the kitchen. We just got up and left.

Q Where did you go?

A Alicia's place, my aunt.

Q Did anybody say anything to you before you left?

A Yeah, they–Freddie told me it was his carida–like girlfriend–carida. Or the way I understand it, there in Texas, it's–well, it means being married and having an affair with another one–carida, but it all depends on where you are at.

Q Freddie said that?

A Yes.

. . .

BY MR. BRAUDRICK:

Q What did he say before he said the word, carida?

A Well, 'cause I asked–I told Willie–well, that's–that's–I told Willie that's a low excuse for a man, 'cause–well, up there, like I said, well, I was talking to Willie at the time. "Anybody hit my wife, I'm going to drag the floor with him."

Q Okay. What did Freddie say?

A Well, that's when he told me it wasn't his wife.

Q And what did he say exactly?

A His carida.

Q Referring to Inez?

A Well, I would imagine so. I think so. . . .

THE WITNESS: Well, the way I understand it, here, everybody says carida is my girlfriend. If she's a girlfriend to me, she's my querida. Out there in Texas, it's a lover. Having an affair with someone that's married.

. . .

Q Okay. What did you do–what did you do when you got to Alicia's house?

A Well, like we got down. We went in the inside the house and we–well, she was waiting for them. I know that much, and then the babies were in the other room and she asked me to go see the babies, and I went to see the babies, and then I was back. And at that time, Freddie and Alicia–I mean–excuse me. Take that off. Freddie and Inez were at the door together.

Q Could you describe what Inez looked like when she was at the door there at Alicia's house?

A Yes, she still had her blouse torn open. Well, her hair, I think, she ran her hands through it.

Q Were her breasts exposed then?

A Yes, sir.

Q Okay. What did you do when they were at the door?

A Well, they stood there with Alicia a little while, then she sent me in to the babies' room again, and she told me, stay there with the babies.

. . .

Q Do you know whether or not Inez and Freddie left the house after they came into the house?

A Freddie did leave the house with Alicia, but Inez did not.

Q Did Freddie say anything before he left the house?

A No, they were going to go get a pack of cigarettes for Inez.

. . .

BY MR. BRAUDRICK:

Q What did you do after Alicia and Freddie left the house?

A Well, I asked Inez to cover up. First place, because she had taken off my coat.

Q She was still sitting there with her breasts exposed?

A Yes, sir.

Q What did she do when you asked her to cover up?

A She said, it was just a little bit. Wouldn't matter and I asked her to cover up, 'cause she was showing all of it, and she asked me if I could find something to put on, and I went–I was looking for a safety pin. Yes, a safety pin, and I don't know if I found a safety pin or a bobbie pin, but I gave her something. I don't know whether it was a bobbie pin or a safety pin.

Q Did she then pin her blouse up, then?

A Yes, sir.

. . .

Q Okay. Then what happened?

A Well, at that time, red lights were outside and Alicia just slammed in the house. Didn't even knock that time, and there was a policeman outside.

Q Okay. What happened then?

A Well, Alicia told Inez that the policemen were outside, and Inez said, "Okay." She got the rifle and stood up, grabbed it by the barrel and stood up and then the other policeman came in. I do not know what his name was. He came in and Inez just handed him the rifle, and Inez told him that she had shot—I don't know whether she said the boy, or whether she gave his name.

(RT 392-410)

CROSS-EXAMINATION

BY MR. GARRY:

Q I asked you one question and that was—and you told me, did you not, that Inez never once asked anybody to hit her, you said that, is that right?

A The first, uh—that is what I said.

Q Isn't that what you told me?

A That she did not start the conversation in the first place.

Q No, no, my question is——

A Later on, she turned on—like I told you, she turned around to Freddie and asked him to hit her.

Q Isn't it a fact, sir, that you told me yesterday morning when I asked you the question, you told me that Inez Garcia never once asked anybody to hit her. Didn't you tell me that?

A No, sir.

Q You didn't tell me that?

A No, sir.

Q I want you to know you are under oath.

A Yes, sir.

Q Do you know that?

A Yes, sir.

Q All right. Now, isn't it a fact that you talked to Alicia during the noon hour?

A Yes, sir.

Q And you told her that you don't remember what had happened and you don't remember who said what, and you asked her?

A No, sir.

BY MR. GARRY:

Q Isn't it a fact you told her that you don't remember what anybody said and you called her to find out if she remembers? And she told you that she didn't remember the details herself and you said then maybe later on, we should be discussing this. Didn't you have that kind of conversation with Alicia?

A I called her and I asked her, but not about this, no, sir. I asked her who was the one that started and she told me that she said it. It might be her and I said I didn't recollect it that way.

Q All right. What is it that you asked her and what is it that she said to you at noon today?

A I asked if she remembered who was the one that started the conversation about hitting each other, whether it was Freddie or Inez and she said she didn't remember. She had put that out of her mind, it might have been Freddie and it might have been Inez, and at the same time, it might have been her.

Q It might have been her, your Aunt Alicia, is that right?

A That is what she told me.

Q All right. Now, why was it necessary, sir, for you to call her?

A Well, in the first place, I called her because like the District Attorney knows, I am desperate to get out of here. I am desperate to get back home.

. . .

Q Did you have a conversation with Mr. Worthington during the noon hour?

A Yes, sir.

Q Please tell the jury what that conversation was about?

A That was a conversation about me and Freddie being together yesterday. . . .

BY MR. GARRY:

Q What else was the conversation about?

A I told him that I was going to call Alicia.

Q Yes. You told Mr. Worthington that. Is that right?

A Yeah, and he asked me not to call her.

Q He told you not to call her?

A Yes, sir.

Q And you asked him for a dime, did you not?

A No, sir.

. . .

Q Why was it necessary for you to say to him that you wanted to talk to Alicia?

A In the first place, he came to me and told me about a little visit I had with Freddie, and I told him, like I am going to tell you the same thing, I said since the beginning, I am going to still keep on saying it because it is the truth and I am not about to stick my neck out for anybody else.

Q Did you tell Freddie you were shot at last week at Soledad?

A Yes, sir.
Q Were you shot at at Soledad?
A No, sir.
Q You lied to him?
A Yes, sir.
Q What are you trying to do, brag?
A No, sir.
Q Do you want to show that you are a big shot?
A No, sir.
MR. BRAUDRICK: Your Honor, I object.
THE COURT: This is not a very fair method of attacking this young man. Let's give him a chance to explain. That is not the method.
MR. GARRY: I will let him explain.
THE WITNESS: That way, he wouldn't——
THE COURT: There is no question asked. Let him ask a proper type of question and the Court will let you answer it.
MR. GARRY: I have no further questions.

CROSS-EXAMINATION

BY MR. WORTHINGTON:

Q You were being quite honest on direct examination here today when you said you don't really remember if Freddie asked anybody to do anything, weren't you being honest?
A Yes, sir.
Q You don't remember, do you?
A Well, sir, it has been a couple of months ago and the way I recollect it, he was the one that started it.
Q Juan, you are telling the truth to the best you can remember, aren't you?
A Sir?
Q You are now telling the truth as best you can, aren't you?
A Yes, sir.
Q And it has been a long time, hasn't it?
A Yes, sir.
Q And when you started out here on direct examination, you were telling the truth the best you could when you said you really didn't remember?
A Yes, sir.
Q And you don't, do you?
A I can't really remember.
MR. WORTHINGTON: I have nothing further.
THE COURT: Re-direct.

RE-DIRECT EXAMINATION

BY MR. BRAUDRICK:

Q Is it you can't remember who brought up the hitting Inez first, is that what you can't remember?

A Yes, sir.

Q You don't know if it was Freddie that brought it up first or Inez or Alicia?

A Yes, sir.

Q Can you remember whether or not Freddie asked for somebody to hit Inez?

A The way I recollect, Freddie was the one that asked Willie.

Q You don't remember whether or not he was the first one who asked?

A I do not remember whether he was the first one or not.

Q Thank you.

RE-CROSS-EXAMINATION

BY MR. WORTHINGTON:

Q Do you recall what Inez said when she came into Rosie's house, what she first said?

A Yes, sir.

Q What was that?

A I shot Mike.

Q Did she say anything after that?

A Yeah.

Q What was that, I shot him five times in the heart and once in the forehead.

Q What did she say after that?

A Like I said, I don't recollect if she said it or if Freddie said it, but I think the way I recollect, Freddie was the one that said it.

Q All right. After she said she shot Mike, did she say why she had shot Mike?

A Well, a little after my aunt asked her why.

Q Your aunt asked, was that the next person that spoke after she explained she shot Mike and how many times?

A Uh huh.

Q Your aunt said why, or something to that effect?

A Yes.

Q Was that Alicia or Rosie?

A Alicia.

Q And then did Inez explain that she shot him because she had been raped by him?

A They tried to rape her, she said.

Q All right. And that was before anybody had any discussion about Inez being hit in the face. Is that right?

A Yes.

Q All right. She said Mike and somebody else had tried to rape her and did she name the people?

A She did not name them.

Q She said the person she shot had raped her?

A No, like I say, she said they tried to rape me.

Q She used the word they?

A Yeah.

Q All right. Then, Alicia said to Inez that you don't look good enough or something to that effect, didn't she?

A I can't recollect that, sir.

Q Didn't she say nobody is going to believe you?

A No, sir.

Q Didn't Alicia say the cops around here don't believe women when they say they have been raped?

A No, sir.

Q Wasn't it Alicia's idea to hit Inez in the face so that the cops would believe her?

A No, we come back to that, like I said, I could not recollect that. Like I said, I recollect that Freddie was the one that started that conversation.

Q That was––

A –but then she might have and then he might have or Inez might have.

Q As a matter of fact, Alicia told Inez that nobody was going to believe her and that somebody ought to do something about it, and it was Alicia who asked your Uncle Willie to hit her, isn't that true?

A Well, I can't remember that part.

Q You don't remember?

A No, sir.

Q Do you remember your Uncle Willie refusing to hit her?

A Yes, sir.

Q Then Alicia asked you to hit her, didn't she?

A After she–I think she turned around and asked Freddie to hit her, and Freddie wouldn't do it.

Q Freddie refused also?

A Yeah.

Q You remember that?

A Yeah.

Q Then, Alicia asked you to hit her?

A They asked me to hit her and I wouldn't do it, and then I turned around and faced the window and she said, hit her.

Q Who, Alicia said that?

A Alicia.

Q Then you did it?

A Yeah, I turned around and hit her.

MR. WORTHINGTON: I have no other questions.

RE-CROSS-EXAMINATION

BY MR. GARRY:

Q Now, sir, why did you hit Inez Garcia?

A Because my aunt told me to.

Q Could you figure out why you were socking her?

A No, sir.

Q Did it make any sense to you?

A No, sir.

Q Don't you think she was in a bad shape enough without you slugging her?

A Yes, sir.

Q But, you went ahead and slugged her anyway?

A Yes, sir.

Q How long have you known your aunt?

A Not very long, sir, that had been my second time that I had seen them.

Q The second time that you had seen your Aunt Alicia?

A The second time that I had seen either one of them.

Q And your Aunt Alicia and Aunt Rosa?

A Yes, sir.

Q And just because your Aunt Alicia said slug her, you slugged her?

A Yes, sir.

MR. GARRY: I have no further questions.

THE COURT: Any questions? I think I will ask this question myself. We are sort of left up in the air, you only had met your aunt twice?

THE WITNESS: Yes, sir.

THE COURT: You thought Mrs. Garcia had already been beaten up or otherwise injured?

THE WITNESS: Yes, sir.

THE COURT: And still simply because the aunt told you to, you slugged her?

THE WITNESS: Yes, sir.

THE COURT: You think that makes sense?

THE WITNESS: Well, sir, it depends on what side of it you see.

When my parents leave me in the care of somebody, I have to do just as they tell me to.

THE COURT: Oh, I see.

THE WITNESS: In other words, when I am in charge of my aunt and uncle, I have to do exactly what they tell me as if they were my father and mother.

(TR 414-433)

The next prosecution witness was John P. Bowden, a criminologist employed by the California Justice Department, who testified that in his expert opinion the shell casings recovered by the police at the scene of the crime were fired from Inez Garcia's .22 rifle. On cross-examination, Mr. Bowden indicated that the bullets recovered had not been fired from a shotgun.

JOHN P. BOWDEN
CROSS-EXAMINATION

BY MR. WORTHINGTON:

Q The markings on the bullets, the casing you stated were consistent with having been fired from a .22 rifle, were they not?
A Yes.
Q They were not consistent with having been fired from a shotgun?
A That's correct.
Q You didn't examine any other bullets that might have been fired from a shotgun, did you?
A No, I did not.
Q Thank you.

. . .

(TR 443)

The prosecution's next witness was teen-ager, David Ferrel, who together with a girlfriend, Dima Gallardo, was chatting on the porch of Dima's house down the block from the shooting.

DAVID FERREL, SWORN
DIRECT EXAMINATION

BY MR. BRAUDRICK:

Q David, how old are you?
A Seventeen–eighteen.

Q What is your occupation?
A I go to Gonzalez High School.

. . .

BY MR. BRAUDRICK:

Q Bringing your attention to March 19, 1974, where were you living? . . .
A Monterey Street in Soledad, 1308 Monterey Street.
Q Okay. Now, bringing your attention—do you know Dima?
A Yes, sir.
Q What is her last name?
A Gallardo.
Q Where was she living on March 19?
A On the corner of First and Monterey.

. . .

BY MR. BRAUDRICK:

Q Okay, now, bringing your attention to close to ten o'clock on the night of March 19, where were you?
A On her porch.
Q Who was with you?
A Just me and her.
Q Do you know Louie Castillo?
A Yes, I do.
Q Did you know Mike Jimenez?
A Yes, I did.
Q Did you see them that night?
A Yes.
Q Where did you first see them?
A They were walking out of Joe Mendoza's house. He lives across the street on the corner and they were leaving his house.
Q Okay. What happened as they walked across the street?
A Well, they walked by and—well, I know them but not real good, but I know them and they said hello and I said hi, and they were walking by, and they were going uptown; and then,——

. . .

BY MR. BRAUDRICK:

Q Okay. Where were they when they said hello to you?
A Right in front of the house.
Q Okay. What happened as they first—first of all, what were you doing—what were you and Dima doing on the front porch?
A We were standing there talking and just talking. That's all. And they passed by, and they kept on walking by after we said hi, and then they got down, I guess, to the other side of the truck, the pickup.

. . .

BY MR. BRAUDRICK:

Q Okay. What happened after they walked past you?

A Well, they walked by—well, like I said, after they passed the truck, I couldn't see them anymore.

Q Okay. What happened after they got up to where the camper-truck was parked?

A Well, I took my eyes off——

THE WITNESS: Well, I didn't see them after they passed the truck, but I just kept on talking and then——

. . .

BY MR. BRAUDRICK:

Q Okay. Did you see any cars in the road?

A Yes, I did.

Q When did you see any cars in the road, before they went past the camper-truck? A No, no cars.

Q Afterwards?

A Well, see—I took my eyes off them when they were walking down toward the truck, and I was just looking across the street, and I just started looking around and I seen a car coming from the left.

Q Okay. Did you recognize the car?

A Yes.

Q Whose car was it?

A His,* Fred's, that is all I know him by.

Q How much longer after you lost sight of Louie Castillo and Miguel Jimenez did you see the car drive up?

A Not very long, a couple of seconds maybe.

. . .

BY MR. BRAUDRICK:

Q What did the car do after it passed First Street?

A It was going down and it was just going, and then before it started stopping, a person got out.

Q How fast was the car going when the person got out?

A Pretty slow, now fast.

. . .

Q Were you able to tell who the person was that got out of the car?

A No, I wasn't.

Q Were you able to tell whether it was a man or a woman?

A A woman, yes.

* The witness pointed to Fred Medrano.

Q Were you able to see the driver of the car?

A No.

Q Could you tell whether the driver was a man or a woman?

A No.

Q Okay. What happened after the woman got out the car?

A Well, she started shooting. That's all.

Q Did you see a rifle?

A Yeah. Well, that is what she was shooting with.

Q Well, were you able to see Louie Castillo and Miguel Jimenez?

A No, I wasn't and that is where the truck was in the way.

Q So, the camper-truck shown in the driveway in People's number 20 was blocking your view of Louie Castillo and Miguel Jimenez?

A Yeah, it was.

Q Was it blocking your view of the women who was doing the shooting?

A No, it wasn't, no.

Q Do you know how many times she shot?

A No.

Q Okay. What did she do as she started shooting the rifle?

A Well, she just started, I guess, walking toward them.

MR. GARRY: I am going to ask that the guessing go out. The answer is not responsive.

THE COURT: Just state what you saw. I realize the word "I guess" doesn't always mean anything to a lay witness, but we don't want guessing here. So, if you will just say what you saw, if you are imagining it or thinking or believing that is what happened, we don't want that. We want just what you saw with your eyes or heard with your ears.

THE WITNESS: Okay.

. . .

BY MR. BRAUDRICK:

Q What did she do after she started walking toward them?

A Well, she like—I didn't know what to do. I just stood away and I was dazed. I didn't see anything like it before, so I really wasn't paying that much attention to everything that was happening.

Q Okay. What did she do after she stoppped shooting?

A She turned around and I seen Louis running toward the park and she fired two shots toward that way.

Q Okay. Would the park be across the street from where the car was?

A Yes, it would.

Q Would that be where it is labeled Community Park on the diagram?

A Uh-huh.

Q Okay. What did she do after she fired the two shots at Louie who was running across toward the park?

A I heard her yelling she wanted the shotgun to go in that direction after Louis.

Q What exactly did she say?

A "Give me the shotgun. I am going after Louis."

Q Who did she say that to?

A The driver.

BY MR. BRAUDRICK:

Q And as she said, "Give me the shotgun," where was she facing?

A The park.

Q The park?

A Yes, facing the park.

Q Okay. Then, what did she do?

A She didn't go anywhere. She got back into the car.

Q Okay. Did you hear anything else?

A No. No, I don't remember.

Q Did you hear anybody else besides her saying anything?

A The driver—no, no, I didn't. I can't remember.

Q Well, did you hear the driver say anything?

A No, I am not sure.

BY MR. BRAUDRICK:

Q You did testify at the Grand Jury hearing?

A Yes, I did.

Q And can you recall stating what the driver said at the Grand Jury when you testified before the Grand Jury?

A Let's see. He said, "No, let's go." That's all.

Q And when did he say that?

A When she wanted the shotgun.

Q Okay. What did the car do then?

A Well, the car was already turned around and it proceeded slowly down and took a left down First Street.

Q After the driver said, "No, let's go," what did the woman do?

A Well, she was, I guess, pulled into the car or something.

MR. GARRY: I object to that guessing again, Your Honor.

THE WITNESS: Oh, well, she was pulled into the car.

THE COURT: Just tell us what you saw or heard, see.

THE WITNESS: She ended up in the car.

THE COURT: All right.

BY MR. BRAUDRICK:

Q Did you see her get into the car?

A No, I didn't because I was looking down toward—I was looking toward the direction Louis ran, Louis Castillo.

. . .

Q All right. Okay. What did you do after she started shooting?

A Well, I told Dima to go in the house and call her dad and I was scared, so I went to the sidewalk and took a glance down toward where Mike was, and I could see somebody laying down but I wasn't sure who it was. I didn't know if he was hurt bad or nothing, so I didn't go close to him. I went to my mom's house and I ran across the street, and my brother and sister-in-law, which were staying with me, I told my brother to come with me and he grabbed his flashlight and I told my sister-in-law to call the ambulance and the police. And we went down there and we seen Mike lying there on the ground, and we looked at him and he was face up, and we went down toward the park to go see if Louis was there, and we didn't find him and that is when Mr. Moran was looking out. And we asked him to call the police too, because the police hadn't arrived yet or the ambulance.

(TR 445-459)

September 16, 1974

BY MR. BRAUDRICK:

Q How close did you get to Mike?

A Well, close because we looked at him and seen how he was, and then I stood back.

Q I show you People's Number Four, a knife, have you seen a knife like this before?

A Yeah, that looks like the one that was lying right next to him.

CROSS-EXAMINATION

BY MR. GARRY:

Q Mr. Ferrel, you say you were outside with Dima?

A (Nodding.)

Q From 8:30, what did you do there?

A We were just talking.

Q Well, I know, but were you standing, were you sitting?

A Yes, just standing up. She was sitting down. I was standing up.

Q What was she sitting on?

A Oh, just a small chair, like one of those (indicating).

Q With arms on it?

A No, without arms.

Q And was the chair facing the street?

A Uh-huh.

Q Was there only one chair?

A Yes.

Q And how close were you standing to her?

A About two feet apart, around there.

Q And the second car that you saw was the car that came north after Mike and Louis walked in front of you on the sidewalk, isn't that right?

A (Nodding.)

Q Answer yes or no.

A Yes.

Q All right. Now, how many people were in that car?

A I am not sure.

Q What did you tell the police how many people were in that car?

A I said I thought I seen three people in it, but I wasn't sure about the third person.

Q Would you describe where you thought you saw the three people?

A By the light in front of Dima's house on the corner.

Q And how far were you from the automobile that you have described that you thought there were three people in the car?

A About maybe ten or fifteen yards, around there.

Q Were the lights on on the automobile?

A Yes, they were.

Q And did it have lights inside the car?

A No.

Q Could you describe the driver of the car?

A No, I couldn't.

Q Is that because it was dark?

A Uh huh.

Q Then, before March the 19th, you knew who Freddie was?

A I—not really knew who he was, but I had seen him.

Q Did you know his name?

A Yes, I knew it was Freddie. That's all.

Q And if you saw him, you would recognize him, would you not?

A Yes, I would, yes.

Q But, when the car went by, you did not recognize——

A Well, cause it was dark.

Q —the driver of the car, that's right?

A (Witness nodded head.) Cause it was dark.

Q Had you ever seen Inez before?

A No, I hadn't.

Q And had you ever seen the third person that you thought you saw before?

A Yeah, I have, but you know, like I thought it was him. I'm not sure if it was him.

Q Who was that third person that you thought you saw?

A Well, it was a guy that lives in Soledad by the name of Bobby Urquidez, Robert Urquidez. . . .

Q You thought you saw him?

A Uh huh.
Q Was he in the back seat or front seat?
A Back seat.
Q Was he on the—behind the passenger's side or behind the driver's side?
A Behind the passenger's side.

. . .

Q My question is, was your eye on the automobile throughout the entire time it was going towards town?
A Yes, I was just looking at it.
Q And were you talking to Dima at that time?
A When the car first started coming down the street, yeah, I was talking to her at that time.
Q What were you talking to her about?
A Can't recall.
Q What did she say to you, and what did you say to her?
A I don't know. I can't remember. It was awhile back.

. . .

Q Did the car at any time—did you notice if the car at any time stopped?
A No, except when it was going up to—towards Mike—was slowing down.
Q It was slowing down?
A Uh-huh.
Q And did it stop?
A I can't remember if it stopped.
Q In other words, you didn't see it stop?
A Yes, I didn't see it stop.
Q What's the next thing that you heard?
A Well, I didn't hear nothing. I just seen a girl getting out of the car.
Q You saw a girl getting out of the car?
A Uh-huh.
Q And did you see the girl getting out of that car or a girl near there that you thought came out of the car?
A No, I seen her getting out of the car.

. . .

Q When you say you were still there, let's put you at F-5* where you were standing. Did you hear anything else?
A Yeah. Well, she wanted the shotgun but the driver said no.
Q What else did the driver say?
A That he wouldn't give it to her.

---

* F-5 refers to a mark on a photograph in evidence showing where on Dima's porch the witness was standing.

Q Now, what did he say, not your conclusions, you see, the difference between what you are concluding and what the person said may be different, and I want to know what she said, and I want to know what the other person said, if you remember the words.

A She said she wanted the shotgun to go after Louis and the driver said, no, let's go.

Q And at that time, was that at F-4.* Is that right?

A Yes.

Q Right next to the automobile?

A Yes.

Q Then, what did—did you see what happened to the person that said give me the shotgun or something?

A Well, she was, I guess she was pulled in the car, I don't know.

Q Now, when you say you guess, I don't want you to guess, I want you to tell me what you saw.

A She was pulled into the car.

Q She was pulled in?

A Yes, or she ended up in the car.

Q Did you see her when you say she was pulled in, did somebody drag her in?

A Probably.

Q You say she was probably drug into the car?

A Yes.

Q Describe that for the jury.

A Describe it, how it happened or what?

Q Yes.

A Well, she was like reaching out to grab the shotgun and she didn't come back out.

. . .

(RT 463-492)

CROSS-EXAMINATION

BY MR. WORTHINGTON:

Q And were you able to see anybody in it the first time you saw it?†

A Well, no, wasn't looking to see who was in it.

Q And when it went by Dima's house, you couldn't see who was in it, could you?

A Well, like I said, I thought I had seen a third person but I wasn't really paying attention to looking at it.

* F-4 refers to a mark on a photograph of the street where the witness indicated Medrano's car was stopped.

† The question refers to Medrano's automobile.

Q So, you don't know how many people were in it when it went by?

A No, I don't.

Q And then you ultimately saw one person that looked like a female to you that you thought got out of the car. Is that right?

A Yes.

Q Now, what made you think that person was a female?

A Well, when I heard her talking that she wanted a shotgun.

Q She had a female voice?

A Yes.

Q Before that, did you think she was a female?

A Yes.

Q What made you think that?

A Her long hair.

Q Did you notice Louis Castillo that night?

A Yes.

Q How long was his hair?

A I don't know. I don't think it was as long as a woman's hair.

Q You don't remember seeing Freddie Medrano on that night, do you?

A No.

Q Now, when the person that you described as a female, yelled something into the car, did you hear somebody answer from the car?

A Just the driver.

Q Could you tell that was the driver answering or could it have been the third person you thought you saw in the back seat?

A No, I couldn't tell, but I am pretty sure it was the driver, though.

Q The best you can tell, it was somebody from within the car. Is that right?

A Yes.

Q Was that a male voice or a female voice?

A A male voice.

Q And she said something like give me the shotgun?

A Uh-huh.

Q Are you sure those are the words she used?

A She said give me the shotgun, I am going after him.

Q After——

A —after Louis.

Q So, she used the name of the person?

A Yes.

Q And then what did you hear the person from in the car—inside the car respond?

A He said, "No, let's go."

Q Now, you testified before the Grand Jury, didn't you?

A I—yes, I did.

Q On April 8, 1974?

A Yes, I testified but I don't know the date.

Q I am referring to page 33, line 22, Your Honor.

Do you remember being asked the question: What were the words as near as you can remember, and giving the answer: Give me the shotgun. I am going to go after him. And the driver said, "No, get in." Do you remember that question and answer?

A Not really.

Q Well, at the time you testified before the Grand Jury, the events were still fresh in your mind, weren't they?

A Yes, they were.

Q And you told the story as accurately as you could remember it at that time?

A Yes.

Q Would you say your memory was better then than it is now?

A Yes, it was better then than it is now.

Q And so if you said the driver had said, "No, get in," is that the best that you remember it now?

A Now, yes. I have tried to put it away from my mind.

Q But, I have refreshed your memory now, have I not?

A Yeah.

Q Is it true then that the driver said, "No, get in."

A I don't know. I can't recall.

Q You just can't recall?

A I am not going to take your words.

Q Pardon me?

A I am not going with your words.

Q You are not quite sure even though I have refreshed your memory from the Grand Jury transcript?

A Yes.

. . .

Q Then after the police arrived did they ask you any questions?

A No. Well, see, I was just standing around then. Louis came running from—I don't know where he came from, but he came running, and he started telling the police what he had seen and who it was and everything.

. . .

Q Well, by the time Louie came out from the park, quite a crowd had gathered around; is this right?

A Well, the officers and—yes, a couple of onlookers.

Q And Louie started telling the policemen everything that he thought had happened?

A Well, everything—well, who did it and who it was and everything.

Q So, he named certain people while this other crowd was there—while you were there too; is that right?
A Yes.
Q Did he name Inez Garcia?
A Yes, I think he did. I'm not sure.
Q Did he name Freddie Medrano?
A I can't recall.
Q Alfred Medrano?
A I don't know. He might have.
Q Did he tell the police that Alfred Medrano owns a car like that old model Chevrolet?
A Yes, I think he did.
Q He told them that while you were there and several other people were there; is that true?
A Just while me and my brother and the officer were there.
Q Could you hear what he was saying?
A Yes, I was standing right next to him.
Q When was the first time the police ever asked you for a statement?
A Well, they just asked me my name and if I had seen it, and I said, "Yes." Then they told me to show up to the police station the following day.

. . .

Q All right. Now, do you know how many people lived in Soledad?
A Not very many, about 5,000 or something like that.
Q That many, 5,000?
A I think it is. I am not sure.

. . .

BY MR. WORTHINGTON:
Q Have you heard any people in Soledad talking about this event since March 19?
A Yes, I have.
Q Would it be fair to say a lot of rumors have been going around town about what happened?

. . .

MR. BRAUDRICK: Objection, Your Honor.
THE COURT: Sustained.
BY MR. WORTHINGTON:
Q Have you talked about this incident to other people?
A No, I haven't.
Q Besides the police?
A No.

Q And the investigators?

A No.

Q None at all?

A None except for some elderly man that went to my house when I had just arrived from work.

Q I think that is the same fellow, the same elderly man described before as my investigator.

A That is the only one.

Q Are you still going to school?

A Yes, I am.

Q And do you and Dima go to the same school?

A Yes, we do.

Q Have the two of you talked about this incident at school?

A No, I don't talk to her at school.

Q Do you still go over to Dima's house?

A Yes, I do.

Q And between March 19 and the time you talked to the Grand Jury, were you going over to her house?

A Yes, I have gone over to her house but I don't talk to her about it.

Q And how about Mr. Moran, have you talked to him about this incident?

A No.

Q Has he addressed you about it?

A No, he hasn't, just that night, he asked me what happened and I just said he got shot, and that was about it, and I stood away.

Q That night he asked?

A That night he asked me, he said I thought I heard a firecracker and I said it wasn't firecrackers.

Q Did you tell me you talked to him after the time that you heard what Louie had to say or before that?

A It was after.

Q After you heard Louie talking?

A Yes.

Q All right. I have no further questions.

(TR 494-510)

RE-CROSS-EXAMINATION

BY MR. GARRY:

Q I have only one question. Mr. Ferrel, you were stunned, were you not?

A Yes, I was.

MR. GARRY: Thank you. I have no further questions.

THE COURT: You say stunned?

THE WITNESS: No, not stunned, but it is the first time I have ever seen it, you know.

THE COURT: I see.

BY MR. GARRY:

Q Isn't it a fact, sir, that you told the Grand Jury when you testified under oath there that you were stunned, didn't you?

A Yes, I said that but I might not be what I meant.

Q But, that is fair that you did say that?

A Yes, I did state that.

Q To the Grand Jury on April 8?

A Yes.

MR. GARRY: I have no further questions.

THE COURT: Anything else, gentlemen?

RE-DIRECT EXAMINATION

BY MR. BRAUDRICK:

Q What did you mean by stunned when you said that to the Grand Jury?

A You know, that I have never seen it before and one thing that I don't see very often and it just, I looked very carefully.

Q All right. Thank you.

THE COURT: That's all, young man, you are now excused.

(TR 511-512)

The prosecution's next witness was Nicholas Bunte who testified that he had sold a shotgun to Fred Medrano sometime before the shooting.

NICHOLAS JAMES BUNTE, SWORN
DIRECT EXAMINATION

BY MR. BRAUDRICK:

Q Mr. Bunte, do you know Freddie Medrano?

A Yes, sir.

Q And how long have you known him?

A Approximately one year.

. . .

BY MR. BRAUDRICK:

Q All right. Now, bringing your attention to March, 1974, did you have occasion to go see Freddie Medrano?

A Yes, I did.

. . .

BY MR. BRAUDRICK:

Q I show you People's Number Twelve for identification. Have you seen this?

A Yes, I have.

Q And when was the last time you saw that?

A In March.

Q And where was that?

A At Freddie Medrano's.

Q Was there anything inside this when you last saw it?

A Yes.

BY MR. BRAUDRICK:

Q What was inside it?

A A twelve gauge Remington pump shotgun.

Q And prior to your going over there that day, whose shotgun was that?

A Mine.

Q And whose case was this?

A Mine.

. . .

Q Okay. What did you do with the shotgun and case when you went to see Freddie Medrano in March?

A I took it to his house and I left it with him.

Q Did you sell or trade it to him?

A Yes.

Q What kind of a shotgun was it?

A It was a Remington. It was a Remington twelve-gauge pump, a Wing Master.

Q Did it work?

A Yes.

Q Do you know approximately what day it was that you went to see him?

A All I can say is it would be approximately the second week in March.

Q Was it before—do you know whether it was before March 19, the day Mike Jimenez was killed in the City of Soledad? . . .

BY MR. BRAUDRICK:

Q Okay. How do you know that?

A Well, at the time of the murder, I was in Santa Cruz and at that time, I had already been there approximately a week and I had left the gun with Freddie before moving to Santa Cruz.

Q Do you know Inez Garcia?

A Yes, I do.

Q Was she present when you brought the gun over, the shotgun over on that day?

A She was in the house.

Q Was it a single or double barrelled?

A Single barrel.

Q And during the four years that you had the shotgun, did you keep it in this case?

A Yes, sir.

. . .

CROSS EXAMINATION

BY MR. GARRY:

Q Mr. Bunte, you talked to us this morning, did you not?

A Yes, sir.

Q And you told me at that time, did you not, that you don't know whether this is the case that the shotgun came in; is that right?

A I said at the time I had not marked the case; therefore, I couldn't definitely say it was my case, but it is one like mine.

. . .

Q Yes. There is nothing on here that shows that this is your case?

A No. Like I said, I have no identification mark on it.

Q All right. Now, you stated that you've known Inez Garcia?

A Yes.

Q When did you meet her?

A In March, I believe.

Q You had never met her before that?

A No.

Q And did you ever talk to her?

A Just at the house I saw her once or twice.

Q You had been to the house on more than one occasion?

A Oh yeah, a couple of times.

Q You say this was the second week in March; is that right?

A I believe so, yes.

MR. GARRY: I have no further questions.

THE COURT: Mr. Worthington.

BY MR. WORTHINGTON:

Q Mr. Bunte, do you recall having ever gone back to Freddie Medrano's house after this transaction that you related in the middle of March?

A I don't recall if I did. If I did, it would probably not be more than once or twice.

Q Well, let's take the period between the time of this transaction and March 19th.

A Okay.

Q Do you recall having gone there?

A Between—from the transaction in between March 19th?

Q Yes.

A Like I said, I don't recall. I believe I could safely say I went there one time after that.

Q You didn't see the shotgun there—the shotgun that you have described at that time?

A No, I didn't.

Q As a matter of fact, after the date that you left the gun that you have described at Freddie's house you never saw it again, did you?

A No, I didn't.

Q Now, after you heard about this killing of Mike Jimenez, did you talk to any policeman?

A Yes, I did.

Q When did that first happen?

A It was a weekend. It would be after—it might be the weekend after the murder. I'm not sure.

Q Just—you keep referring to this as a murder. Let's just call it a shooting.

A All right. After the incident.

Q All right.

A I had called Monterey County Jail. I had read in the newspaper where there was a .22 automatic rifle and a shotgun supposedly in Freddie's car. Now, I was interested in this time in buying my shotgun back. When I found this out, I called Monterey County Jail to find the whereabouts of my shotgun.

Q You just assumed that from what you read in the newspaper that a shotgun you left with Freddie might be involved in some way?

A Yes.

Q You don't know what the source of information was from the newspaper at all?

A No, I don't.

Q All right. But as a result of what you read in the newspaper, you went and talked to—actually, you said a policeman, but was it a deputy sheriff?

A A sheriff—a Sergeant Ralston in the Monterey County Police Department—or Monterey County Sheriff's Department. I called him from Santa Cruz.

Q All right. And did you relate to him——

A Yes.

Q —this possible connection?

A Yes, I told him why I was calling, and I wanted to know the whereabouts of the shotgun, and if at all possible, I was going to leave $30 on Freddie's books and get my gun back.

Q Just assuming that they had.

A Assuming, yes.

Q He told you they didn't have any shotgun?

A They said they didn't have any weapons whatsoever. That the Soledad Police Department would be the ones to contact.

. . .

Q Did you mention Louie Castillo's name this morning when you talked to us in the room in the back?

A Yes, I did.

Q And you got the information from some source that Louie Castillo——

A No, I didn't get any information from any source. That was my own thought.

Q —that Louie Castillo knew where this shotgun was, right?

A I had no knowledge of any way of anybody finding out that I gave that shotgun to Freddie, and this was just a guess on my part. I don't know.

Q Well, were you aware that Louie Castillo had a key to Freddie Medrano's apartment?

A No, I wasn't.

Q Were you aware Louie Castillo lived in the same apartment?

A No.

(TR 520-524)

The prosecution's next witness was Rosa Almanza who lived across the street from Freddie Medrano's apartment. The prosecution sought through her testimony to establish that Freddie Medrano and Inez Garcia left together in Freddie's car after the fight in the apartment.

ROSA ALMANZA, SWORN

DIRECT EXAMINATION

BY MR. BRAUDRICK:

Q Whereabouts do you live?

A Pardon me?

Q Whereabouts do you live?

A Where do I live?

Q Yes.

A 1760 Monterey Street.

Q Do you know defendant Freddie Medrano?
A I saw him.
Q Do you know Inez Garcia?
A I just saw her there.
Q Whereabouts in relation to where you live did they live?
A Not very far, it is about the size of the courtroom, I would say.

. . .

Q So, basically, you lived across the driveway from them?
A Yes.
Q Now, bringing your attention to the night of March 19, did you see Freddie Medrano's car?
A Yes.
Q I show you People's Ten-A and Ten-B, does that appear to be photographs of his car?
A Yes.
Q Whereabouts did you see his car?
A In front of the door.
Q And where were you when you saw somebody out by his car?
A I was out of my house at the back door of my bedroom.
Q Were you looking through a window?
A Yes.
Q Who did you see—how many people did you see?
A At the time, I didn't see—I just saw a figure walking to the car, but that is all I saw.
Q Okay. What did you see after that?
A After that, I didn't see anything until later when I went in to my bedroom and started reading, and I heard some noise and I walked and I looked out the window and the car drove off and that is all I saw.
Q And did you see anybody in the car?
A I saw a couple of figures.
Q Who did it appear to you to be in the car?
A I don't know, I wouldn't know who it was.
Q Isn't it true that it was dark at this time?
A Yes, it was dark.
Q Did you see people get into the car?
A No, I didn't see them get in.
Q Can you recall giving a statement to the officer Santos in March of 1974?
A Yes, I did give a statement but I don't remember the month.
Q And you recall telling Officer Santos that when you walked back to the clothes line while you were walking back into the house, you saw two persons getting into an older model car that you saw there?
A I don't recall.
Q Okay. I show you a copy of the statement that you gave to the

police, would you take a look at that and see if it refreshes your memory? Does that refresh your memory?

A I remember that I didn't see the two persons getting in——

. . .

BY MR. BRAUDRICK:

Q How many people were in the car when the car drove away?

A I saw two people.

Q Could you tell what sex the people were?

A Not necessarily, I don't think so.

Q In the car that drove away was Freddie's car?

A Yes.

Q Did you see anybody else near his car that evening?

A I don't recall.

. . .

Q Did you see anybody get into the car?

A No.

. . .

BY MR. BRAUDRICK:

Q Were you able to tell who it was that was walking out by the car?

A It looked like Fred.

Q Did you see Inez Garcia?

A No, I didn't.

Q Do you have any idea of what time it was when you saw the car drive away?

A No, I know it was after nine some time.

Q Okay. Thank you.

THE COURT: Cross-examine.

. . .

CROSS-EXAMINATION

BY MR. GARRY:

Q You live right next door to where Inez was staying. Is that right?

A Yes.

Q And you heard what you thought to be a party next door around eight-thirty or nine o'clock?

A Yes.

Q And then soon after that, right after that, you went outside to hang your clothes?

A I went out to take some clothes off the clothes line.

Q That is when you saw the car leaving?
A No.
Q How soon after that?
A It was a while later.
Q About ten minutes or fifteen minutes?
A I really wouldn't be able to tell you the time.
Q But, you did not see Inez Garcia?
A I did not see her.
Q Thank you. No further questions.
THE COURT: Mr. Worthington.

CROSS-EXAMINATION

BY MR. WORTHINGTON:
Q Mrs. Almanza, do you recall talking to me on August 14?
A Talking to whom?
Q To me?
A Yes.
Q And do you recall telling me that after you went out to the clothes line, you went back in and laid down in your bed in the house?
A Yes.
Q In your house?
A Yes.
Q And you were reading a book then, weren't you?
A Yes.
Q You weren't paying too much attention to what was going on next door. Is that right?
A No.
Q You had gone out to the clothes line about 8:30. Is that right?
A Approximately that, I wasn't really looking at the time, but it was dark and it was already late in the evening.
Q It was dark, but this was now on March 19?
A Yes.
Q We were on daylight saving time at that time, but was it getting dark about six o'clock?
A Yes.
Q Or seven?
A I don't know. I don't remember.
Q All right. Do you recall whether it was completely dark?
A Yeah, it was dark.
Q All right. And then the next thing you noticed was when you looked out your bedroom window and saw Freddie's car leave, is that true?
A Yes.

Q You recall telling me as close as you could remember that was right around nine o'clock?

A Yeah, I wouldn't tell you the exact time because I do not know it.

Q But, when you told me it was right around nine o'clock, that was as close as you could come?

A Yeah, as near as I could remember, yes.

Q You didn't see anything else that you thought was unusual in any way, did you?

A No.

MR. WORTHINGTON: No further questions.

. . .

(TR 525-532)

The prosecution's next witness was Dima Gallardo who together with David Ferrel witnessed the shooting from her front porch.

DIMA GALLARDO, SWORN

DIRECT EXAMINATION

BY MR. BRAUDRICK:

Q Dima, how old are you?

A Sixteen.

Q And do you go to school?

A Yes.

Q Where do you go to school?

A Gonzales High.

Q Do you know David Ferrel?

A Yeah.

Q Now, going back to March 19th, this year, whereabouts were you living?—

A The day it happened?

Q Yes.

A On my front porch.

Q No, where were you living?

A With my father.

Q And where was that?

A 1299 Monterey.

. . .

Q And David Ferrel lived across the street?

A Yeah.

Q What time did you see David Ferrel that night?

A Came over about 9:00.

Q Where were you with him then?
A On the front porch.
Q Okay. Now, do you know—do you know who Defendant Freddie Medrano is?
A (Witness nodded head.)
Q Do you know him personally?
A No.
Q Did you know who he was on March 19th, 1974?
A Yeah.
Q And do you know Louie Castillo?
A Yeah.
Q Do you know Mike Jimenez?
A Yes.
Q Did you have occasion to see them that night?
A What?
Q Did you see Louie Castillo or Mike Jimenez that night?
A Yes.
Q Where did you first see them?
A They were passing by my house.
Q Okay. Where were you then?
A On the porch.
Q What were they doing?
A They were just walking by.

. . .

Q Okay. What did they do as they walked by you?
A They just said, "Hi," and they kept on walking.
Q They kept walking towards town?
A Yeah.
Q That would be—on the diagram that would be on the left side towards Pine Street?
A Yes.
Q Did you see any cars?
A No.
Q Did you see any cars drive up after they walked by?
A Yes.
Q What kind of car drove up?
A A blue old car.
Q i show you People's 10-A and 10-B, photographs of the old model Chevrolet. Does that appear to be the car that drove up?
A Yes.
Q Do you know how many people were in the car when it drove up?
A No.

Q Where was Louie Castillo and Mike Jimenez when the car drove up?
A By the alley, I guess.

BY MR. BRAUDRICK:

Q Okay. What did the car do as it drove past your house?
A Just drove by, and then when it saw them, it stopped.
Q Okay. What happened after the car stopped?
A A girl got out and started shooting.
Q What was she shooting with?
A A rifle, I guess.
Q Could you tell how many people were in the car then?
A No.
Q Could you see Louie Castillo or Mike Jimenez?
A No
Q What did you do when she started shooting?
A Nothing. I just stayed there.
Q And where were you when she started shooting?
A Still on the porch.
Q In People's number 21. What did the—what side of the car did the girl get out of?
A Passenger's side.

. . .

BY MR. BRAUDRICK:

Q Could you tell whether or not it was a pistol or rifle?
A Well, there was a big one. It wasn't small.
Q Do you know how many times the girl shot?
A More than once.
Q What did the girl do after she stopped shooting?
A She turned around and started shooting at Louie.
Q Okay. When did you see Louie?
A After he took off running toward the park.
Q Where was he when you first saw him after the shooting started?
A I couldn't tell you, because of the camper.
Q When the shooting first started, you could not see Louie Castillo and Mike Jimenez?
A No.
Q After the shooting started, then you saw Louie Castillo?
A Run across.
Q When you say run across, did he run across the street?
A Yeah.
Q Okay. What did the girl do then?
A She just turned around and started shooting at him and the car made a U-turn.
Q Car made a U-turn?

A Yeah.
Q While she was shooting at Louie?
A Yeah.
Q Could you see how many people were in the car then?
A I could just see, I guess, the driver and the passenger.
Q When the girl was out shooting at Louie, how many people were in the car?
A One.
Q That would be the driver?
A Yeah.
Q Now, you can't identify who the driver was, can you?
A No.
Q You can't identify who the girl was?
A No.
Q Do you know about what time this took place?
A About twenty minutes to ten.
Q What happened after Louie Castillo ran across the street and into the park?
A She started shooting and then she got into the car and they left.
Q Do you know what side of the car she got into?
A The passenger's side.
Q Did she get—was this after the car made a U-turn?
A Yes.
Q Did you hear the girl say anything at any time?
A No.
Q How about the driver of the car?
A No.
Q Now, how much time was it between the time that you said hello to Louie Castillo and Mike Jimenez, until the time the car drove up?
A A couple of seconds, I guess.
Q How much time was it between the time you said hello to Louie Castillo and Mike Jimenez until the time the girl started shooting?
A About a minute.

. . .

Q What did you see—did you see where the car went after the girl got out of the car?
A It turned off on First Street.
Q And what did you do then?
A I just stayed there.
Q Did you ever go down to where Mike's body was?
A No.
Q Are there any street lights on that night?
A No.

Q Where are the street lights located, do you know?

A On the corner of my house and on the corner of Pine.

Q So, it would be—the one is on First and Monterey Street and one is on Pine and Monterey Street?

A Yes.

Q Was it dark?

A Yes.

CROSS-EXAMINATION

BY MR. GARRY:

Q Miss Gallardo I have a few questions to ask. Was David Ferrel with you all the time that the shooting was going on?

A Yes.

Q And how long did he remain with you after that?

A Not very long.

Q Well, a minute or two?

A Yes.

Q Now, how do you know what time it was?

A I had barely went in to see what time it was.

Q I see. What time was it when you looked at the time?

A Twenty til.

Q How much after that was it that Louie and Mike came by?

A About two minutes.

Q Was it at least five or ten minutes later that these two came by?

A I couldn't really tell you.

Q Well, do you recall testifying at the Grand Jury hearing on April 8, 1974?

A Yes.

Q Now, do you recall what you said to the Grand Jury as to how long it took after you looked at the clock?

A I said a few minutes.

Q I beg your pardon?

A I said about five minutes.

Q Page 26, Your Honor, of the Grand Jury testimony beginning with line 22 and ending with 3 on page 27: I am going to read your testimony that you gave, Miss Gallardo. Q Do you know what time it was? A It was—well, when I went in to see what time it was, it was twenty minutes until ten. Q Twenty minutes until ten? A Yes. Q And when was that in relation to the time that Mike Jimenez came by? A That was before it happened. Q How long before, have you any idea? A About five or ten minutes. Q You gave that answer, did you not?

A Yes.

Q Was that true?
A Yes.
Q And your memory was a lot fresher in April than it is now in September 16th, is it not?
A Yes.
Q Is that correct?
A Yes.
Q How long—strike that. Would you tell the jury, Miss Gallardo, what you were doing out on the porch?
A Talking.
Q All right. Were you standing or sitting?
A Standing.
Q You were standing. Is that right?
A Yes.
Q You were sure you were not sitting?
A I am positive.
Q Was David Ferrel standing or sitting?
A Standing.
Q Was there a chair there?
A Yes.
Q And you were both standing. Is that right?
A Yes.
Q During the time that David was there, did you sit down at any time?
A No.
Q Were you looking in that direction?
A After it happened?
Q Yes.
A No.
Q Now, you were quite frightened when this happened, were you not?
A Yes.
Q Stunned?
A Yes.
Q And you were in shock, isn't that right?
A Yes.

. . .

Q Now, was the car lights on when you saw the automobile?
A I didn't notice.
Q And did you ever see the lights on in the automobile?
A I can't remember.
Q Did you and David have any conversation at all while the shooting was going on?
A No.

Q He didn't say anything?
A No.
Q And you didn't say anything?
A No.
Q And you were standing next to him when the shooting was going on?
A Yes.
Q And were you standing next to him when this person got into the car?
A Yes.
Q Do you have good hearing?
A Yes.
Q And you didn't hear anybody say anything, did you?
A No.

MR. GARRY: I have no further questions.

THE COURT: Mr. Worthington?

MR. WORTHINGTON: Thank you, Your Honor.

CROSS-EXAMINATION

BY MR. WORTHINGTON:

Q You are indicating the car was on Monterey Street at First Street. Is that right?
A Yes.
Q And that just got almost to your house and that is when you first saw it?
A Yes.
Q And then the car passed by. Is that right?
A Yes.
Q Were you and David talking at that time?
A Yeah.
Q After the car passed by, did you go back to whatever you were talking about?
A No.
Q Do you recall if you were talking just before the car came up?
A Yeah.
Q Do you recall whether or not you stopped talking?
A We stopped talking after he passed by.
Q After it passed by?
A Yes.
Q When the car passed by, you didn't make any particular impression and you kept right on talking. Is that true?
A Yes.

Q And as a matter of fact, you weren't paying any attention to the car at all?

A Yes.

Q That is true, you weren't paying any attention to it?

A (Nodding.)

Q I have no further questions.

. . .

(RT 533-556)

The prosecution's next witness was Rosa Bracamonte. She testified concerning what transpired in her apartment after the arrival of Freddie Medrano and Inez Garcia the night of the shooting. Her testimony is offered to corroborate Juan Carbajal's earlier testimony and lay a foundation for her sister, Alicia Alcaraz', testimony to follow.

ROSA LINDA BRACAMONTE, SWORN

DIRECT EXAMINATION

BY MR. BRAUDRICK:

Q Mrs. Bracamonte, where do you live?

A 300 Monterey Street, Apartment 5.

Q In the city of Soledad?

A Uh huh.

Q Are you any relationship to Juan Carabajal?

A He is my nephew.

Q Any relationship to Alicia?

A She is my sister.

. . .

THE COURT: How old are you?

THE WITNESS: Twenty.

THE COURT: Twenty?

THE WITNESS: Yes.

THE COURT: He is seventeen?

THE WITNESS: Uh huh.

BY MR. BRAUDRICK:

Q Now, bringing your attention to March 19, 1974, that evening, did you and your husband have a fight at your house, a quarrel?

A Yes.

Q Were the police called?

A Yes.

Q Who was there during the quarrel?

A It was my—me, my husband, Alicia and Juan.

. . .

BY MR. BRAUDRICK:

Q Did you know Inez Garcia?
A Yes.
Q And how long before March 19 did you know her?
A About two weeks before.
Q And did you know Freddie Medrano?
A Not really.
Q Did you know who he was?
A Yeah.
Q Did you see them that night after the police left?
A Uh huh.
Q Where did you see them?
A At my house.
Q Did they come inside the house?
A Yeah.
Q Who came in first?
A Inez.
Q Did Freddie come in after her?
A Yeah.
Q I show you People's Fourteen for identification, a manila envelope containing a blouse. Can you recognize this blouse?
A Yeah.
Q And where have you seen it before?
A Inez was wearing it.
Q Now, when she first came in the door, was the blouse ripped?
A Yeah.
Q Like this?
A No, it wasn't that much, no.
Q How much was it ripped?
A Oh, take off about maybe that much (indicating).
Q It was ripped that much?

THE COURT: Let's see what you are indicating. About an inch and a half–two inches, maybe.

BY MR. BRAUDRICK:

Q Okay. Now, what did Inez say when she came in the house?
A That she had shot Mike.
Q What else did she say?
A I can't remember.
Q Did Freddie say anything then?
A No, he was pretty much quiet.
Q Okay. What happened after she said she shot Mike?
A Well, there was a lot of confusion then. I wasn't paying too much attention. There was some words said after that, but I can't really

remember what it was.

Q What was it about?

A Well, about what happened that night.

Q Okay. At this point, were you still involved in a quarrel with your husband?

A Yeah.

Q What happened after the words that were said that you can't remember?

A Umm–I think my sister said that it didn't look like she was raped or something like that.

Q Inez say anything to you or say anything about being raped?

A She said they tried to rape her.

Q Okay. Did she say that after she said she had shot Mike?

A Uh huh.

Q Okay. What happened after she said that?

A I think Alice said that it didn't look like she had really been raped. . . .

BY MR. BRAUDRICK:

Q Okay. Are you sure that she said that?

A Uh huh.

MR WORTHINGTON: The answer was yes?

THE WITNESS: Yeah.

BY MR. BRAUDRICK:

Q Okay. What happened after your sister said that?

A Then something was said for her to be hit.

Q Do you know who said that?

A No, 'cause me and my husband were talking and came out–that, you know, then I remembered afterwards that–that Inez said that, you know, "well, shouldn't I get hit so it looked like I was, you know, I was raped," or something like that.

Q Okay. What happened after Inez said that?

A Well, somebody said to hit her?

Q Do you know who said that?

A No.

Q Did you say that?

A No.

Q Okay. Then what happened?

A Freddie was asked to hit her and he said he wouldn't be able to do it, so we told Juan to hit her, and he hit her.

Q Now, this was the blouse, People's Fourteen for identification, was it ripped more while Inez was in your apartment that night?

A Uh huh.

Q Do you know whether or not it was ripped more before she was hit by Juan?

A Yeah, it was ripped already before.

Q Ripped more than it was when she came in?
A Yeah.
Q What did Inez have on when she came in the house?
A A pair of green pants and that blouse.
Q What did she have on when she was hit?
A She just had my nephew's jacket.
Q Okay. What happened after Juan hit her?
A I told her if she wanted an aspirin?
Q Where did she go then?
A She went in the kitchen.
Q Where did you go?
A I went to go give her the aspirin.
Q And how much time was there between the time she came in the house and the time that she was struck by Juan?
A I would say about maybe five minutes.
Q Okay. What were they doing during that five minutes?
A They were talking things over, you know, about the shooting and all.

. . .

(RT 556-566)

CROSS-EXAMINATION

BY MR. WORTHINGTON:

Q And your sister? Was she there when the fight started?
A Yeah.
Q And Juan was there when your husband came in, wasn't he?
A Uh-huh.
Q And at that time, was your husband living with you?
A No.
Q And he came in in a drunken condition, didn't he?
A Yeah. Well, I didn't know it then till—until he said so later on.
Q But, the minute he walked in, he got in an argument with Juan?
A Not right away.
Q Well, you remember talking to me two days ago, don't you? Saturday?
A Yeah.
Q And at that time you said your husband wasn't living with you on March 19th, hadn't been living with you on March 19th?
A Uh-huh.
Q And you said that he and Juan got in a fight because Juan was there, and he thought that Juan was staying with you; is that right?
A What Willie said?
Q Didn't you tell me that the cause of the fight was over the fact

that your husband wasn't living there, and he'd come home and here was this strange man that he couldn't remember?

A Willie said that.

. . .

Q You don't remember?

A What do you mean, messed up, how much messed up?

Q That is what I am asking you? What kind of condition was her hair in?

A In good condition.

Q Pardon?

A Good condition.

Q It was in good condition?

A Yes.

Q Her blouse was torn when she walked in, wasn't it?

A Yes.

Q In fact, it was torn so much that Juan threw his coat at her to cover up her breast?

A Not then.

Q When did he do that?

A After it was ripped.

Q He didn't throw that coat at her the minute she walked in?

A No.

Q Now, do you remember talking to me Saturday and telling me that you really don't remember what happened that day at all?

A Yeah.

Q You told me that, didn't you?

A (Nodding.)

. . .

BY MR. WORTHINGTON:

Q And you told me that you would remember that Inez said she shot somebody?

A Yeah.

Q And she even named that person or said because they raped me, or they tried to rape me, or words to that effect, didn't she?

A Yeah—well, not right then, after she said that.

Q Well, after she said she had shot somebody, didn't Alicia ask her why?

A No.

Q You don't remember what was said next?

A No, I just know parts of what was said.

Q All right. Would it be fair to say your memory has faded on this?

A Yes.

. . .

BY MR. WORTHINGTON:

Q Has it?

A Not all of it.

Q All right. Has anything happened to refresh your memory since Saturday?

A Well, it is about the same.

Q Have you been in the jury room in the back?

A Yeah.

Q Just before testifying this morning?

A Yes.

Q And Alicia is back there, too, isn't she?

A Yes.

Q Have the two of you been talking at all?

A Yes.

Q Have you been talking about this incident?

A Yeah.

Q All right. And has that tended to refresh your memory?

A Yep.

Q Basically, when you told me Saturday you don't know what happened, you were telling me the truth, isn't that right?

A No.

Q You weren't telling me the truth?

A No.

Q Pardon?

A I just was like trying to get you off my back, in other words.

Q I was questioning you some way and you wanted to get me off your back?

A I don't like too many questions except I am here today and I have to do it.

Q I told you I was representing Freddie Medrano, didn't I?

A Yes.

Q And he was charged with murder and he is on trial for his freedom, didn't I?

A You didn't say that.

Q Didn't I tell you that I wanted to just get the truth from you, if you could remember?

A That I don't remember.

MR. BRAUDRICK: Objection, Your Honor, we are going into matters that are purely collateral now as to his conversation with her as to what he told her and the important thing——

MR. GARRY: I hardly think that is collateral.

THE COURT: It is perhaps to the principal issue but it is material for impeachment and it will be received for that limited purpose. Continue.

BY MR. WORTHINGTON:

Q Did I tell you that?

THE WITNESS: I can't remember if you told me that or not.

Q Rosa, I ask you as much as you could remember about that, didn't I?

A I was kind of high that day.

Q You were kind of high when I was talking to you?

A Yeah.

Q Were you kind of high on March 19 when these events occurred?

A No, I hadn't been drinking at all.

Q You hadn't been drinking?

A No.

Q What were you high on Saturday?

A Beer.

Q And you intentionally withheld information from me, is that what you are telling this jury?

A Yeah, I wasn't sworn to anything and why should I tell you anything?

Q I see. You didn't tell me you were withholding information, did you?

A No.

Q So, it was not true when you said you don't remember these events?

A All that I had been telling you.

. . .

BY MR. WORTHINGTON:

Q When you talked to me on Saturday?

A Uh huh.

Q You told me you really don't remember anything, you were telling me a lie, weren't you?

A Yeah.

Q Okay. Now, have you stopped telling lies and started telling the truth?

MR. BRAUDRICK: Objection, it is argumentative.

MR. WORTHINGTON: I don't think so, Your Honor.

THE COURT: In view of what she just stated, maybe it is a fair question.

THE WITNESS: If I am telling a lie right now?

BY MR. WORTHINGTON:

Q Yeah, that is the question, are you telling a lie now?

A No, I couldn't afford to.

Q You couldn't?

A No.

Q When did you stop lying and start telling the truth?

MR. BRAUDRICK: Objection, argumentative.

THE COURT: Well, I think that is immaterial. Sustained.

. . .

Q Now, everything you were telling me here is true; is that right?
A Yeah.
Q And you remember all these events, now?
A Yeah.
Q At least to the extent you have testified to here?
A Uh-huh.
Q You don't remember in particular who said—who first mentioned the idea of Inez getting hit in the face, do you?
A Cause when me and my husband were talking the other night, he said that Inez suggested it—was the first to suggest it.
Q You don't remember that of your own independent recollection do you?
A No.
Q You are testifying to what your husband says he remembers?
A No, then I said after—cause Officer Perez was there, and then I go, "Yeah, now that come to think of it, that's what happened."
Q Now, I don't think I have a clear answer. You mean that Officer Perez was there at your house recently?
A Yes.
Q This is the man sitting right here in the corduroy coat and he told you what happened that night?
A No, he really more or less to come to tell us to come to court today.
Q Did you talk to Officer Perez today?
A Today? No.
Q I'm sorry. I don't understand. When did you say you talked to Officer Perez?
A Think it was the same day you came.
Q Well, I was there Saturday, two days ago, and you talked to Officer Perez that day; is that right?
A No, I don't know what day it was.
Q Well, was it close to that day or day before, day after?
A Close to it.
Q Just in the past few days, then, you have talked to Officer Perez?
A Uh-huh.
Q What did he tell you?
A I was drunk by then.
THE COURT: What's that?
THE WITNESS: I was drunk by then.
THE COURT: Oh, you were drunk by then.
THE WITNESS: Yes.

BY MR. WORTHINGTON:

Q Was that approximately the same time you talked to me, then?
A Yes.
Q Or was it a different time you were drunk?
A No, it was the same day.
Q Same day. Okay. Now, did you tell Officer Perez the truth that day?
A Oh, yeah. I like to rap with him.
Q You do like to rap to Officer Perez?
A Uh-huh.
Q Okay. And you didn't withhold any information from him?
A No.
Q Did he tell you what Juan had said on the witness stand the day—couple of days before?
A No, I read in the newspaper.
Q Oh. Did you take your testimony that you are giving us today from what you read in the newspaper?
A No.
Q Did it influence you in any way?
A No.
Q Do you recall whether you talked to Officer Perez after you talked to me or before?
A It was after.
Q Afterwards, and the things he said to you tended to refresh your memory about what happened; is that right?
A Well, I told him mostly the same thing I told him before.
Q Was that the same thing that you told me?
A No.
Q All right. Is it the same thing you are telling the jury today?
A Yeah.
Q It is?
A Uh-huh.
Q Now, do you remember what kind of a physical condition Freddie was in when he came into the house?
A No.
Q Well, how did his face——
A Oh, physical?
Q How did his face look?
A Oh, it was beaten up.

. . .

Q Okay. Now, when Inez came in, she also looked like she had been beaten up, didn't she?
A No.
Q Did you take a look at her pants?
A Yeah, more or less.

Q Did you inspect her?
A No. What do you think I am?
Q As far as you could tell, you just couldn't tell whether she had been beaten up or not; is that right?
A I have been beaten, and I never looked that good.

. . .

BY MR. WORTHINGTON:
Q How long have you known Freddie?
A I don't know him too well.
Q Would it be fair to say you don't like Freddie Medrano?
A Oh, he's okay.
Q He's all right?
A Uh-huh.
Q How about Inez?
A She's okay.
Q Are you jealous of her?
MR. BRAUDRICK: Objection, Your Honor.
THE COURT: Well, I suppose that might affect her attitude unless there is some basis for it. Do you have any basis for the question?
MR. WORTHINGTON: Yes. She just said she never looked as good as Inez when she's been beaten up.
THE WITNESS: Physically.
THE COURT: I don't know if it has anything to do with jealousy.
MR. WORTHINGTON: Well, I'll withdraw that.

. . .

BY MR. WORTHINGTON:
Q Well, let me ask you this: Did you withhold information from me Saturday because you dislike me personally?
A Yeah.
Q That was the reason, or was it because you didn't want to help Freddie in any way.
A Oh, I'll help Freddie. Doesn't bother me none.
Q Wouldn't bother you if you helped him some?
A No.
Q Wouldn't bother you if by withholding information it would hurt him?
A Why would I want to hurt him?
Q That's what I'm asking.
A If I would withhold information? I don't have no reason to.
Q You talked to Louie Castillo since this incident occurred?
A Oh, yeah.
Q Has he talked to you about the incident?
A No, just what happened up here.

Q He told you about how he testified here?
A Yeah.
Q Is that right? Did he tell you what the contents of his testimony was?
A About him using and you know——
Q Did he tell you that Inez had accused him of helping to rape her?
A No, he didn't tell me that.
Q Did he tell you he was pretty unhappy when he left here?
A No, he didn't.
Q Did he ask you to help him out a bit, to make up some good sounding stories?
A No.
MR. WORTHINGTON: No further questions.

. . .

(RT 569-588)

The prosecution's next witness was Alicia Alcaraz, Rosa Bracamonte's sister. She gave her version of what happened in Rosa's apartment after Freddie Medrano and Inez Garcia arrived shortly after the shooting.

ALICIA ALCARAZ, SWORN
DIRECT EXAMINATION

BY MR. BRAUDRICK:
Q Alicia, where do you live?
A 1416 Metz Road.
Q Is that Soledad?
A Soledad.
Q Do you know Juan Carbajal?
A Yes, he is my nephew.
Q Do you know Rosa Bracamonte?
A She is my sister.
Q And Willie Bracamonte?
A My brother-in-law.
Q Do you know the defendant Freddie Medrano?
A Yes.
Q And do you know Inez Garcia?
A Yes.
Q How long have you known Inez Garcia?
A Well, I have seen her in Soledad, but I've only known her a short time, ever since she moved in with a girl-friend of mine and that is when I got really to know her.
Q Okay. How long have you known Freddie Medrano?

A Well, when Inez was over there he used to start—he went over there too, and really I got to know him was when they were being roommates, Freddie and Inez were sharing their apartment and that is when I really got to see more of him, but I had only seen him once before that.

Q Okay. How did you get to see more of him?

A Well, I used to go visit Inez.

Q Did you ever do any favors for them?

A Well, I did a lot of favors for that little group.

Q Did you ever meet any members of her family?

A Yes, a brother-in-law.

Q When was that?

A Oh, it was about a week or so before this happened.

Q Okay. What was the occasion for you meeting him?

A Well, her brother-in-law was coming down to see her and she didn't want it to look bad for her family so I made out like I lived there with them so her family wouldn't get the wrong impression about her sharing the rent and the apartment where they lived, her and Freddie.

Q Okay. Did you have your children over there?

A Yes, I had my three children over there so it would look like I lived there and wouldn't look bad for her.

Q Okay. Bringing your attention to March 19, 1974, when Mike Jimenez was killed, did you have occasion to go to your sister's house on Monterey Street, your sister Rosa?

A Yes, I was down there.

. . .

Q Do you remember how long after Sergeant Perez left the house that Inez and Freddie came to the house? . . .

Q Okay. What happened when they got to the house?

A Well, just when they knocked on the door and Rosie answered it—well, she opened the door and Freddie and Inez came in and that is when Inez told me that she had shot Mike.

Q So what happened after Inez said she shot Mike?

A Well, I asked her why, and she said that Mike had tried to rape her or raped her, I am not positive of which, but I know rape was the main thing.

Q Did she say that Mike had tried to rape her or that Mike had raped her?

A I can't really be sure, but I know it was either one; like I said, I was a little upset at the time.

Q Okay. What happened after she said that?

A Well, I couldn't really say for sure, my memory is a little vague, but we started talking and somehow it came out that I said it didn't look like she had been raped.

Q You said that?

A Yes, I am almost sure.

BY MR. BRAUDRICK:

Q Okay. What happened after that?

A Well, like I said, the conversation was more or less on that topic and I really don't remember what happened next. The only thing I do remember is that somehow either Inez, Freddie or someone in the room said something about like I said she didn't look like she was raped, so somebody tore the blouse because she ripped it about two inches from the top, it was a knit blouse and it was ripped about two inches, about an inch or so from the top.

Q Did somebody tear the blouse then?

A Yes.

Q Do you know who did it?

A No, I am not sure.

Q Okay. So, it was torn an inch or two?

A Yes.

Q Then, somebody tore it the rest of the way?

A Yes, a little bit more.

Q Where was Juan when the blouse was torn?

A Well, I guess he was just looking.

Q And do you know where Freddie was?

A Well, we were standing more or less in a huddle. There was the door facing you and I was facing the door and there was my brother-in-law was sitting on the chair and Freddie was standing next to it and Inez was next to him and my nephew was on my side and I was in front of Inez and my sister was on the other side of me, so somehow we all got—we were all in those positions, so I really couldn't say who tore or who did what.

Q Okay. What happened after the blouse was torn?

A Well, like I said, somebody said to sock Inez and we told my brother-in-law and he wouldn't do it, and we told Freddie and Freddie wouldn't do it, so I just turned around and it seemed normal to just tell the next man in the room to sock her and he just turned, you know, and lined her up and socked her which I really didn't think he would do it.

Q Who was that?

A My nephew Juan.

Q And the blouse was ripped before Juan hit her?

A Yes.

Q What did Inez do when she was struck by Juan?

A Well, he hit her pretty hard; I mean, she sort of swayed back and she sort of lost her knees sort of.

Q Okay. What did you do?

A I don't remember after that, you know, we all huddled around her to catch her, you know, because we thought she might fall or something. . . .

Q All right. Did Freddie say anything when he came in the house?

A Not really, Freddie is kind of a quiet person. I don't really remember.

Q Did he say anything at any time that you can recall now while he was in the house that night?

A No, not really.

Q You can't recall?

A No, I can't really remember.

Q Okay. How long did you stay in the kitchen?

A A couple of minutes, not very long.

Q Where did you go from the kitchen?

A I think we went back to the living room.

Q Okay. What happened when you got in the living room?

A Well, I am not positive what, but I figured more or less that that is when I told her that, you know, it would be better if we went over to my house because my kids were at home and they were asleep and I was a little worried for them and I didn't want the police to find Inez or Freddie at my sister's house and I said if anything happens it would be better if they were at my house so I told them if they wanted they could follow me to my house.

. . .

Q Okay. What did they do when they got inside your house?

A Inez was walking around with her rifle in her hand. So, I told her to sit down. She sat down next to the heater, and she leaned the rifle against the wall.

Q Did Inez say anything when she got in your house?

A It was more or less the same answers had been said at Rosa's. That she had shot Mike and that was because he had raped her or tried to. I couldn't really be sure.

Q What did Freddie do when he got into your house?

A He walked in and sat down on the sofa and just more or less shook his head and I think Juan had to go get some paper. Freddie's nose—there was some blood trickling down his nose, but he was mostly just shaking his head, you know, like he couldn't believe this was really happening.

Q Could you describe the condition of his face when he came into Rosa's house?

A Well, he had some scratches on his nose, and I'm not sure whether it was his cheek or forehead, but he had some scratches on his face.

Q What kind of scratches did they look like to you?

A To me, finger nail scratches, or——

Q Now, what did Inez do after she set the rifle down?

A She was mostly walking back and forth. She was just pacing the floor. She was, I guess, a little nervous over the whole thing.

Q What was Freddie doing?

A He was just sitting there. Just, I guess, he was mostly just like he couldn't believe it. He just would say, "wow."

Q Did you have any conversation with Inez after she set the rifle down?

A No, I just kept telling her, "why?" I couldn't really believe that it had happened. To me, it just didn't seem like it was true. I mean, her and Mike were very good friends. I couldn't believe it. I thought it might be a joke or something of this sort.

Q Did you stay in the house after you first went in it?

A Repeat that?

Q Did you stay in the house––

A Inez wanted some cigarettes, because she was nervous. So, they asked me–I–if I would go get them some, or if Juan and me could go get them. Go to the store and get her some cigarettes. So, I told her I would go with Freddie to get the cigarettes.

. . .

September 17, 1974–10:15 A.M.

BY MR. BRAUDRICK:

Q Did you talk to Freddie about going to get cigarettes?

A Yes. I told him for me and for the two of us to go get the cigarettes instead of taking my nephew, Juan.

Q What did he say?

A He said it would be okay.

Q Well, what did you do then?

A Well, I told him that cause his car was parked right in front of the house next to the road–I told him it would be better to get it out of the way. Hide it behind the house in case the Jimenez brothers might show up or whatever. So, I was afraid something had happened. They might come to the house and my kids were in the house. I was also afraid for them–to leave them by themselves in case something–I mean they found them. They think they would be in the house. You never can tell what would happen.

. . .

Q Who moved the car?

A Freddie did. I moved mine out of the way so he could–well, I moved my car first. I went and moved my station wagon which was parked back there. Then I moved my car out of the way so he could park it real close to the house where it wouldn't be seen if anybody was passing by the street.

. . .

Q Where did you go to?

A We turned—well, right there where the accident had happened, the block before it where the projects are. I don't know the name of the street, and I saw—when I stopped there, I saw the police cars and I—that's when Freddie told me that that's where it happened, and so instead of going over there, I said, "I got to go back home." And I turned south again. That's when Freddie said something like there's some cigarettes at the house—at the apartment, and if I would go get them. So, I started going towards the apartment. When I saw—just as we're getting to the end of Fifth Street, I saw the police car driving into the driveway of the apartment, and that's when—and I turned back.

Q Driving into whose driveway at whose apartment?

A Freddie's and Inez's apartment.

Q After you saw the police car turning in there into Freddie's and Inez's apartment, where did you go then?

A I drove north and went into Third Street up again to try to get back home, and we just—I just stopped at the stop sign when I saw a police car coming. So, I just kept going. I thought they wouldn't stop me, and just as I passed the stop sign, they put all the lights on me; and so, I got to the side and Freddie told me it was okay, that not to resist the officers. So, I just stopped and that's when they got Freddie out of my car.

. . .

Q What happened after the police pulled you over?

A Well, I had guns and lights all shining in my face. So, an officer got Freddie out of the car and another one told me to get out of the car; and so, they locked up my car and said they were going to take me home.

They took Freddie in one of the cars, and the other officer was going to take me home, and they asked me if I knew where Inez was, and I told her that she was at my house, and so they told me that she was armed and dangerous, and that sort of got me nervous. So, they drove over to my house, and by the time we got there, there was all kinds of police cars surrounding my house, and I told one of the officers to please let me go in because I knew she wasn't violent or anything. That I knew she was going to surrender herself.

So, Chief Jimenez let me go into the house, and he was just outside the door and I told them to come in. That she—that she said for them to come in and get her.

Q Okay. What happened when Chief Jimenez went into the house?

A Well, she handed him the rifle and that was it, and they took her out.

Q Did this appear to be—I show you People's number 11. Does this appear to be the rifle that she had there? Does it look similar to you?

A Yes.

Q I show you People's 16 which is a photograph of Inez Garcia. Is that similar to the way she looked when you saw her that night?

A Yes.

Q Was she wearing—is she wearing a wig in this picture?

A I think so.

Q Was she wearing a wig that night?

A I'm pretty sure.

. . .

(RT 590-610)

CROSS-EXAMINATION

BY MR. WORTHINGTON:

Q Let me try to refresh your memory from what you said yesterday so we can be sure it is correct. At 594 of the reporter's transcript line 12, the question was asked: "So what happened after Inez said she shot Mike? Answer: Well, I asked her why, and she said that Mike had tried to rape or raped her. I am not positive which, but I know rape was the main thing." The best you can remember, was that the sequence?

A Yes.

Q First she said she had shot Mike and then you asked her why and she explained why, that it had to do with an attempted rape or actual rape?

A Uh-huh.

Q Now, did she say that Mike was the person who did it? Do you remember if she named the person who did it?

A Yes, it was Mike.

Q Did she say that anybody else had assisted Mike?

A No.

Q Did she mention that anybody else was involved in any way, whether she mentioned the name or not?

A No.

Q Did she say anything about Louie Castillo that night that you can remember?

A Yes, she had said—what she really told me was that she had shot Mike and Louie and some other people from what I got.

Q That is the way you understood it?

A Yes.

Q Okay. Now, when all this was happening you were still upset, weren't you?

A Yes.

Q You were upset from that fight that you had, at least to some degree, been involved in yourself; is that what had upset you?

A Yes.

Q When she spoke these words about having shot Mike, did you know who she was talking about?

A Yes.

Q You knew that was referring to Mike Jimenez?

A Yes.

Q Was that the only Mike that the two of you knew?

A The only that I knew that she knew.

Q Your understanding of this relationship before March 19 was that they were friends?

A Yes, they were very good friends.

Q And you found it difficult to believe that she had actually shot him?

A Yes.

Q And you also said that you didn't believe that she had actually shot him?

A Yes.

Q And you also said that you didn't believe that she had been raped?

A No, I didn't believe it.

Q You did say that you did not believe that?

A Yes, I still say that I don't believe Mike would do something like that.

Q And is it still, other than you know it has happened now and she is on trial here for this, it is still difficult for you to even believe she shot him, isn't it?

A They were such good friends and it was such a closely knit group between all those people that it is very hard to comprehend that it would happen to such a–it is like they were something like a little family.

Q So, when you say that you didn't and don't believe that she was raped, you mean it in the same way that you mean it is impossible for you to believe that she actually shot him?

A I mean Mike was a very sweet and understanding person and he never told me anything out of line. He never told anybody anything unless it was provoked.

Q And that is what you knew about him at least, isn't it?

A Yes.

. . .

Q All right. Now, would it be fair to say, Alicia, that even when you gave the first statement about the 20th or the 21st of March that the sequence of events was not perfectly clear in your mind?

A Well, it was mostly because my mother had left very strict orders—she is always protecting my little sister and I didn't want to say what had happened in her house because I was supposed to protect her.

Q I see. And you also—your mother at that time was in very bad condition?

A She has been—she had been that way for quite a few years.

Q All right. And for a number of reasons then, would it be true to say that your mind wasn't completely clear on exactly what had happened that night on March 19th?

A I do know what happened, the parts I wanted to remember, I would remember.

Q All right. You are not completely sure of who said what right now as you sit there now, are you?

A No, I am not too sure.

. . .

Q Now, Alicia, yesterday on direct examination, the District Attorney asked you about the blouse being ripped and I am referring to page 570, I'm sorry, 595, at line 15—well, go back to line 13 and I will go back—excuse me. I will go back to line 12 of the question. Okay. What happened after that?

A Well, like I said, the conversation was more or less on that topic and I really don't remember what happened next. The only thing I do remember is that somehow either Inez, Freddie or Juan in the room said something about, like I said, that she didn't look like she was raped, so somebody tore the blouse because she had it ripped about two inches from the top, it was a knit blouse and it was ripped about two inches, and an inch or so from the top and then you were asked the question, Q Did somebody tear the blouse and then answer Yes.

Q And you were asked, do you know who did it, and you said, no, I am not sure. Do you remember that line of questioning yesterday and giving those answers?

A Yes, more or less.

Q Now, Alicia, I know your memory isn't completely fresh on this now, but do you recall having told me when I talked to you on August 24 that you were fairly certain that it was you who had ripped Inez's blouse?

A Yes, I told you that but like I told the District Attorney right about now I am telling anybody anything because I just want to be rid of you people.

Q You are not sure what happened and you would just as soon be done with all of it?

A Yes. I have my children to take care of and with you people, all of you being over at my house, they are getting a little sassy and need more of my attention.

Q Do you recall telling me last Friday that you really could not remember whether anybody had ripped the blouse at all after she got to your house?

A No, I couldn't, until I really started thinking about it because I knew when she came in that it wasn't that far down; otherwise, my nephew would have been looking at her quite a bit more than he had.

. . .

BY MR. WORTHINGTON:

Q Is this something that has come to your mind recently then?

A Yes.

Q Your recollection about whether or not that blouse was ripped at all was something that has just recently come into your mind, is that right?

A Yes.

. . .

CROSS-EXAMINATION

BY MR. GARRY:

Q Now, how long have you known Inez Garcia?

A Not very long.

Q Isn't it a fact that you have known her about three years?

A No, I'm sorry, but I haven't.

Q You have known her ever since you have known Minga, have you not?

A I have seen her which there is quite a bit of difference between seeing a person on the street and talking to them.

Q Well, when did you first see her then?

A Oh, it has been along about——

Q Three years ago?

A I wouldn't really know. Quite awhile. About two years.

Q You knew her when she was living at the Motor Lodge?

A I met her, which she knew how to make a custard and that sounded delicious and I asked her once if she would ever cook it for me.

Q Did she?

A One time when she lived at the apartment, she cooked it and I tasted it, and it was delicious.

Q This was at the Motor Lodge?

A No, it was when she was living at the—on Monterey Street.

Q On Monterey Street?

A Yes.

Q Did you know her when she lived at the Jimenez Camp with Minga?

A Yes.

Q And how long did she live at the Jimenez Camp with Minga?

A A couple of months.

Q Did she ever take care of your children?

A Oh, yes. . . .

BY MR. GARRY:

Q Now, on this evening in question, the 19th of March, were you at the apartment, at Freddie's apartment?

A Yes.

Q You were there until about nine o'clock, weren't you?

A No, a little earlier than that.

Q You left about a quarter to nine?

A I couldn't say for sure.

Q Well, isn't it a fact that both Mike and Louis were there at the time?

A Yes.

Q And you left because you thought the party was kind of getting out of line. Is that right?

A Yes.

Q And did you—would you tell the jury what you mean by the fact that the party was getting out of line?

A Well, as I have stated before, Mike had been drinking quite a bit and when he came in, he was already half-way drunk or drunk, and he had a fifth of peach brandy which he was trying to get everybody to drink and Inez had a little bottle of whiskey which he also drank.

Q Is that Mike that drank that?

A Yes, he gave us—oh, I would say about a half a cup of the peach brandy and the other bottle he drank it just by himself because I remember that Louie was trying to get some from him and he wouldn't give anybody any of the drink that was in there.

Q When you talk about Louie, you are talking about Louie Castillo?

A Yes.

Q And when they started talking about sex and that you are my girlfriend and so forth, you split. Is that right?

A I wouldn't call it sex. It was mostly saying—joking about who was anybody's pet or who liked somebody.

Q And at that point, you thought the party was getting out of line and you got out of there?

A No, I thought Mike was getting a little too high.

Q And you got out of there?

A Yes.

Q I see. Now, Inez told you that they tried to rape me or they raped me. Isn't that right? They used the word "they"?
A Yes.

. . .

(RT 611-633)

The prosecution's next witness was policewoman Yvonne Moranda who assisted in the booking of Inez Garcia the night of the shooting.

YVONNE MIRANDA, SWORN
DIRECT EXAMINATION

BY MR. BRAUDRICK:
Q Mrs. Moranda, what is your occupation?
A Police woman.
Q And by whom are you employed?
A Soledad Police Department.
Q Now, on March 19, 1974, what was your occupation?
A Police woman.
Q On the night of March 19, 1974, in the early morning hours of March 20, did you recover some clothing from Inez Garcia?
A Yes, I did.
Q I show you People's Fourteen, it is a blouse. Does that appear to be the blouse that you saw?
A Yes, that was it.
Q And when you took it from her, was it ripped like that?
A Yes, it was.
Q Who did you give the blouse to?
A Sergeant Perez.
Q I show you People's Sixteen, did you take this photograph of Inez Garcia that night?
A Yes, I did.
Q Do you know about what time?
A Oh, it was approximately eleven—no, it was probably about twelve or one o'clock, I think, I can't recall what time it was.

. . .

BY MR. BRAUDRICK:
Q I show you People's Twenty-five for identification. Did you recover these blue jeans from Inez Garcia that night?
A Yes, I did.
Q Who did you give the blue jeans to?
A Sergeant Perez.
MR. BRAUDRICK: I move to introduce People's Twenty-five,

Your Honor.

THE COURT: There being no objection, it will be received in evidence as People's Exhibit No. Twenty-five.

BY MR. BRAUDRICK:

Q Did you do anything to the pants?

A No, I didn't.

Q To change them in any way?

A No.

Q Thank you. I have nothing further.

THE COURT: Cross-examine.

MR. GARRY: If Your Honor please, I have subpoenaed Sergeant Moranda as my witness and I will be going into matters that were not covered directly on cross-examination.

CROSS-EXAMINATION

BY MR. GARRY:

Q You did not take her panties, did you?

A No, I didn't.

Q And you did not take what she had on her feet?

A I can't recall.

MR. GARRY: I want to put these togs in for identification first, Your Honor.

THE COURT: All right. Defendant's Three, for identification.

BY MR. GARRY:

Q I show you Defendant's for identification Three, and ask if you recall her wearing those?

A Yes, I do, but I can't recall taking them from her?

A I see. Thank you.

MR. GARRY: I have no further questions at this time, Your Honor.

. . .

(RT 634-637)

The prosecution's next witness was officer Richard Perez who testified to his arrival at the scene of the shooting and his recovery of evidence from the scene of the shooting, Fred Medrano's car and his apartment.

RICHARD JAMES PEREZ, SWORN
DIRECT EXAMINATION

BY MR. BRAUDRICK:

Q Sergeant Perez, how long have you been a policeman with the City of Soledad?

A Approximately six and a half years.

Q Were you employed as a policeman on March 19, 1974, for the City of Soledad?

A Yes, I was.

Q That evening, did you have occasion to go to the residence of William and Rosa Bracamonte?

A Yes, I did.

Q About what time did you get there?

A I believe I got there approximately 9:45.

Q And why did you go there?

A I was called there on a domestic disturbance.

Q How long were you there?

A I can't be exact, I believe it was about ten minutes.

Q Okay. Had you completed your job at their house?

A No, I didn't.

Q And why did you leave?

A I was advised by Officer Armstrong that he had a shooting on Monterey Street by the park, he had a man shot.

Q What did you do then?

A I advised the people there that I had to leave due to a shooting and I went to the location of the shooting.

Q And where is the location of the shooting?

A It was on Monterey Street in the alley way between Pine and First Street.

Q That is across the street from the Community Park?

A Yes, it is.

Q What did you find when you arrived at the location?

A When I arrived at the location, I observed a man laying in the alley way and he was bleeding profusely around the face area.

Q Did you recognize the man?

A Yes, I did.

Q Who was that person?

A Miguel Jimenez.

Q I show you photograph, People's Number Two, does that appear to be a picture of Miguel Jimenez at approximately the time you arrived there that night?

A Yes, sir.

Q What did you do after you got there?

A As soon as we arrived there, we secured the crime scene and they had already called for the ambulance, and I assigned Officer Armstrong to keep the people back.

Q I show you People's Number Four, have you seen that knife before?

A Yes, sir.

Q And where did you first see it?

A It was lying next to the body of Jimenez.

Q Was it in the location as shown in the photograph?

A Yes, sir.

Q That would be People's Number Two?

A Yes, sir.

Q And have you kept the knife in your possession since then?

A Yes, I have.

Q Did you recover any other evidence at the scene?

A Yes, sir.

Q What sort of other evidence did you recover?

A I recovered, I believe, eight shell casings, .22 and two spent rounds.

. . .

Q Now, did you take measurements of the area of between 1201 Monterey Street and 1299 Monterey Street?

A Yes, I did.

Q And what was the distance between the porch on 1299 Monterey Street which would be at that time where Dima was living and what was the distance between the porch and the other side of the street?

A From the porch to the other side I believe was eighty feet.

Q All right. What was the distance between the porch and the location where you found the knife?

A The location from the porch to the body I believe was 111 feet.

. . .

BY MR. BRAUDRICK:

Q I show you People's Ten-A and Ten-B, are those photographs of Freddie Medrano's automobile?

A Yes, they are.

Q Did you search that car?

A Yes.

Q When did you search the car?

A On the 19th, it was checked and re-checked again at Doc's Towing.

MR. BRAUDRICK: Your Honor, I would like this plastic bag containing one round of .22 caliber ammunition marked for identification.

THE COURT: Twenty-six.

BY MR. BRAUDRICK:

Q I show you People's Twenty-Six, have you seen this before?

A Yes, I have.

Q And where did you first see that?

A I seen this on the 19th in Medrano's vehicle at 1416 Metz Road.* . . .

BY MR. BRAUDRICK:

Q Do you recall about what time you found that?

A Approximately eleven-thirty or eleven-forty-five.

Q Now, later on the night of the 19th or the early morning of the 20th, did you have occasion to go to the apartment where Inez Garcia and Freddie Medrano lived?

A Yes, I did.

Q About what time did you go there?

A I am not sure without checking, but I believe it was about 1:45 or 2:00 o'clock, around there.

Q And had Mrs. Garcia consented to a search of her house?

A Yes, she did.

BY MR. BRAUDRICK:

Q I show you People's Number Thirteen which is a box containing numerous rounds of .22 caliber ammunition, where did you first find this?

A That was on the headboard of the bedroom.

Q Whose bedroom?

A Medrano's.

. . .

(RT 637-653)

Officer Perez' direct examination was interrupted in order to allow testimony by Dr. Konrad Titus who performed the autopsy on Miguel Jimenez and Police Chief Benjamin Jimenez who was present when Inez Garcia surrendered herself into custody.

DR. KONRAD WOLFGANG TITUS, SWORN
DIRECT EXAMINATION

BY MR. BRAUDRICK:

Q Dr. Titus, what is your occupation?

A I am a physician.

Q And are you licensed to practice medicine in California?

A Yes, I am.

---

* This is Alicia Alcaraz' address.

MR. GARRY: We will stipulate, Your Honor, please to the doctor's qualifications.

MR. WORTHINGTON: We will.

MR. BRAUDRICK: As a forensic pathologist, his specialty.

MR. GARRY: Yes.

THE COURT: All right. So noted.

BY MR. BRAUDRICK:

Q Now, bringing your attention, Doctor, to March 20, 1974, did you have occasion to perform an autopsy on Miguel Jimenez?

A Yes.

Q And who was present at the autopsy?

A Officer Perez, I believe, from the Soledad Police force, a deputy coroner and I forget which one and Mr. Terry, the owner of Terry's Mortuary.

Q Could you give a general description of the body of Miguel Jimenez?

A The body appeared to be that of a large, rather overweight, young Mexican-American male.

Q And did you perform an autopsy on the body?

A Yes, I did.

Q Were you able to determine the cause of death?

A Yes, it was a gunshot wound of the head.

Q What was the point of entrance of the gunshot wound?

A The left eye.

Q Did you recover anything from the head?

A Yes, the bullet was recovered and was given to a Detective police officer.

Q Given your experience as a pathologist and medical doctor, what would you expect to happen to somebody when receiving a wound such as Mr. Jimenez received to his head?

A I believe that this wound is a fatal wound but not instant; depending on what he is doing at the time, he could have collapsed or he could have walked a few steps and then collapsed.

Q Were there any other wounds on the body?

A Yes, there were two abdominal wounds which I interpreted as being gunshot wounds: One on the right side of the abdomen and one on the left side on the abdomen, entry and exit wound, and they were very superficial, just through the fatty tissue. And there was an abrasion of the right thigh in the front which I also interpreted as possibly being a grazing type of wound from a bullet.

Q Were there any other bruises or wounds on the body?

A No, I did not detect any others.

Q I show you People's number 7 for identification. Is that a photograph taken of Miguel Jimenez at the time of the autopsy?

A Yes.

Q And I show you People's number 33. Is this also a photograph taken at the time of the autopsy?

A Yes, it is.

Q Now, you say the fatal wound was to the left eye?

A Left eye.

. . .

(RT 655-657)

CROSS-EXAMINATION

BY MR. GARRY:

Q Dr. Titus, you extracted some blood from the body, did you not?

A Yes, I did.

Q And for the purposes of determining the content of blood alcohol?

Q And you have been told, have you not, that there was .16 blood alcohol—–

A Yes, I have.

Q –in his system?

A I read the record, yes.

Q I see. Are you capable of telling us the significance in meaning of .16 blood alcohol?

A Well, it means that alcohol was consumed and that there is a metric amount of alcohol present in the dead body at the time of the autopsy. Everything else, I believe, would be a speculation.

Q On your part?

A On the toleration. That's all.

MR. GARRY: Thank you very much. I have no further questions.

. . .

(RT 657)

BENJAMIN JIMENEZ, SWORN
DIRECT EXAMINATION

BY MR. BRAUDRICK:

Q What is your occupation?

A Police officer with the City of Soledad.

Q Are you any relation to Miguel Jimenez?

A No, I'm not.

Q Bringing your attention to March 19, 1974, did you have occasion to see Inez Garcia?

A I did.

Q And when you saw her, did you take the rifle from her?

A I did.

Q I show you People's Number Eleven. Does that appear to be the rifle that you took from her?

A Yes, it does.

Q And who did you give the rifle to?

A Sergeant Perez.

Q Now, did you check the rifle after you took it from Inez Garcia?

A Yes.

Q What did you find when you checked it?

A I found that the chamber was open, and it had a spent cartridge crosswise, and a live round was in the chamber.

Q How would you commonly describe what you found? With the spent––

A It was jammed.

. . .

Q Now, after you took–after you took the spent cartridge that had been filed, that was jammed out of the rifle, what happened?

A The chamber closed and then I put them in the envelope and gave them to Sergeant Perez.

Q When you got the rifle, this cartridge was jammed in the chamber?

A Right.

Q You took this out then, and what did you find in the chamber?

A Live round.

Q So the live round was after the empty cartridge?

A Yes.

. . .

(RT 660-662)

Upon the conclusion of Chief Jimenez's testimony, Officer Perez resumed the stand to conclude testimony for the prosecution's case.

CROSS-EXAMINATION

BY MR. WORTHINGTON:

Q Officer Perez, I would like to show you People's Exhibit No. Twenty-six again, could you describe again for the jury what this piece of evidence is?

A A .22 shell.

Q All right. Has that shell been fired?

A No, it has not.

Q All right. So that is a shell similar to the ones that are in this box, that is People's Number Thirteen.* Is that right?

A Yes, sir.

Q It looks just like it did when it was taken out of that box and you have looked at it and that is the case. Is that right?

A Pardon?

Q It looks just like it did assuming it was taken out of this box, it looks just the same, it hasn't been fired or it hasn't been placed in a gun so far as you know?

A I couldn't say if it had been placed in a gun or not.

Q You can definitely say it has not been fired?

A Yes, sir.

. . .

BY MR. WORTHINGTON:

Q Now, you say you found that unfired .22, you call it a round, don't you?

A Yes, sir.

Q You found that unfired .22 caliber round in the right-hand floor of Freddie Medrano's car?

A Yes, sir.

Q And you found that at about 11:15, did you say, p.m., March 19?

A I believe the first time I stated it was about 11:45, but it was close to about 11:15.

Q At any rate, it was after the shooting, wasn't it?

A Yes, sir.

Q It was after you arrested Freddie and Inez?

A Yes, sir.

Q So, you have no way of knowing when that round got into the car?

A No, I do not.

Q So far as you know, it could have gotten into the car after the shooting occurred?

A It could possibly.

Q Does it show any markings to show that would indicate to you that it was ever placed in the rifle and ejected from the rifle?

THE WITNESS: Visible markings?

BY MR. WORTHINGTON:

Q Yes.

A Not to the naked eye.

CROSS-EXAMINATION

* This refers to the box of shells found on the headboard in Fred Medrano's room.

BY MR. GARRY:

Q Sergeant Perez, I believe you testified that about 1:30 in the morning you went to the premises at 1760-A Monterey Street; is that right?

A Yes, sir, approximately 1:30, 1:15, around there.

Q Whatever time it was, it was early in the morning on the 20th?

A Yes, sir.

Q And with you was Officer Santos?

A Yes, sir.

Q Now, was Chief Jimenez with you?

A No, sir, he was not.

Q You knew, did you not, that Chief Jimenez had been there earlier with Mrs. Garcia?

A No, sir, I did not.

Q You did not know that?

A No, sir.

Q Were you not coordinating with the Chief of Police as to what was going on that evening?

A For a time I had left to transport Mr. Medrano to Salinas.

Q Now, this People's exhibit number 12 was not in Mr. Medrano's automobile, was it?

A No, sir.

Q And you don't know whether Mrs. Garcia had already indicated what she had observed at the premises to Chief Jimenez——

MR. BRAUDRICK: Objection, Your Honor. Calls for hearsay.

BY MR. GARRY:

Q –at the time you went down there?

THE COURT: Overruled.

THE WITNESS: I–could have possibly.

BY MR. GARRY:

Q I beg your pardon?

A I could have possibly. I can't say for sure if I did or didn't.

Q Isn't it a fact that Chief Jimenez told you that Mrs. Garcia had gone to the premises and also had given permission to have the premises searched by the police, and that she had said someone had come in there and cleaned up the premises after she had left?

A She had stated that someone had cleaned up the premises to me.

Q She said that to you?

A Yes, sir, while we were at the house.

Q At what house?

A At her house.

Q At her house?

A Yes, sir.

Q You mean at 1760 Monterey?

A Yes, sir, she accompanied us.

. . .

Q Let's start over again. . . . Who went with you to the premises?
A Officer Santos, Officer Miranda, and the defendant, Inez Garcia.
Q And Officer Miranda is the person who testified here today—
A Yes, sir.
Q —earlier? And we asked her to come back?
A Yes, sir.
Q And Mrs. Garcia at that time told you that somebody has cleaned this place up since she was there last; isn't that right?
A Yes, she had.
Q And was she quite indignant over it? Wasn't she?
A She was persistent of the fact.
Q Quite persistent about it?
A Yes, sir.
Q And what else did she tell you while she was at the premises?
THE WITNESS: I believe she pointed out the bedrooms, which was hers and which one was Freddie's.

BY MR. GARRY:

Q And she also pointed out that she hadn't quite unpacked her things yet, did she?
A Yes, sir, they were still in cartons.
Q What else did she tell you about the premises?
A I remember her telling us somebody had cleaned it up, and I believe emptied out the garbage. I'm not sure.
Q And she was surprised about this, wasn't she?
A Yes.
MR. GARRY: I have no further questions. Thank you.

. . .

THE COURT: That's all, Mr. Perez. Anything further now?
MR. BRAUDRICK: No, Your Honor. The People rest.

. . .

THE COURT: Ladies and gentlemen of the jury, this is the conclusion of the People's case.

. . .

QUESTIONS FOR STUDY AND ANALYSIS

THE PROSECUTION'S CASE

ARMSTRONG'S TESTIMONY
(Pages 12-13)

1. What is the significance of Mr. Garry's question whether Armstrong had purchased a shotgun from Inez Garcia?

LIPSKY'S TESTIMONY
(Pages 13-14)

1. What is the significance of Lipsky's testimony that Jimenez was still alive when placed in the ambulance?

CASTILLO'S TESTIMONY
(Pages 14-42)

1. What is the significance of Castillo's admissions on cross-examination that he has lived off the streets, trafficked in heroin and sold some bogus heroin to an undercover agent to the prosecution's contention that the fight between Freddie and Louie was over dope?
2. What is the strategy of Mr. Garry's cross-examination?
3. Why does Mr. Garry carefully establish the amount of alcohol that Castillo consumed prior to the fight?
4. What importance should be attached to Castillo's admission that he did not tell the Grand Jury that the fight with Freddie was over dope? Is Castillo's explanation as to why he first mentioned the dope connection two weeks before trial to the D.A. credible? (pp. 31-32)
5. Why does Mr. Garry ask Castillo whether he knifed Conutro Gonzales? (p. 32)
6. Is Mr. Garry successful in discrediting all of Louis Castillo's direct testimony? What problems still remain for the defense, if any?
7. What is the meaning of Castillo's laughing and sneering when Mr. Garry asks him whether he raped Inez Garcia?
8. What is the strategy and effect of Mr. Worthington's cross-examination?

SOLIS' TESTIMONY
(Pages 42-80)

1. Much of Solis' testimony is offered by the prosecution to corroborate Castillo's testimony. Compare the differences, if any, between Solis' and Castillo's testimony on the following points:
   (a) the meaning of the term "home town boy."
   (b) events immediately after the fight in the apartment.
   (c) whether Inez went outside with Louie and Mike after the fight and if so, for how long.
   (d) whether Inez's blouse was torn.
   (e) what was said during the telephone call from Mendoza's house to Inez after Louie and Mike left.
   (f) the presence of a shot-gun in the apartment the day of the fight.
2. What is Mr. Garry's strategy in cross-examining Solis?
3. What reason does Solis advance for why Inez would want to kill Mike Jimenez for Freddie Medrano? Is this reason consistent with the prosecution's theory of the motive for the crime?
4. What is the significance of Solis' testimony before the Grand Jury that there was no mention of drugs in the argument and fight between Freddie and Louie and Mike? (p. 67) Does Mr. Garry establish a credible motive for Solis' change of testimony?
5. Why does Mr. Garry ask Solis whether he had ever seen Mike Jimenez throwing knives? (p. 70)
6. Do Solis' admissions that he has lied under oath on some matters to the police, the defense attorneys and the court completely discredit all his damaging evidence against Garcia and Medrano?

MORAN'S TESTIMONY
(Pages 80-84)

1. What facts is the district attorney trying to establish by Moran's testimony?
2. Is Mr. Garry trying to discredit or to clarify Moran's testimony concerning what he saw and heard?

CARBAJAL'S TESTIMONY
(Pages 84-96)

1. Of what significance to the defense is Carbajal's statement "I am

desperate to get out of here"? (p. 91)

2. Why did Mr. Worthington ask Carbajal not to call his aunt? (p. 91) Does his admission that he talked over his testimony with her impugn the accuracy of his memory?
3. What is the strategy of Mr. Braudrick's re-direct examination? (p. 93) Does he re-habilitate the damaging portion of Carbajal's testimony?
4. Does Mr. Worthington extract new admissions from Carbajal on his re-cross-examination? Do we get a clue as to Alicia Alcaraz's role that night? (pp. 93-95)
5. Why does Judge Lawson ask for clarification of Inez Garcia's physical condition after Mr. Garry's re-cross-examination?

FERREL'S TESTIMONY

(Pages 96-108)

1. Does Mr. Garry succeed in throwing doubt on Ferrel's ability to remember accurately what he saw the night of the shooting?
2. What is the strategy of Mr. Worthington's cross-examination? Does he successfully hint that what Ferrel saw and heard might in part what others say happened? Compare Ferrel's testimony with Dima Gallardo's (pp. 117-124) *Supra.*
3. What is the point of Mr. Garry's re-cross-examination? (p. 108)

BUNTE'S TESTIMONY

(Pages 109-114)

1. Do the defense attorneys succeed on cross-examination in limiting the possible conclusions to be drawn from Bunte's inference that there was a shotgun in Medrano's car the night of the shooting?
2. What does Mr. Worthington hint at in probing Bunte's discussions and relationship with Louie Castillo? (pp. 111-113)

ALMANZA'S TESTIMONY

(Pages 113-117)

1. Why is the time of the sighting of Medrano going to the car so important? Are the defense attorneys successful in countering the prosecution's inference that Mrs. Almanza saw Inez and Freddie leave their apartment together shortly before the shooting? What

are the other possibilities as to what she might have seen?

GALLARDO'S TESTIMONY
(Pages 117-124)

1. Compare Dima Gallardo's testimony with David Ferrel's (pp. 96-108). What are the differences in what they saw and heard? Are the differences material ones? On what points, if any, does Dima's testimony corroborate Ferrel's testimony?
2. What is the defense strategy for discrediting Dima's otherwise damaging testimony? Is the cross-examination completely successful in countering the damage?

BRACAMONTE'S TESTIMONY
(Pages 124-134)

1. Compare Rosa Bracamonte's testimony with that of her nephew Juan Carbajal (p. 84) *infra* and her sister, Alicia Alcaraz's testimony (p. 134) *supra.* What material differences are there in their testimony about what occurred after Freddie and Inez arrived at Rosa's house after the shooting?
2. Does Mr. Worthington succeed in establishing on cross-examination that Rosa is hostile to Inez or Freddie? Does Worthington indicate a reason for Rosa's animosity against Inez?

ALCARAZ'S TESTIMONY
(Pages 134-145)

1. Is Alicia's memory intentionally selective when it comes to recalling the events after Inez's and Freddie's arrival at her sister's house after the shooting?
2. Why does Alicia state "right about now I am telling anybody anything because I just want to be rid of you people"? (p. 142)
3. Is there evidence that Alicia is slanting her testimony with respect to either or both of the defendants?
4. Are Alicia's statements about Mike Jimenez's behavior at the Medrano apartment before the fight (p. 144) consistent with her statement on cross-examination that "Mike was such a sweet understanding person" (p. 141)? What accounts for the difference?

DR. TITUS'S TESTIMONY
(Pages 149-151)

1. What is the significance of Dr. Titus's estimation that Mike Jimenez "could have walked a few steps and then collapsed"? Compare this conclusion with Inez Garcia's description of what Jimenez was doing when she shot him.

CHIEF JIMENEZ'S TESTIMONY
(Pages 151-152)

1. What is the significance to the prosecution's case that Inez Garcia's rifle jammed with a live bullet in the chamber?

OFFICER PEREZ'S TESTIMONY
(Pages 146-149, 152-155)

1. What is the significance of the .22 bullet found on the floor of Medrano's car after the shooting. What possible inferences are there as to how and when it could have gotten there?
2. What is the significance of Inez Garcia's observation to Perez that Medrano's apartment had been cleaned-up when she returned with the police after the shooting? Who had an opportunity to clean the apartment?

THE CASE FOR THE DEFENSE*

The first defense witness was Dr. Jane Oldden, a psychiatrist, who testified as to Inez Garcia's social, emotional, and psycho-sexual case history and to Inez Garcia's statements to her of the events that culminated in the shooting of Mike Jimenez. The defense sought by Dr. Oldden's expert testimony to explain Inez Garcia's state of impaired consciousness at the time of the shooting in light of the emotional trauma and effects on her that were triggered by the rape.

September 18, 1974
DR. JANE OLDDEN, SWORN
DIRECT EXAMINATION

BY MR. GARRY:

Q Do you want to get your notes together first, Dr. Oldden? I wonder if you would briefly give us the bibliography about yourself, your background?

A Well, at present, I am in private practice of psychiatry in San Francisco. I am assistant clinical professor at the UC Medical School in psychiatry. I am on the teaching staff at Mount Zion Hospital. Previous to this, I–I am a board certified psychiatrist and previous to this, I took my residency ten years ago now, two at UCC and one year at Harvard. Previous to that, I practiced internal medicine for twenty years. I am board eligible in internal medicine.

Q And where did you have your medical training, Doctor?

A I graduated from Women's Medical College in 1941 and did my undergraduate work at Cornell University.

MR. BRAUDRICK: Your Honor, I am willing to stipulate that she

* Mr. Worthington's opening statement has been omitted.

is an expert for purposes of testifying here in psychiatry.

THE COURT: A qualified psychiatrist?

MR. BRAUDRICK: Yes.

BY MR. GARRY: And board certified?

MR. BRAUDRICK: Yes.

. . .

Q What is the field of psychiatry?

A Well, the field of psychiatry is the study of emotional illness, even though people talk about it as mental disease, we still use that phrase. I think it is easier to conceive of it as an emotional study of emotional illnesses, study of feelings and how the feelings motivate behavior and the conflicts that arise in people which fall in certain categories which we describe as certain different types of illnesses and I guess one main concept is that in psychiatry your major general condition is anxiety, which represents conflicts between unconscious parts of your psyche and conscious parts of your psyche. So, anxiety is to the emotional illness what pain is to the medical diseases. You have anxiety in all emotional illnesses and manifested in different ways. We have different categories for that.

Q Now, you said you were board certified. Would you tell the jury and the court what is meant by being board certified?

MR. BRAUDRICK: Your Honor, I stipulated that she is an expert.

MR. GARRY: I know, but no one knows what that means.

. . .

Q Now, Dr. Oldden, at my request, did you examine Mrs. Inez Garcia?

A I examined Mrs. Garcia at three different times.

Q And would you tell us what history you obtained from her?

A I saw her first on the 22nd of July and at that session—before I go into this, I think in order to share with you my findings and the basis for my conclusions, that it may be necessary for me to discuss certain aspects of Mrs. Garcia's life that ordinarily—

THE COURT: I think you are only allowed to answer the questions, madam witness.

THE WITNESS: All right. Okay.

THE COURT: You might also admonish the jury whatever she relates that the defendant Garcia told her as evidence is not evidence, but is received by her for the purpose of treatment, observation, examination, et cetera, but not for the truth of the facts stated. Proceed.

BY MR. GARRY:

Q Now, what you are referring to, Doctor, is that there will be certain confidential matters that were divulged to you. That it's necessary for you to divulge in order to be able to give a proper diagnosis and evaluation; is that what you are telling us?

A Correct.

Q With that in mind, I believe that Mrs. Garcia, by the very nature of submitting to you, has literally waived all of these rights. So, you may feel free to give us whatever history you have received from her.

A I first saw Mrs. Garcia on July 22nd and at that session—I first saw Mrs. Garcia July 22, and at that hour's session, we primarily talked about background because I wanted to get an impression of her total personality and her development, and in the subsequent hour, we focused more on the present situation that she's in.

Briefly, just to share with you some of the background, she's the second of six children, and she was brought up in Spanish Harlem primarily by the—the most active parent was her mother who seems to be a very self-reliant and stable person, and the father apparently was not present at all times, though Inez says that he was very warm and gave her things that she wanted when she did see him. So, she identified with him, and in her own way built up a very positive image of him.

She had various difficulties in her early childhood which resulted in her spending a year at the Hudson School for Girls in New York State, which is a youth—part of their youth division there, and in that report which I got and which supplemented what she told me about it, she was examined at that time, and at that time, she was thirteen—fourteen years old 'cause she spent a year there. She was illiterate at that time, and her examination—her IQ test showed that she was what they call mildly defective in intelligence, but they realized since she couldn't read or write that the tests we usually give would not necessarily be accurate as a measure of her intelligence. They described her then as a very negative person and angry young adolescent on admission there, and pointed out she had very basic core problems of self-hatred and self-alienation, and this is important because this has continued, but is not as obvious as it was when she was an adolescent and was in this situation.

At any rate, she related well there. They gave her some medication to calm her down. She spent a year there, and in the report from there, they said she related well to her peers and to the staff and it's interesting, because this is fairly characteristic of various other reports, in the sense that when her emotions do break through and she gets impulsive or acts out or gets melodramatic, she appears one way. When she's not under pressure, she's very cooperative and compliant and normal until —I mean, an intelligence not necessarily based on intellectual achievement, but based on good common sense and the use of her experiences.

Following her discharge, and now I'm going into the past record as it came out following her discharge from the Hudson School. Her mother summoned—served a summons on the father for lack of support, and Inez saw him dragged from the home by the police, which upset her deeply, and she was admitted to Bellevue Hospital on their adolescent service for a brief time. Actually for about two weeks, because she threatened to jump off the roof, because she was so upset by seeing her father taken away from the home by the police. And on that admission, she was evaluated at Bellevue and said to be emotionally unstable personality adolescent turmoil. In other words, there was no evidence of psychosis, no evidence of hostility in a paranoic sense or unreal sense, no break with reality, though they described her social judgment as being poor and felt she was unrealistic in her reaction to her family situation.

After that, she didn't return to school and she had been attending as far as I know parochial schools before that and was then indeed a highly religious person already and has continued to be a very devoted Catholic. At that time she was fourteen when she was discharged from Bellevue Hospital, and she met a young man who was actually living in one of her mother's properties—a tenant in one of her mother's properties on the West Side of New York City, and she got married and he was twenty-two years old, and shortly after that, they went and moved in Florida which is where she now lives.

At that first session with me, it was clear that she was rather compliant and very cooperative and very gentle in manner.

. . .

BY MR. GARRY:

Q Then, you can refer to the medical records and I will ask you about the medical records; so, if you will continue with the history, doctor.

A The history as I got it from Miss Garcia, to continue, she had married her husband and they went to Florida to live, and she had some difficulty in achieving sexual gratification, though, she feels very warm toward her husband and looks upon him as a person that she owes—as she puts it—a wife should cause no problems for her husband, and a good wife is a silent wife.

Q That is what she told you?

A These are quotes. However, they lived together and she gave birth to a child when she was 19 years old and about this time she was upset because she discovered her husband was unfaithful to her. And a few years following this, she got divorced from her husband in order to free him to marry a woman whom he had impregnated because she felt the child should be legitimized and have a name. All of these things fit in with the fact that when I spoke to Mrs. Garcia, she emphasized the fact that while she was very disturbed by the situation she was in, she was much more disturbed in general by the fact that the children all over the world are molested and are in serious situations. The scene that is important to her is this emphasis on the welfare of children.

Now, the second time I saw her, which was about a week later in July, we then focused on the situation here where she had come to Salinas to be near her husband who was in Soledad.

. . .

Q Just tell us the history as though no one has ever heard of anything.

A She brought her 11-year-old son with her and came to this area in order to be able to visit her husband whom she was at that time divorced from but still very warmly attached to him and very much a part of the emerged extended family of her family and his family who lived back in Florida. So, she visited her husband and they have been remarried in Soledad since her coming here. She worked with the farm workers in Salinas and was very concerned again about the welfare of the children there. She was concerned about sexual abuse. She was concerned about physical abuse. She was concerned about the neglect that she saw, and naturally, some of her criticism was not well received by the people there. She, in fact, had been arrested for assault on some woman who was beating a child. She had sent her son back to Florida and was herself planning to join him on the 7th of April. On the 19th of March she had just moved into that apartment on Monterey with a friend named Fred and three hometowners as they call themselves visited her there. There was a fight that ensued and which Fred, the person who she was sharing this apartment with, got badly beaten up. Subsequent to that, she went outside to try to appease the two young men who were being very argumentative and in essence, treating them like intruders and talking about the fact that they weren't hometowners on their own territory, and one of these men hit her and tore her shirt, and they threatened to rape her, and one of these men raped her. Now, at the moment of the actual rape, she blocks out the penetration and this fits in again very well with what is seen psychologically when somebody is severely shocked they tend to have an instant amnesia or blocking out of recall of what happened. Subsequent to the rape, she went inside, loaded her .22 gun, called her brother-in-law in Florida, received a phone call from the two men who had left threatening her and advising her not to report this to the police. She went out and accosted them on the street which would be probably a half an hour after the fight and the rape and when she met them, one of the men had a gun—had a knife and threw it at her and she fired at him and fired six shots at him and killed him. Following that, she went to the house of her friend and told the friend about what happened and with her friend asking her to do it, reported it to the police. Mrs. Garcia was very anxious, though she maintained she was able to be articulate and coherent and intelligent as she talked to me. She was appropriately anxious for her situation at this time and also very appreciative of the help she was getting. She was having flashbacks at night of the actual scene and having a very hard time sleeping. She had lost 25 pounds in the four months that she had been in the Salinas jail and was suffering from other evidences of anxiety such as dizziness and lack of appetite and insomnia. I gave her some tranquilizers to help her sleep at night and then I saw her again on the 6th of August. And at that time, she merely substantiated some of the areas of herself about her dependence upon this very extended family. She identifies, I think, to some extent with the children she is so concerned about in the sense that her dependency and suggestibility if you add up all the qualities that you see in her which is histrionic expression of her feeling.

. . .

Q Was there anything in there about bed wetting in the history that you obtained?

A Actually Inez did not directly give me a history of bed wetting. I have heard about it from other sources, and it has been a repeated symptom throughout her life which occurs under stress.

Q Do you consider without giving us any conclusions right now, because we'll come to your diagnosis, but do you consider that to be relevant to your diagnosis?

A The bed wetting or enuresis is definitely a symptom expressive of her underlying condition, yes.

. . .

Q Now, Doctor, would you tell us about the medical records that you examined, that you consider to be significant?

A Yes. I mentioned some of them, and I'll include the rest. The fact that she was in the training school for girls for a year when she was fourteen; the fact that she was briefly in Bellevue Hospital and that these reports—the first giving—emphasizing the feelings of self-destruction and self-hatred, and considering her adjustment reaction of early adolescence; the importance of both these reports is—and the one—the emotionally unstable personality with borderline defective intelligence—the gist of both these reports is that she was not psychotic, that she had no break with external reality; that her problems, her conflict and anxiety arose from a conflict within her own psyche between her own conscience and feelings on the way she thought or judged the world to be, and that's the essence of her conflict and not one of a break in reality, nor delusions, not paranoid, no hallucinations. That's important, too, because later on, she stays briefly in Jacks Memorial Hospital, and they were——

. . .

Q Thank you. Now, we can go on to Florida and Jacks Hospital there.

A In Jacks Memorial Hospital, she was—came to the emergency room four times. Some time after the baby was born in 19—probably 1962—it was hard to decide for the date on these xerox copies of the records. Two of the admissions were for—two of the examinations were medical things, and one was because she had drunk some disinfectant secondary to discovering her husband was unfaithful. She had a gastric labage* and was discharged.

There again, another example of where she was seen by physicians and treated, but not considered to be psychotic and out of touch with reality even though upset. . . . Discharged home and again this was an impulsive melodramatic histrionic expression of her feelings of jealousy and anger and despair, and the difficulties in her marriage.

Then in 1963, she had threatened to kill herself and her baby and her husband because again of trying to work out the difficulties in her marriage with her husband. She was only in the hospital at that time for 48 hours and left the hospital against medical advice, but again in their record there was no evidence that she had any symptoms of break with reality.

Q When you talk about a break with reality, you consider that to be relevant, do you not?

A Yes, I do. . . .

A The reason I'm emphasizing that is because in understanding her underlying emotional problem, I'm inferring she has a neurosis, and from a psychosis—and she at no time was thought to be psychotic. That is, totally out of control as far as the real world around her in a sense of hallucinations or delusions, but that her anxiety mounts whenever she has something that triggers her feelings, because in essence she presents herself somewhat as a saint or thinks of herself that way in a—I use that word just to convey the idea to you that she has a very high ideal about herself. She has a very high ideal about taking care of children and in finally settling her marital problems; she did it in a way, or thought it through in a way which again fits in this rather noble view of the meaning of life. She divorced her husband, and I am sure this was difficult since she is a Catholic, in order that the baby he had impregnated this other woman with, had a name. Interestingly enough, she brought this little girl who is now five or six, to Soledad to visit her husband—the child's father—for two weeks while she was here in Salinas. So, she not only has high ideals, but she acts on them.

Q Continue with the hospital reports.

A The other reports are merely manifestations of anxiety about hepatitis at one time that her son had, and she was worried that she was getting it. That is an appropriate sort of thing. The final report I had was on an examination done on her in July of 1974 and was a medical examination. And again, the physical examination essentially is that

---

* A washing-out of her stomach.

any physical illness was absent but she showed marked effects from this severe anxiety in which the described dizziness, weight loss of 25 pounds, difficulty sleeping, which I mentioned, and abdominal cramp and lack of appetite, bad dreams; and at that time, the only abnormality was an increased thyroid production which you see when a person is under extreme stress and is extremely anxious. I bring this out because Mrs. Garcia has a presence about her and this is all described in what we called hysterical neurosis, sometimes called label indifference (phonetically), meaning the patient is disconnecting from their feelings—whether they be anxiety feelings or sexual feelings and assumes a very calm air which is very deceptive to many people. She presents a very calm air and that is the way she likes to think of herself as being even though she may be in turmoil, so that is really the significance and relevance medical records. As far as just summing up some of these things that we have been talking about—by the way, her illiteracy I think is very interesting. She did go to school until she was fourteen in New York, and whatever I can get from the past records and from what I observed, her lack of learning to read and write is related again to an emotional block. She can learn to read or write in my opinion or could, but for some reason, chooses not to which keeps her of course in a rather separate world from the world of advertising and billboards; and when you think about being able to read in our society, it would tend to let her function more in her own idealized world rather than reading daily reports in the newspapers about what the world is really like. So, while that is not a psychotic withdrawal from reality, it is some kind of emotional distortion to refuse to read or write in our society because she does drive a car and I have a lot of patients who read and write but they feel too insecure to drive a car. She has driven a car since she was 16 and has memorized all the traffic signs so she knows what they mean even though she has never allowed herself to read. To summarize then my diagnosis of her is she has what we call a psycho neurosis of a hysterical type and briefly we have gone over the fact that her major problem is a conflict within her own mind which basically has expressed in the early records she has a core of self-hatred and self-alienation which she covers up with great emphasis on her appearance. She has a hundred and twenty pairs of shoes. She cares a great deal about how she looks. She wants to look well even though she may not feel well and about her frigidity and her sexual feelings and the denial of them. Again, you know, she rationalizes that children are important and her own sexual feelings or sexual gratification are not important, so her frigidity has been a problem in the sense that she also wanted to have more children and obviously can't have more children if you are frigid as was pointed out to her by the doctor. The melodramatic histrionic way of expressing her feelings when they are touched off by her father being dragged out of the house by the police, by her husband's infidelity, those are the very melodramatic expressions of the way she feels and isolated almost from the general way she sees herself. She is very suggestible which is also typical of psychoneurotic hysterical type and she is also manipulative and part of that is that kind of immaturity or childlike quality manipulating the world around you when you can't really understand it and relate to it from your own feelings. Okay. And the person like this with this kind of an illness, one of the characteristics, there are two types of hysterical neurosis. The one she exemplifies is what we call people who suffer from disassociative episodes and when something triggers them by some violent act or something that really touches on the feelings that they are trying to constantly suppress, they are thrown into a real struggle within themselves. I said it is not so much the outside world as within themselves to handle their angry or sexual feelings; and in this struggle, they very often go into a disassociative episode by which I mean they are no longer relating to the world around them so much or their position in that world by their immediate reality. They are relating to their own intrapsychic structure which is what happened to her in my opinion when she described to me her feelings and reactions to what happened to her the night of the rape. I guess I could best summarize it in how I describe this by this paragraph. By the time I saw Mrs. Garcia on August 6th, I felt clear about her emotional problem of psychoneurosis hysterical type. I also felt given her view of herself and her religious reinforcement of her neurotic values that only something as extreme as rape would project her into violent retribution, and her story was consistent with the reality of being raped. On the initial aggressive inner action and realization that Louie and Mike were threatening her life by using the sexual assault and by a fight between the hometowners and outsiders and her acceptance of the actual penetration as inevitable when she passively removed the rest of her clothes and then the actual amnesia or blocking out of the act itself which was, as I said before, a common reaction to extreme anguish and that for her only a sexual act would provoke.

Q Doctor Oldden, was Mrs. Garcia in the state of consciousness when she—can you tell us whether she was in a state of consciousness when she fired at Mike Jimenez?

A She was in a state of impaired consciousness which is what I meant by so-called disassociative act. She, after the rape and in the whole subsequent events until she fired, she was indeed engaged in the internal conflict between the feeling that she was demeaned and defiled and permanently damaged by the rape so that she was not thinking about the consequences in the sense of the world around her or what the world around her would judge the consequences of her act, and she was in an impaired consciousness. To explain this better would be disassociative acts are like sleep walking or periods of two or three hours of amnesia that people go through when the internal conflict is triggered off, and they can't disengage their energy from what is going on inside and relate what is going on around them, and they may block out what is happening for two or three hours.

Q You may cross examine.

(RT 701-723)

CROSS-EXAMINATION

BY MR. BRAUDRICK:

Q You testified—you have testified in court before, haven't you?

A Yes.

Q Have you testified for Mr. Garry before in any of his cases?

A No.

. . .

Q In terms of your evaluation of her, you were mostly concerned about what happened on March 19, 1974, weren't you?

A On the contrary, I deliberately on the first session wanted to find out what kind of a person this was and how does she function dynamically and what is her psyche like.

Q How about in the later sessions you had with her?

A In the later sessions again, I was not so much interested in the specific incident on March 19 but how she reacted to it and what it meant to her and what it meant to her as far as her whole relationship with her religion, her family and her culture.

. . .

Q How many months was it after that particular incident* that you first saw her, after the incident in March?

A Oh, I saw her July the 22nd.

Q So, that was in—that would be what, April, May, June, four months afterward?

A Correct.

Q And that was after she had been interviewed by the police. It was after she had been interviewed by the Public Defender's office and been represented by the Public Defender. That was after she retained Mr. Garry as her attorney, and that would have occurred sometime in May. Is that correct?

A Yes.

Q And after she had been represented by the attorneys for a total of four months, isn't that correct, that you first saw her?

A That's correct. I saw her July 22 for the first time.

---

* The shooting of Mike Jimenez.

Q And you did state on direct examination that she is very suggestible, didn't you?

A Yes.

THE COURT: When you use the word suggestible, meaning subject to influence by other people?

THE WITNESS: Yes.

THE COURT: All right.

BY MR. BRAUDRICK:

Q And you were aware that she hadn't mentioned anything about having actually been raped to the police?

A I was well aware of that. As I say, on my first hour spent with her I did not go into that myself because I realized that was probably difficult for her to deal with even at that time. Very often the patients when they are very upset by something, just to talk about it puts it in a more frightening perspective for them and makes it more real. It is a way of denial not to talk about it, about a trauma and it is a form of denial of the event.

Q Now, did you believe everything that she told you?

A I think I answered before that I don't believe everything anyone tells me.

Q Well, I am asking you did you believe everything that Inez Garcia told you?

A Belief is a funny word. I accept the core of what she told me as being valid.

Q What don't you accept?

A There is nothing that I don't accept specifically. I have no specific disbelief or I don't discount any of it. I put it in perspective of what I feel she is functioning at dynamically.

Q What does that mean?

A It means that as I tried to say before in the history in any evaluation which is hard to explain to people, unconsciously she has this bad image of herself, wrapped up with that are her feelings of suppressing both her sexual and aggressive feelings. She projects a very—how can I explain it—idealized moralistic black and white view of things. She, in that sense, could be said to be naive. She sees herself or she attempts to present to herself or be the kind of person that she would like ideally to be. This presents a conflict, and of course, in a situation where she is being both physically and sexually attacked, she is bound to get connected with some of her feelings which really frightens a person like this.

Q Now, I believe you stated on direct examination that only something such as rape could bring her to act violently. Is that correct?

A Well, I didn't say that.

Q Did she tell you about any other incidences where she reacted violently?

A I had a history of her angry behavior. I have a history of her being arrested for assaulting someone.

Q And who was it that she assaulted?

A I don't know the specific name of the person, but it was a woman who she felt was abusing a child.

Q Did this take place in Soledad?

A I assume it is in this area somewhere. I don't know specifically whether at Soledad or not.

Q Did it take place while she was living in Soledad?

A While she was living in this area, yes.

Q Would it change your opinion any if you found out that actually in the situation involving the child, the other person was arrested and that she was later arrested in a fight in a bar, would that—if you had that information change anything?

A Not necessarily. I would have to know what she was arrested in the fight in the bar about.

. . .

Q Now, her children weren't living with her on March 19, 1974, were they?

A No.

Q Why not, do you know?

A She had sent her son home to Florida. She told me she planned to join him in April. I didn't ask her specifically why she sent him home.

Q Now, you stated she was frigid. Is that correct?

A She had sexual difficulties and she had difficulties reaching an orgasm, yes.

Q Did she state to you that she was faithful to her husband?

A No, she didn't state that.

Q What did she say? Did she say anything about sexual relations since her husband went to prison?

A She didn't discuss any extra-marital relations.

Q Did you ask her about it?

A Again, specifically, we explored her relationship with people and what she was doing, and she didn't—I don't think I specifically said, did you have any extra-marital relations in a period of time.

Q Did she state to you whether or not she had any?

A No, she did not state that she had any extra-marital relations.

Q Again, your evaluation of her, would you expect her to have had any?

A My evaluation of her would lead me to think that she would avoid sexual activity.

Q And that would be because of her thinking of herself as a saint and being a very religious person, is that why?

A And because she very much thinks of herself as a mother and wanted more children and yet she avoided sexual relations with her husband and that implies a conflict, even though there was a period of time, of course, when they were legally separated, they were divorced, actually.

Q Did she tell you whether or not she went to church every Sunday?

A She does go to church every Sunday.

Q And what religion does she state that she was?

A Catholic religion.

Q Would you expect her to lie to anybody being a religious person?

A That is difficult. I would expect anybody would lie at certain times. I don't think that your religious training necessarily interferes.

Q I am talking about specifically her.

A I think that lying for her would cause her anxiety.

Q It would be a difficult thing for her to do?

A (Nodding.)

Q Did she relate to you an incident when her family visited her from Florida and she had a friend of hers come over and stay at the house so that her family wouldn't think she was living with Freddie Medrano, in which the friend brought over her children and toys and scattered some toys around the house? Did she tell you anything about that?

A She mentioned a visit from her mother and her sister, but she didn't mention the fact that she tried to deceive them.

. . .

Q How about your opinion that she acts on her high ideals, would that alter that opinion that you have?

A No, because people can have very high ideals and they can't always live up to them. When I spoke of high ideals, I were merely speaking of the way she functions emotionally, I wasn't saying that she was in any sense a perfect human being.

. . .

Q All right. Now, let's go into what she said regarding what occurred on March 19. Did she tell you how she spent that day on March 19? Did she go into that at all?

A No.

. . .

Q She didn't talk about what occurred before they came to the house, that is the question I asked you.

A No.

Q She didn't. All right. Now, what did she say to you regarding her relationship between Luis Castillo and Mike Jimenez before March 19?

A She implied some difficulty, but it wasn't specific that there was anything more than what she implied to me was that she was having difficulty, not just with Mike and Louie but with the other people and with the people around Mike and Louie. There was no—she didn't express any specific relationship with Mike and/or Louie. They were just part of this group of people that she was having difficulties with.

Q Part of the group of people she was a part of, isn't that right?

A Where she lived?

Q Yes.

A Yeah, but that she was not really a part of it.

Q And she didn't tell you anything specific about her relationship with those people?

A Nothing more specific than she actually got into a fight with a woman about a kid being abused.

. . .

BY MR. BRAUDRICK:

Q Okay. What did she tell you happened when she came to the house, meaning Louie and Mike when they came to the house?

A She told me that they came in and were presumably going to visit socially and that initially started off with their coming in regarding having a social visit with her and Fred, and I think there was another person present whose name I don't know, maybe not, and at any rate that she described there was an argument in which they were talking from the point of view of their being there as hometowners and both she and Freddie being outsiders and they emphasized this and got into an argument in which they beat up Fred, and that is what she said. . . .

Q Did you ask her what the fight—did you go into what hometown boys or anything like that meant? Did you ask any questions about that?

A I asked some questions about that and it came out around again that she was in disagreement with the way they were dealing with their kids.

Q Oh, I see. In other words, she told you that the issue was the hometowners weren't treating their kids right, or something like that?

A No, the issue was they were hometowners and she wasn't and she was an intruder and as an intruder she didn't have the right to tell them what to do and that was the gist of the argument.

. . .

Q Did she say anything to you about trying to break the fight up or trying to stop the fight in the house?

A I believe she did.

. . .

Q In the house about trying to break up the fight while it was going on.

A That was my understanding from what she told me that she was trying to intervene, you know, successfully between Fred and Louie and Miguel and then she went outside after Louie and Miguel to try to get them to calm down and that was my understanding.

Q Okay. What did she tell you occurred outside?

A She said that she was beaten and her blouse was torn and they kept threatening her and kept saying we are hometown boys and they kept emphasizing the sort of territorial hometown business and threatened her with rape and then raped her.

. . .

BY MR. BRAUDRICK:

Q What I am trying to find out is how badly she told you she was beaten and so far, you have told me——

A —That her eye was bruised and her blouse was torn at which point she was afraid and she submitted and took her clothes off.

Q Did she say who tore her blouse?

A I believe it was Miguel.

Q Did she say how many times they hit her during the beating?

A She didn't tell me the number of times she was hit.

Q Well, was she hit more than once?

A The implication was she was hit badly and roughed up and her blouse was torn preliminary to raping her and that was how she described it.

Q And did she say anything about receiving any bruises on her face?

A She said her eye was black.

Q Did she tell you anything about being hit later on that night?

A No.

Q She didn't tell you about being struck at someone's house after the shooting?

A No.

Q Did she tell you anything about having her blouse ripped after the shooting at a friend's house?

A No.

Q Did she say anything—now, she told you after she was beaten that she said they were going to rape her?

A (Nodding.)

Q And what did she say, okay, or something like that, and they took her clothes off?

A She took off the rest of her clothes and she felt very badly about doing that. She told me——

Q Badly about what?

A Submitting, she felt she should have fought harder. Apparently Miguel was a very big person the way she described him.

Q Did she say who raped her?

A I understood she said Louie.

Q She told you that Louie raped her?

A Yes. . . .

Q Okay. Did you go into—did you ask her any questions about exactly what Louie did to her?

A Yes, and she said to me that actuai penetration was something that she blocked out, once she took her clothes off and submitted that it was like a passive sort of thing that she blocked out.

Q In other words, she doesn't know whether Louie inserted his penis inside of her?

A It was as though she described it to me actually blocked any emotional reaction. She didn't hesitate to tell me that he did indeed rape her and that is why she took her clothes off and he raped her and she blocked any sensation or any—well, as I said, in a person who is very upset, they block out something at a certain point.

Q Well, was she able to remember whether or not Louie performed an act of sexual intercourse with her?

A That she stated definitely.

. . .

Q All right. What did she do after Louie raped her. . . .

A She put her clothes on and went in the house, at least so she said to me and loaded the gun.

Q What did she tell you she done then?

A She said she phoned, I guess, someone in Florida.

Q Did she tell you what that conversation was about?

A That she had actually said that she was going to defend herself and that she had been raped—I am not sure—well, maybe she said that she had been beaten and they had tried to rape her, I don't think she told them she was raped, actually, but the implication was there, but she didn't come out and say it from what she said to me.

Q And what did she do, did she say where Freddie was during the time?

A She said that Freddie was either there when she came in—I got the impression that Freddie knew she had been raped but was on his way out to continue the fight with Louie.

Q She told you that Freddie knew she had been raped? . . .

A It was very difficult for her to use the expression I have been raped because to her that meant that she was defiled and that she would have to acknowledge this to other people and it was very difficult.

. . .

Q Did she tell you then what happened after the phone call to Florida?

A I think she told me that she also got a phone call from Louie and Miguel.

Q Did she tell you what they said to her?

A Heard the threat and not to report what happened. . . .

Q And this is a very important part of what her later mental make-up would be at the time of the shooting, isn't it, her mental state at the time of the shooting, the things that Louie and Mike were saying to her over the phone would have a great effect on her, wouldn't it?

A The major effect would be the sexual aggressive assault and the only other—I mean, the additional effect of their calling her would probably increase the fear and anger, but I think her whole reaction was the immediate reaction to having been assaulted sexually.

Q Did she say anything to you as to why Freddie left?

A She said Freddie went out to again accost them and to continue the fight.

BY MR. BRAUDRICK:

Q Did she say whether Freddie drove a car or walked?

A No.

Q Did she tell you whether or not she went with Freddie?

A I believe she said they went separately. I believe that she told me that Freddie went ahead of her or went before she went.

. . .

BY MR. BRAUDRICK:

Q Did she tell you what her intention was when she left the house with the loaded rifle to look for Louie and Mike?

A Yes, she said that she intended to settle her account, to defend herself, to kill the guy that had raped her.

Q So, she left the house with the intention to kill?

A That is what she said.

. . .

Q Okay. What did she say happened when she found Louie and Mike?

A She said that she saw them and Freddie was there too, and that I guess it was Miguel that had the knife and that she saw the glint of a knife and that he threw the knife and that she shot the gun and that she shot it repeatedly.

Q He threw the knife at her?

A That is what she said.

Q Did she say how close the knife got to her when he threw it?

A She didn't say that.

Q Well, she did say that he definitely threw the knife?

A She said that he threw the knife.

. . .

Q Now, you stated that she was in a state of impaired consciousness after the rape. Is that right?

A That's right.

Q If the information that you received, if she lied to you about the rape would your conclusion be different?

A I would—my conclusion would be that she was in a state of impaired consciousness in order to commit such a violent act, you know, whether indeed your question being whether the rape provoked it or the fight provoked it or something else provoked it, knowing her she still must have been triggered by something very profound and disturbing in order to act that violently. She is not a violent person. She is a hystrionic and melodramatic person.

Q She is not the sort of person you would expect to get into fights?

A Fights, yes, you know, hair pulling and kicking but not killing.

Q Couldn't you make that same conclusion about most everybody?

A No, no, there are people who suffer from certain conditions where they can indeed be said to be in a state of readiness or violence almost at all times.

Q Well, you are differentiating between violence with a rifle and violence with one's fist, aren't you?

A No, I am differentiating between the kind of angry acting out that was characteristic of her behavior and the kind of person who is really harboring a homicidal feeling; you know, who really accepts it as part of their style.

Q Well, she harbored homicidal feelings before?

A She doesn't harbor them, she advertises them and that is different.

Q Well, when she went into the hospital in Florida she had homicidal feelings about her husband and her child.

A She was angry and expressed wanting to kill herself and the child and her husband, but it was nothing in the record that suggested this was actually a plot or a plan or any definitive act.

. . .

Q Do you believe that she confided in you and told you everything?

A I doubt that she told me everything because I don't think she tells anybody everything.

Q But, she did confide in you and tell you about a rape, isn't that right?

A That's right.

. . .

Q Did she tell you why she didn't report the rape to the police?

A She didn't want—she did indeed talk to me about the fact that she couldn't talk about the rape to the police, that she didn't want to talk about the rape to the police.

Q Did she tell you why?

A She told me that she felt so badly that she did not want to talk about the rape.

BY MR. BRAUDRICK:

Q Did she relate to you what happened after her friend called the police?

A Nothing specific. The inference was she went to the police station. I didn't hear anything further.

Q You didn't ask her any questions about what happened after she went to the police station?

A Yeah, I was curious as to what they did at the police station.

Q Okay. What did she tell you?

A She talked to them and she wasn't examined. She went to jail. They put her in jail.

. . .

Q . . .Would you say she was in an excited state when she was shooting?

A I tried to describe the fact that in her particular kind of condition if you trigger off negative feelings about herself which are primarily unconscious and covered over by this reactive formation of being concerned about children and welfare and, you know, what I term as a saint-like idealized virgin, if you trigger her that negative feeling which would be provoked by such an act as rape being a hysterical person who was striving always to suppress this sensuality and their aggression then you could indeed throw her into a state where she is emotionally relating to her own inner conflicts is what I am saying, so in that sense, you know, when you say was she excited, she was unquestionably at a very high level of energy and anxiety and tension, or whatever, excitement, but mostly because of the threat to her interpsyche conflicts is what I'm trying to get across, so she blocked out her best judgment or what is right in the eyes of society and she takes it upon herself to defend herself. So, when you say excited state that goes back to when I said she was disassociated from, you know, she was—her awareness of what she was doing was grossly impaired by triggering the conflict in her.

Q She knew how many times she shot, though, didn't she?

A What?

Q She knew how many times she shot, though, didn't she?

A Yeah, it's interesting that in a disassociated state like this, the people can sort of remember things, but they're not connecting with their judgment and their awareness of what they are doing is impaired by an almost survival kind of excitement. When you saw she was excited, yes.

Q You would expect her in this excited state to be shooting well, assuming she can shoot well?

A Oh yes, oh yes, oh yes.

Q She'd be able to?

A When you are surviving, you do very well, you know.

Q She was able to hold the rifle steadily, aim it, pull the trigger once, twice, three times, four times, five times, six times, seven times, eight times, ten times or whatever it was; is that correct?

A If she's excited and full of adrenalin, which she would be at that time, then her performance should be compatible with her skill.

Q And you would expect her to remember how many times she fired or who she shot? What she did after the shooting and so on?

A Yes, there is no reason why when the frame of reference of her own intrapsychic conflict of defending herself she couldn't remember very sharply of whatever details occurred because of adrenalin, because of when you are full of adrenalin, you remember everything like that as far as numbers of shots.

Q This excitement came as Miguel threw the knife at her?

A The excitement came when she was raped. It started then.

Q That's when she formed the intent to kill?

A That's when she—that's when she got primed. That's when, as I say, she got triggered into this conflict of her own about the badness in her and the badness about her sexuality or her aggression, and she went out to defend herself.

. . .

(RT 724-810)

RE-DIRECT EXAMINATION

BY MR. GARRY:

Q Doctor Oldden, the question came up as to what extent Inez Garcia reported the rape or the attempted rape to the police. Remember that?

A Yes.

Q Now, from your experience as a doctor and as a psychiatrist for many years, is there anything unusual about women who had been raped and not reporting in detail to the police?

A No.

Q Could you tell the Court and the jury the extent of persons who are raped and report to the police?

MR. BRAUDRICK: Objection, Your Honor, beyond the scope of direct and no foundation.

THE COURT: No foundation for that. How could she possibly know how many people have been raped or haven't been raped.

MR. GARRY: There has been studies made on that.

THE COURT: Let's get a foundation.

MR. BRAUDRICK: I also object to being beyond the scope of cross examination.

THE COURT: I wouldn't pass upon that, but certainly I'd like to know what studies she's made.

THE WITNESS: In my experience––

THE COURT: Let's find out.

MR. GARRY: First, let me ask the question––

THE WITNESS: I'm saying in my experience––

MR. GARRY: Let me first ask you a question. Have you made a study of rape in women in relationship to the reports that I made by women who are raped to the police?

Have you made a study of that and studies that have been made?

A I'm familiar with literature on it and also have had experience on that, yes.

Q Would you tell that experience and literature?

MR. BRAUDRICK: I would object. That is not a proper––

THE COURT: This is not experience but training I'm interested in. If this is a subject of expertise, let's find out.

BY MR. GARRY:

Q Tell us the literature or texts that you have––

A In the literature–in the standard literature text–comprehensive textbooks of psychiatry and in other standard texts, the issue of rape has been studied and has been found that only one out of ten women––

MR. BRAUDRICK: Objection. Going into it.

THE COURT: Don't you understand me? I said investigation into your expertise on the subject. The time has not yet arrived for you to express an opinion on the principal question. I'm going to give the district attorney an opportunity to ask you questions on this further, because you're qualifying now in a field that I suspect is only collaterally a part of pscyhiatry. I'm not at all sure that all psychiatrists are qualified to say this is true or is not true. Now, I would want to find out further.

BY MR. GARRY:

Q How does this fit in with your expertise as a psychiatrist as to the question of rape and the number of rapes and the reports that are made to police by women who have been victims of rape?

A I feel sort of hemmed in. I was going to say that in my expertise as a psychiatrist both from the current reports on it and my own experiences. Is that suitable for me?

THE COURT: You haven't reached the point to qualify yet without first giving the opponent an opportunity of examining you.

MR. GARRY: I'll let Mr. Braudrick voir dire.

MR. BRAUDRICK: I don't think any foundation has been laid yet, so I would object to anything further at this time.

BY MR. GARRY:

Q What has been your experience as a psychiatrist on the questions of rape, Dr. Oldden.

A Among my patients, I have treated people—many people who have been raped in my own experience.

And——

THE COURT: I want to know what studies she's made on the subject, and I haven't heard yet what studies she's done. What's the extent of it? What experience have you conducted? What books have you read? What degrees have you taken in the subject?

THE WITNESS: I haven't done any experience or taken any degrees in the subject of rape, but I have been very interested in the subject and kept up in the——

At this point in Mr. Garry's voir dire of Dr. Oldden there was laughter in the courtroom from spectators in the court room and while the judge admonished the spectators for the disruption, Inez Garcia jumped out of her seat and directed the following outburst at Judge Lawson.

. . .

DEFENDANT GARCIA: Why don't you find me guilty and put me in jail? I killed the mother fucker because I was raped and I'll kill him again. You're acting like an old—you pig.

. . .

Following this dramatic outburst Judge Lawson declared a recess. Dr. Oldden was excused as a witness and no further testimony was taken that day.

September 19, 1974—10:15 A.M.

The defense's next witness was Dr. Sandy Carter. Dr. Carter testified that Freddie Medrano was being treated for tuberculosis on March 19, 1974.

DR. SANDY CARTER, SWORN
DIRECT EXAMINATION

BY MR. WORTHINGTON:

Q Dr. Carter, would you state your occupation, please?

A I am a physician presently working at Silas B. Hayes Army Hospital at Ford Ord.

Q You have any specialty? . . .

THE WITNESS: I am a specialist in internal medicine.

. . .

BY MR. WORTHINGTON:

Q Fine, thank you very much. And performing your duties as a physician, did you recently examine Alfred Medrano?

A I spoke with him approximately three weeks ago.

. . .

BY MR. WORTHINGTON:

Q Based on all of the information that you had at your disposal, you have concluded that Mr. Medrano was suffering from pulmonary tuberculosis in January of 1973, did you not?

A From reviewing those records, yes.

Q All right. Now, could you describe what the symptoms of pulmonary tuberculosis are?

A They can be variable with manifestations of systemic complaints of fever, weight loss, or weakness, or they can be related directly to the lungs, if that's where it is involved and coughing up blood, or shortness of breath or chest pains, along that line

Q And do the records indicate whether or not he has finished that specified course of therapy?

A They did not indicate because the end of the therapy was supposed to be through 1975.

Q Through 1975. All right. Did Mr. Medrano tell you that he was still taking his medication when you saw him in August of 1974?

A He said that he stopped taking it approximately one or two weeks before I saw him, I think. I think he said he had run out of them.

. . .

Q Based on all the information that you have at your disposal, is it your conclusion that Mr. Medrano was suffering from pulmonary tuberculosis on March 19th, 1974?

A It's felt his disease was in a latent stage at that time.

Q In other words, the disease was there but the symptoms were not present. Would that be a layman's description of what it amounted to?

A When he was seen in the out-patient clinic at that time in March,

'74, it was felt that the disease was latent, that it was nonactive. He was not suffering any symptoms from it.

Q At that time do the records indicate that he was still taking his medication?

A It did.

. . .

(RT 819-836)

The defense's next witness was Walter Stephens, an educational psychologist who testified to his I.Q. testing and evaluational sessions with Inez Garcia.

WALTER STEPHENS, SWORN
DIRECT EXAMINATION

BY MR. GARRY:

Q Mr. Stephens, what is your occupation?

A I am an educational psychologist employed by the Salinas Union High School District in Salinas, California. . . .

Q And precisely what do you do there?

A Currently I am assigned to handle all the psychological work at Salinas High School and Washington Junior High School and the special education program at North Salinas High School. This is some counseling with children but primarily diagnostic evaluations and especially for placing children in classes for educable mentally retarded and diagnosing pupils with severe reading problems for the purpose of placing them in special remedial reading programs.

Q Now, Mr. Stephens, at the suggestion of my office did you have occasion to examine Mrs. Inez Garcia?

A I did, sir.

Q And what was the purpose of the examination?

A I was told that Mrs. Garcia was—even though she was 30 was unable to read with any fluency or write and was unable to tell time, and I was to make a determination of her mental level and to find how it was possible for someone that age to have presumably attended school and to be unable to read and write.

Q Did you do that?

A Yes, I did, sir.

Q Would you tell the court and jury what you did in that connection?

A I administered the Wechsler Adult Intelligence Skill commonly known as the WAIS, both verbal, and I administered the Bender Motar-Gestalt Test, the Rorschach Diagnostic and I think the blots and two reading tests, the Gray's Oral per Form A, and the Wide Range Achievement Test, the reading portion.

Q Now, would you take each one of those tests that you gave and tell us what they signify?

A The WAIS is a standardized adult intelligence skill. It, incidentally, has included a selected sample of the minority non-Caucasian population in its standardization group. It gives both a verbal and nonverbal measure. Mrs. Garcia received 81 nonverbally which tests above even the range that is considered retarded or on the broadest definition of that. She received only 75 on the verbal. However, there is a good deal of what is known as scatter. For example, certain types of items which are much affected by education are quite low. Information which is the sort of thing like who is president of the United States, she would get one like that, but the more difficult ones you tend to pick up in school. If you can't read, you don't pick them up, or her arithmetic is quite low for the same reason. Her digit span, which is memory for numbers, is very low which I would attribute to a very high level of emotional tension in taking tests. Mrs. Garcia finds taking tests in which she is evaluated kind of threatening, apparently, so I would tend to disregard that. . . .

. . .

Q Mr. Stephens, are you able to tell us what the prognosis is of Mrs. Garcia's ability to be able to read and the reasons why she is not reading or cannot read?

A I think the prognosis, if they went about it the right way, is very favorable. I base that on the fact she learned to tell time. She'll have to go about learning to read the right way, and I discussed that. She has certain—developed certain procedures and complications which she can't ever read. That way she has to do it somewhat differently. I think the prognosis of her learning to read is very good; and as to the causes of her not learning, that's difficult to tell. There may have been a mild perceptual problem.

Q What does that mean?

A That is this trying to tell the words apart, and nobody knows why people have this. I can keep the Court tied up for three days on counting theories, but there are some people who when they look at a word have perfectly good vision. Things that look somewhat alike, they can't tell them apart. There are, unfortunately, a lot of words in English that determine the meaning like this, that, there, them, that. They look alike, and they have great deal of difficulty in doing that. This makes it harder to learn to read.

I doubt if her problem was really very severe, or I'd get more traces. Now, but if she did have this even mildly and was also upset and there was turmoil—I don't have her history. I do know her history. I do know she was—she told me she had been institutionalized, and usually a person doesn't get institutionalized without a great deal of turmoil preceding it. That's an inference I make. Then she may have been turned off.

She stated she was in a special class. I have no idea what kind of special class it was, because all sorts of things in school are called special classes and I would think that she probably just got turned off, but I don't know certain things about the history. I don't know if her school attendance was irregular. If it was irregular, then even the slightest problem causes you trouble, but I don't know that her attendance was irregular.

Mrs. Garcia didn't want to be questioned. I guess she had been questioned by a great many people, so we agreed we'll stick to the tests, and I took a brief educational history and, otherwise, didn't inquire, and she was tired of being questioned.

Q Did you arrive at any conclusion as to whether she is retarded or not?

A I arrived at a definite conclusion that neither by the standards of the State of California, nor by the current standards of the American Association for Mental Deficiency could she be considered retarded.

MR. GARRY: All right. I have no further questions.

. . .

(RT 839-849)

The defense's next witness was Father Eugene Boyle, a Catholic priest. The defense sought to present to the jury through Father Boyle's testimony what the duties and responsibilities of a devout Catholic are to rape and what are the attitudes of Spanish-American Catholics toward rape. The defense also sought to show the reaction that Inez Garcia would have and the reticence she would have in talking about the rape to the police or friends and what shock and effect the rape would have on her as a person.

EUGENE BOYLE, SWORN
DIRECT EXAMINATION

BY MR. GARRY:

Q Father Boyle, what is your profession?

A I am a Catholic priest.

Q And would you tell me your background as a Catholic priest?

A Well, first of all, I went to the seminary when the seminary had eleven years, starting in high school and going all the way through our seminary. I have been a priest, ordained priest, for 28 years. I have served as assistant pastor with the Diocese Mission Band which I did traveling and speaking. I directed a Vallombrora Retreat Center in Menlo Park for eight years. I was a pastor of the Inner City Parish in San Francisco for four years. I worked with—I, at that time while I was in both the Inner City Parish and also the Vallombrora Retreat, I also taught social ethics at the St. Patrick's Seminary in Menlo Park. In the last two years, I was director of justice and peace for the National Federation of Priests Council and also director of the Field Education for Jesuit School of Theology in Berkeley.

. . .

BY MR. GARRY:

Q Father Boyle, I have had the court reporter type up the question that I asked you and the question that I am asking you now is: Would you tell the court and the jury as to the Catholic Church's attitude towards rape and the responsibility of a person who is a devout Catholic when they are about to be raped, what their obligations are and in particular if you can talk about the Spanish Church aspect that you are familiar with.

. . .

BY MR. GARRY:

Q Would you answer the question now, Father Boyle?

A As I have already said, the Catholic Church has very strict codes of sexual morality and this has shown itself throughout history. Most of the text books that I studied were actually written by those whom we would call in the Latin tradition of the Church, most of them were at that time French or Spanish, and I would say that the attitude would be, Number One, that a person would have to try to resist, you know, even to the point of death, and I am not saying that is what is written in the book itself, but so strict is the, you know, the whole notion and the idea of resistance that that would almost be expected, in fact, as I said this morning,* such actions would be honored, for example, and have been honored even recently in the part of, say, virgins resisting attack. I mention Saint Maria Guerretti. I mentioned the last century, but I am a little stale on this, I think really it was certainly the latter part of the last century and I think it might even be in this century and somebody might be able to confirm that for me. But, she is a saint who was held up as someone who resisted to the point of death an attack upon her virginity. Also, in Catholicism, we do have—there are not as many married saints as there are saints who are virgins, but nonetheless,

* Father Boyle had given his testimony earlier in the day in a hearing out of the presence of the jury to determine if it was admissible. The prosecution strenuously objected to Father Boyle's testimony.

there are married saints and certainly one of the aspects and one of the virtues held up for that canonization would be the fact that they were faithful to their husbands. In the Catholic morality, certainly that which was taught up until just a few years ago, the marriage debt as it is spoken of, is owed by the woman to her husband as the husband to her, as the husband to his wife, and to no one else, and that a person would certainly be expected to resist strenuously any attack upon that particular right of the husband to that violation.

THE COURT: Cross-examination.

CROSS-EXAMINATION

BY MR. BRAUDRICK:

Q He's saying that as a Catholic Church's attitude, if a woman is going to be—is being assaulted by a man with the intent to rape, that she has to resist until she dies?

A I say she's certainly supposed to resist strenuously that particular attack and that has been the attitude. Now, the point is, it's certainly the case of some, you know, might not do that, but certainly there would be within the teaching itself as viewed by persons who have this particular kind of understanding that she would—she would be expected to resist to that point, and I think the very fact women are canonized because of that. I admit when you are talking about canonization, I talk about extraordinary——

. . .

Q Now, the attitude you are talking about, is that a present-day church attitude that a woman must resist until death, if a man attempts to rape her?

A I'm not saying that it would be any kind of teaching of the Catholic Church. I do believe that there would be persons who were imbued with a particular sense of their honor—their virtue if they were virgins; their honor, if they were married people that they would feel that this is what they should do. I'm not saying this is any official kind of teaching. Once again, as I said today, so much—any religion——

Q You're not saying it's an official teaching but yet you haven't done any kind of cultural investigations. You are not a sociologist, not an anthropologist. How can you testify to things that aren't——

A I wonder if one has to be an expert in sociology or an expert in anthropology to be able to imbue and to understand the feelings of people and the way they act. I don't think we need—one doesn't have to be an expert. So therefore, what I am saying—I would like to finish this, if I could—I have been associated with families. I have been a priest who has that kind of associations with people and I do believe that I have understood and imbued the feelings that they have.

. . .

Q And you are saying that if a man points a gun at a woman and tells her to take off her clothes, that he's going to rape her, that she has to resist, that she has to be shot?

A I'm not–no, I'm not saying that she has to be by any meaning. You know, but I think there would be some who would actually be imbued with the sense of the protection of their virtue or their honor, that they would believe that that's the way they would have to act.

I'm not saying–no, I'd like to be very clear. I want to answer your question, you know, there's no official teaching that says if there's a gun pointing at you, therefore, you have to die instead of undergoing this. You know, what I'm saying is that the teaching is such that there are many who would understand this. That that's precisely the way they would act.

Q You are not testifying as to church doctrines?

A I'm testifying as to church doctrines in the only way church doctrines ever live and that is in cultural incarnation. I mean, there's no such thing as a theoretical church doctrine. You know, there's no–you know, when it comes right down there, it's a life thing and therefore incarnated in some kind of cultural or flesh or whatever, you know.

. . .

BY MR. BRAUDRICK:

Q How many times have you met Inez Garcia?

A I met her once before yesterday.

MR. BRAUDRICK: Thank you.

. . .

(RT 860-877)

The defense's next witness was William Hyers, the manager of the Soledad Motor Inn where Inez Garcia had lived. Mr. Hyer's testimony was offered to show Inez Garcia's good reputation in the community and Louie Castillo's reputation for abusive behavior.

WILLIAM RAY HYERS, SWORN
DIRECT EXAMINATION

BY MR. GARRY:

Q Mr. Hyers, where do you live?

A At Soledad–Soledad Motor Lodge.

Q And what do you do there?

A I'm the manager.

Q And how long have you been the manager at the Soledad Motor Inn?

A Well, since a year ago—oh, about the first of June.

Q And do you know Inez Garcia?

A Yes, I do.

Q And over what period of time have you known Inez Garcia?

A Well, all that time up until she left there shortly after the first of the year.

. . .

BY MR. GARRY:

Q Did you know Castillo's aunt who lived there?

A Yes.

Q And did she have difficulty with Louis Castillo?

A Yes.

. . .

BY MR. GARRY:

Q Do you know the reputation of Mrs. Garcia for good character in the community there?

MR. BRAUDRICK: Objection, your Honor.

THE COURT: Wait a minute, what kind of good character, do you mean good character with respect to truth, honesty, integrity or with respect to assaultive behavior?

MR. GARRY: Truth, honesty and integrity.

THE COURT: All right.

THE WITNESS: Yes.

BY MR. GARRY:

Q And what is that reputation, good or bad?

A It is, as far as I know, or have heard, it was good.

Q Thank you. Now, do you know the reputation and character of Mr. Castillo, Louis Castillo for abusive behavior? . . .

BY MR. GARRY:

AQ And what is that reputation, good or bad?

A Well, it was bad.

MR. GARRY: Thank you. I have no further questions.

DIRECT EXAMINATION

BY MR. WORTHINGTON:

Q Have you heard from other people in the community as to his reputation for violence and aggressive conduct?*

---

* referring to Mike Jimenez.

THE WITNESS: Yes, I have heard other people say something.

BY MR. WORTHINGTON:

Q What do you understand of his reputation in the community of Soledad for violence and aggressive conduct?

A Just hearsay that it was–

Q That is exactly what we want.

A That it was bad.

Q He had a bad reputation?

A Yes.

Q And specifically as to violence and assaultive conduct?

A Right.

Q That is the same as to Louie Castillo?

A Yes.

(RT 879-892)

The defense's next witness, Clifford Martin, worked as a security guard and he testified as a character witness for Inez Garcia.

CLIFFORD W. MARTIN, SWORN
DIRECT EXAMINATION

BY MR. GARRY:

Q Mr. Martin, where do you live?

A At 263 Front Street, Soledad, California.

Q And would you tell us what your occupation is?

A At the present time, I work in a liquor store, and I work at the Soledad Motor Lodge.

Q And have you been at one time associated with the Soledad Police Department as a security guard?

A Well, not with the Police Department, but as a security guard in Soledad City.

Q I see. And do you know Inez Garcia?

A Yes, I do.

Q Do you know what her reputation is for truth, honesty and veracity?

A Yes, I do.

Q What is that reputation?

A She is very honest.

Q Do you know what her reputation is to clean living and not running around with men?

MR. BRAUDRICK: Objection, your Honor. Irrelevant.

MR. GARRY: I think it is very relevant in view of what he's insinuating.

THE COURT: I don't think so. We are trying a murder case, and not a rape case. Objection sustained.

MR. WORTHINGTON: Your Honor, for the record, I want it clearly reflected we want that evidence in. We think it bears on Mr. Medrano also.

THE COURT: Objection sustained to you, sir, also.

MR. GARRY: Now, do you know the reputation of Mr. Castillo and Mr.—–strike that. Do you know Mr. Jimenez—–Mike Jimenez and also Louis Castillo?

A Yes, I do.

Q Do you know their reputation for abusiveness and violence?

MR. BRAUDRICK: Objection as to abusiveness. I think violence is proper, but not abusiveness.

MR. GARRY: Well, I think they run hand in hand, your Honor.

THE COURT: Probably a distinction without a difference, but I think you are correct. Violence. Answer as to violence.

MR. GARRY: Do you know the reputations of violence?

A Yes, sir.

Q What is that reputation?

A Both of them seem to tend to be violent when they are drinking.

Q Over what period of time have you known Inez Garcia?

A Since she moved to Soledad.

Q Be about three years?

A Yes, sir.

MR. GARRY: I have no further questions.

THE COURT: Mr. Worthington?

MR. WORTHINGTON: Mr. Martin—–Your Honor will correct me if I am repeating myself but I don't believe this question was asked. Do you know the reputation of Louie Castillo for truth and veracity?

A As far as truth, I could never believe anything he said. . . . nobody trusts him.

MR. WORTHINGTON: Mr. Martin, on one of the nights after you were working after the 19th, when you were working in a bar, did you hear a comment to the effect that the Jimenez friends would stick together on their stories?

MR. BRAUDRICK: Objection.

THE COURT: Sustained. That's obviously hearsay, counsel. . . . And I'll admonish you not to ask a question like that again. You know better.

. . .

Q Do you recall anybody making any statements about the stories and the testimony that would be given at trial? . . .

THE WITNESS: Several people made statements about the case.

MR. WORTHINGTON: Do you know if the person who made this statement or any of these kinds of statements that you have described were people whom you had previously seen in the presence of the Jimenez family?

A Yes, sir.

Q All right. And were they or were they not?

A I had seen them with Mike.

Q And did you know them to be friends of Mike's?

A Yes, sir, they went around together.

Q Now, you cannot specifically identify who made such statements?

A Not by name, no.

. . .

BY MR. GARRY:

Q Sir, do you know the reputation of Miss Inez Garcia for chastity? Do you understand what I mean by chastity?

A Yes, sir.

Q Do you know what her reputation is?

A Yes, sir.

Q What is that reputation? Good or bad?

A Very good.

MR. GARRY: Thank you.

THE COURT: Cross-examine.

CROSS-EXAMINATION

BY MR. BRAUDRICK:

Q Do you consider yourself a friend of Inez Garcia?

A An acquaintance. Not a close friend.

MR. BRAUDRICK: Have you ever heard of men spending the night with her?

MR. WORTHINGTON: I object. That calls for hearsay.

THE COURT: What?

MR. BRAUDRICK: I'm asking him if he's every heard of any men spending the night with Inez Garcia.

MR. GARRY: Now, this opens up the very area that I wanted to go into in the——

MR. BRAUDRICK: Your Honor, when it comes to reputation, I can ask that question.

THE COURT: Certainly true when reputation is placed in evidence. I have had grave doubts whether it should have been, but I permitted it. I suppose if I did permit it, I should admit cross-examination on the basis for reputation. Objection overruled.

THE WITNESS: I believe several men from a band stayed one night at her place.

BY MR. BRAUDRICK: Have your heard of any other men spending the night with her?

A No, sir.

Q What was the name of the band, was that DocoMingos?

A I can't recall.

Q Was Max Perez one of the people in the band?

A I believe so.

MR. BRAUDRICK: I have nothing further, your Honor.

THE COURT: Carry on.

RE-DIRECT EXAMINATION

BY MR. GARRY:

Q Yes. Mr. Martin, you don't know whether any of these men ever had sex with her or not, do you?

A The conversation came up in the Little Mexico where I was a security officer at the time and one of the men said that they all slept in the front room and Inez and her boy slept in the bedroom.

Q Inez and her boy slept in the bedroom?

A Her boy.

Q And these men slept in the front room?

A Yes, sir.

Q Is that right?

A Yes.

. . .

BY MR. GARRY:

Q Mr. Martin, is it a fact, is it not, that you have on several occasions guarded the doors of Mrs. Garcia?

A Yes, sir.

MR. BRAUDRICK: Objection.

THE COURT: Now, that was one that was ruled out.

MR. GARRY: That is what I asked your guidance on.

THE COURT: You didn't tell me what you were going to ask.

MR. GARRY: I'm sorry, that is the only area.

THE COURT: That is stricken from the record and the jury is admonished to disregard it. There are several reasons why that is a bad question other than the ones you are now adverting to.

MR. GARRY: That is the only question I would be interested in, your Honor.

(RT 893-911)

The defense's next character witness for Inez Garcia was Ida Mae Williams.

IDA MAE WILLIAMS, SWORN
DIRECT EXAMINATION

BY MR. GARRY:

Q Miss Williams?

A Yes.

Q Where do you live?

A I live in Soledad, California.

Q And do you know the defendant Inez Garcia?

A Yes, I do.

Q And how long have you known her?

A About three years.

Q All right. Now, calling your attention to a––what kind of party was that?

DEFENDANT GARCIA: A Miracle Maid party.

BY MR. GARRY:

Q A Miracle party, do you remember a party that you went to on Monterey Boulevard?

A Yes, I do.

Q And did you go there with Inez?

A Inez and my boy friend.

Q And someone referred to you as her sister?

A Yes.

Q And you passed as sisters as to each other?

A We do.

Q But, you are not blood sisters?

A No, we are not.

Q You are sisters in––

A Love.

Q In love and affection. Is that right?

A Yes.

Q Since you have known Inez Garcia, where have you known her? Where have you––have you lived with her?

A She has lived with me some times.

Q Where?

A At Soledad Motor Lodge.

Q And do you know her reputation for truth, honesty and integrity?

A Yes, I do.

Q What is that reputation, good or bad?

A Good.

Q Now, do you know her reputation for chastity, do you understand what I mean by chastity?

A Would you explain, please?

Q Chastity means being sexually clean and not fooling around with men?

A No, she don't fool around with men.

Q All right. And is her reputation good or bad in that regard?

A It is good.

Q Okay. Thank you. You may examine.

THE COURT: Cross-examine.

CROSS-EXAMINATION

BY MR. BRAUDRICK:

Q You have known Inez for three years?

A About three years, yes.

Q And you consider yourself like a sister to Inez?

A I do.

Q Okay. Thank you.

. . .

(RT 912-914)

The defense's next character witness was police officer Yvonne Moranda who had earlier testified for the prosecution as to her contact with Inez Garcia on the night of the shooting.

YVONNE MORANDA, SWORN
DIRECT EXAMINATION

BY MR. GARRY:

Q Mrs. Moranda, I believe you are a Sergeant in the Soledad Police Department.

A No, I am just a police officer.

Q A police officer?

A Yes.

Q And have you known—how long have you known Inez Garcia?

A I would say about maybe a year and a half. She is an acquaintance because her boy was in Scouts when mine was in.

Q And you were both active in Scouting together?

A She was going to be a leader but something happened and she couldn't be a leader after all.

Q And calling your attention—well, let me ask you this: Do you know her reputation for truth, honesty and integrity in the community?

A As far as my opinion, she is very honest.

Q Now, on the night in question when you were with her, were you not? As an officer?

A Yes.

Q And could you tell the court and jury whether she was in a state of shock at that time when you saw her?

A Yes.

MR. GARRY: I have no further questions, your Honor.

THE COURT: All right. Cross-examine.

CROSS-EXAMINATION

BY MR. BRAUDRICK:

Q You had known her a year and a half before you saw her that night, isn't that correct?

A Yes, off and on, you know, as an acquaintance.

Q So, when she saw you, she saw somebody that she knew?

A Yes.

Q And you were on duty as a police officer at that time?

A Yes, I was. Q And what time was it when you first saw her, can you recall?

A I think it was about eleven o'clock, between eleven and one o'clock.

Q That was directly after it happened?

A Right, on March 19, yes, I walked in when the Chief was questioning her.

Q You are not a medical doctor, are you?

A No.

Q So, you can't really tell whether somebody is in a medical state of shock, can you?

A No.

Q Thank you.

. . .

(RT 915-917)

The defense's next witness was officer Richard Perez. The defense sought through his testimony to show that defendant Freddie Medrano requested protection after the shooting.

RICHARD PEREZ, SWORN
DIRECT EXAMINATION

BY MR. WORTHINGTON:

Q Officer Perez, you are employed by the Soledad Police Department and you were on March 19, 1974, weren't you?

A Yes, sir.

Q Did you on that night–did you take Alfred Medrano into custody?

A On the 19th, no, sir, I did not.

Q Did you take him into custody on the 20th?

A He was taken into custody by Officer Armstrong and Detective Santos.

Q Were you present when they took him into custody?

A At the scene, yes, sir.

Q You saw Alfred Medrano?

A I believe they were putting him in a patrol car at the time I arrived.

. . .

Q Was there some other reason why you were with him?

A On that particular night, he requested that if we would stand by while he took his belongings from his apartment at 1760 Monterey Street and if we would follow him to his aunt's house on Benito.

BY MR. WORTHINGTON:

Q Did he tell you that there had been threats?

MR. BRAUDERICK: Objection, hearsay.

THE COURT: Sustained.

. . .

(RT 917-920)

SEPTEMBER 23, 1974–10:00 A.M.

The defense's next witness was Dr. Penelope Ellis, a psychiatrist, who had been hired by the defense to examine Fred Medrano.

DR. PENELOPE K. ELLIS, SWORN
DIRECT EXAMINATION

BY MR. WORTHINGTON:

Q Dr. Ellis, would you state your profession?

A Yes, I am a physician. I am a psychiatrist.

Q And how long have you specialized in the field of psychiatry?

A I have specialized in the field of psychiatry for the past seven years.

. . .

Q Now, could you give me a history—relate to the jury the history that Mr. Medrano gave you as to his past life, and then if you could, the facts that he related as to the events of March 19, 1974? . . .

A Freddie Medrano was born in Missouri. He's twenty-five years old. He was raised in Texas where he went when he was one year old. His father was a labor contractor. His mother died when he was only nine months old. He was raised by his grandmother. He had no further contact with his father. He has one sister who's twenty-seven. He went to high school in Brownsville, Texas, as far as the sophomore year. He then joined the Job Corps for nine months. He doesn't have any history of juvenile delinquency in high school. He went into the Army one month after his nineteenth birthday and was in the Army for five years and four months. He received an honorable discharge. He was an infantryman for two years, serving in Vietnam. He was an M.P. for two and a half years.

Q M.P. is military police?

A Military Police.

Q Thank you.

A And he spent about six months in Army hospitals with tuberculosis for which he's still being treated. In fact, when I saw him in my office, he had yellow eyeballs from the medication he was on. I guess it's a kind of drug hepatitis.

Q He did tell you that he had never shot anybody face-to-face. Is that correct?

A That's correct.

Q And did he describe——

A ——he said he had a great aversion to doing anything like that.

Q Now, if you explain then just briefly what Mr. Medrano related to you as to the events that occurred on March 19, 1974.

A All right. He said—he started off saying that he had driven to Gonzales—I should say that I was particularly interested in talking to him about anything that might have impaired his consciousness like drugs or blows or that kind of thing. He said that he had driven to Gonzales and had had four or five joints of marijuana and this was just ordinary marijuana and didn't appear to be remarkable.

Q This was before—the four or five joints were before he went to Gonzales?

A Right.

Q Did he say that he shared those with other persons?

A Yes, there was somebody with him, but I don't know who it was.

Q All right.

A He then came back to the house and was in his bedroom and he split three or four joints of marijuana with Chofero. He said this was a very intoxicating marijuana and it cost him $45 a lid and that three or four people could get high on one small joint.

Q What is a joint?

A A joint is a small cigarette.

Q Then, did he tell you what happened after that?

A Yes, he said that Inez called him and said that dinner was ready and he went in to have dinner and Louis and Mike were there and started making insulting remarks. One of them got behind his chair and kept saying things that were like "You are not a hometown boy," and in a threatening sort of way and saying that they had knifed somebody and that they could do that to him too. He said it ruined his appetite while they were still behind his chair.

Q He was sitting at the dinner table at that time, is that what he told you?

A Yes, Inez prepared the meal and I think Chofero was sitting on the sofa in the dining room.

Q This person you refer to as Chofero, I told you that later that is Cris Solis, the person that goes by the nickname of Chofero?

A Solis, all right, Cris Solis. He then went outside to talk the thing over.

Q Did he say who he went outside with?

A Louis.

Q Okay.

A He said Louis came at him and hit him on the left side of the jaw.

Q With his fist?

A With his fist. He said that he felt stunned, that he felt dazed, and that it was like a dream and it felt unrealistic because it was happening too fast. He didn't seem to remember at all what he did after being hit. He said, "I might have gone to my car, but it was very very fuzzy."

Q Was Mr. Medrano able to account for that four or five minutes?

A No, he was not able to account for it.

Q In what way do you think that is significant?

A I think it is significant that he had a period of four or five minutes of amnesia after he was hit on the jaw.

. . .

Q Now would it be fair to say at the time you were talking to Freddie Medrano his memory appeared to be rather vague on a lot of facts concerning what occurred on March 19, 1974?

THE WITNESS: I felt that he was vague. I felt that his memory was definitely spotty.

. . .

Q Were you able to evaluate him when you talked to him with

regard to his veracity? That is, whether he was telling you the truth the best he remembered it?

A It was my impression that he was telling me the truth, yes. He seemed to be very definitely telling me the truth.

. . .

Q Is it possible to suffer concussion as you have described by being hit by a person who weighs three hundred pounds, assuming that person throws a blow at the head with a fist?

A Oh, yes. You can get it from lesser injuries.

Q From lesser than? In your opinion, would a blow to the side of the face such as Freddie described to you occurred when he was outside with Louie Castillo, would that kind of a blow–could that cause a concussion?

A Yes, I think so. It sounded to me as though he had received a concussion because he felt very dazed. He had a puddle amnesia for that four or five minutes. There's just no–really no recollection of what happened to him during it.

Q And with the kind of blows he described to you from a person who weighs 300 pounds and was pounding down on his head when he was on the ground, would that kind–would this kind of blow be able to cause a concussion?

A Yes.

Q All right. Now, when a person suffers a concussion, is it possible for him to be placed in a condition where he is not aware of what he is doing?

A Yes, he could still be conscious. That means he is not nacomic (phonetic), he can move his arms and legs and can do some things, but the higher ability to use judgment and to use reason and to lose his immediate memory would be very severely impaired. The immediate memory is what you have about what is happening now in contrast to what happened ten years ago.

Q Based on the information that you have at your disposal, did it appear that Freddie suffered a concussion both at the time that he was struck by Louie outside the apartment and when Mike Jimenez struck him inside the apartment?

A I would think so, because he appeared dazed and confused to some witnesses after the fight that was inside the apartment and he felt dazed, and I guess he felt dazed, he seemed dazed and dizzy after the fight inside the apartment and he felt dazed after he was hit by Louie outside the apartment.

Q And I told you, did I not, that a witness testified here that Mr. Medrano appeared to be dizzy after he got up from the beating that Mike Jimenez gave him?

A That must have meant he was falling around?

. . .

Q And were you also advised that Freddie Medrano suffered a bloody nose as a result of this beating?

A Uh-huh.

Q Would that be consistent with your conclusion that he suffered a concussion?

A It would reveal a blow to the head.

Q All right. Now, could you describe the effect of the use of marijuana on a person's central nervous system in particular with regard to his level of consciousness?

A Yes, marijuana in a light amount would cause a person to feel rather like in a daydream, to have lightened sensations of taste, hearing, hunger, they would have a disorder of time perception, and time would go usually slower. In the moderately larger dosage, I think he had quite a bit of marijuana, one of the more striking things is the loss of immediate memory and I think that one thing you notice when somebody has been smoking that one sentence does not follow another. They can't seem to remember as far back as the last sentence of what was happening to them or like an example, somebody will have eaten a sandwich or he will look down and he wouldn't even remember having taken a bite and there is a bite gone from it and that is what a loss of immediate memory is. A lot of studies have shown that this loss of immediate memory and the ability to be connected from one sentence to another sort of comes and goes and you can remember some things and not remember other things.

Q Now, is marijuana a depressant?

A Yes.

Q And would you say that it is additive to the effects of a concussion or do they oppose each other?

A The effects are almost the same, so I am sure they would be additive. The reasoning and judgment are impaired and immediate memory is very—is a very strong sign of a concussion and also a very pertinent factor of smoking marijuana in a moderate dose.

Q And does marijuana in particular seem to have the effect of making it difficult for a person to remember sequence of events and to get his timing accurate?

A Yes.

Q And does it affect the person's ability to know the length of time—the time interval that elapses between the occurrence of two events?

A Yes, both the time sequence and the place will be affected.

. . .

Q All right. Now, based on all of the information that you had at your disposal, your examination of Freddie Medrano and the facts that I have related to you that have been testified at this trial, did you form a conclusion as to his level of consciousness at the time that these events occurred on March 19, 1974?

A Yes, I think it was impaired.

Q All right. Would you say that he was aware of what he was doing on that date from the time the first blows were received from Louis Castillo outside the apartment?

A He seemed to be partially aware.

Q And was he exercising rational judgment of the ability to control his conduct?

A He didn't appear to me to be.

CROSS-EXAMINATION

BY MR. BRAUDRICK:

Q Do you think he was capable of deliberation and premeditation?

. . .

A I sincerely doubt it.

Q You doubt it, but you don't know. Is that correct?

A No, I don't know for sure.

. . .

Q You don't know what the effect of marijuana is upon Mr. Medrano, do you?

A I questioned him if he had ever had any side effects as some people have like getting paranoid and he said he never had. He said he usually got mellow, passive, and nonagressive.

. . .

(RT 926-1021)

The defense's next witness was Inez Garcia's husband, Juan Garcia Cardenas. The defense sought through his testimony to demonstrate Inez Garcia's attitudes toward sex, her frigidity in her sexual relationship with her husband, and how repulsive to her sense of morality was the idea of having sex with a man other than her husband.

JUAN JORGE GARCIA CARDENAS, SWORN

DIRECT EXAMINATION

BY MR. GARRY:

Q Mr. Cardenas, why is your name Cardenas and not Garcia?

A That's my mother's name.
Q Cardenas is your mother's name?
A Yes, and Garcia, my father's name.
Q And you call yourself your mother's name; is that right?
A In Cuba, we use both father and mother's name. The first one we use our father name and the second our mother name.
Q Now, you are in prison, are you not?
A Yes.
Q And you have been in prison how long, Mr. Cardenas?
A For about three year.
Q And your top sentence is what? Five years?
A Five years.
Q And you are about eligible for parole; isn't that right?
A Yes.
Q Now, your home is where?
A Miami, Florida.
Q And you were born where, Mr. Cardenas?
A Cuba–Havana, Cuba.
Q You have been in the United States how long?
A For eleven–twelve–thirteen years.
Q And you left Cuba after the Revolution; is that right?
A Yes, about three years after.
Q And you are considered to be an anti-Castro person?
A Yes.
Q And you have differences of political views of Fidel Castro?
THE COURT: I don't see this is material at all to the case.
MR. GARRY: Well, I just want it for background, your Honor.
MR. BRAUDRICK: Objection.
MR. GARRY: Now, you are the husband of Inez Garcia, are you not?
A Yes.
Q And how long have you been married to Mrs. Garcia?
A About twelve years.
Q And you have a child?
A Yes.
Q And there for a while, you were divorced from her, were you not?
A Problem is between men and women, once in a while.
Q And you got a divorce or she got a divorce?
A Yes.
Q And you remarried again, did you not?
A Yes.
MR. GARRY: I show you a certificate of matrimony that's been issued by Reverend Gagnon, the Chaplain, and ask you is this the time that you and Inez Garcia remarried?

A Yes, sir.
Q Would you tell the jury what date that is?
A This is 21st day of December, 1972.
Q '72?
A Yes.

MR. GARRY: I offer this into evidence, if your Honor please.

THE COURT: Received and marked Defendant Garcia's Number Five.

BY MR. GARRY:

Q Mr. Cardenas, did you hear from Mrs. Garcia as to what happened on March 19, 1974?

A Yes, I hear was——

THE COURT: Wait a minute. That's the answer to the question–I don't know.

MR. GARRY: My next question is, what did you hear her say? What report did you get through her as to what had happened on that day?

MR. BRAUDRICK: Your Honor, I object to hearsay.

THE COURT: No grounds for that. What she told her husband happened. Objection sustained.

BY MR. GARRY:

Q Did Father Gagnon tell you what she said that had happened?

MR. BRAUDRICK: Objection.

THE COURT: Sustained.

MR. GARRY: Well, I'm just asking the questions. I'm not saying what the question was, your Honor.

. . .

BY MR. GARRY:

Q Would you tell the Court and jury Inez Garcia's attitude and ideas toward sex?

. . .

MR. GARRY: Do you understand the question?

A Yes.

Q Would you answer it?

A She's not very expressive and the way that I feel she's frigid, and cause even sometime we been in our room. She feel ashamed even being naked right there in front of me.

Q Being what?

A Naked. She feels ashamed and she try to cover and things like this.

Q Is she a very religious person?

A Yes.

MR. GARRY: You may cross examine.

CROSS-EXAMINATION

BY MR. BRAUDRICK:

Q Do you love your wife?

A Yes.

MR. BRAUDRICK: I have no questions.

. . .

(RT 1036-1043)

The defense's next witness was Soledad police officer Prescott Skinner. The defense sought through his testimony to relate the circumstances surrounding why Inez Garcia left the Jimenez Labor Camp and her involvement in a dispute over her son's welfare with another woman in a bar alluded to by Mr. Braudrick in the prosecution's case. After an offer of proof out of the presence of the jury by Mr. Garry, the judge ruled that officer Skinner's testimony was inadmissable as hearsay.

The defense's next witness was Cameron Smith, a graduate student in psychology, who testified about her research with rape victims. The defense sought to show through her testimony that Inez Garcia's reluctance to talk to police about the rape was a normal reaction among rape victims.

CAMERON SMITH, SWORN
DIRECT EXAMINATION

BY MR. GARRY:

Q Would you state your full name, please?

A Cameron Smith.

Q And where do you live?

A Santa Cruz.

Q And what do you do, what is your occupation?

A I am a Ph.D. graduate student in psychology at the University of California, Santa Cruz.

Q All right. By the way, how old are you?

A I am thirty-one.

Q Now, would you tell us what your background is?

. . .

Q And prior to your—and in your work as a graduate student have you done any work with the police departments?

A Yes, I have.

Q And would you tell us what work you have done with the police department and which police department?

A I participated and I aided two San Francisco psychologists who were setting up crisis intervention programs for the Richmond police which would give the policeman some different skills in helping rape victims and also things such as family fights.

Q And thereafter what did you do?

A I started—as a result of being involved in that program I interviewed several rape victims that came to the police department and I became curious as to what happened to rape victims and I spent the entire summer interviewing hitchhikers that came through Berkeley, California. I talked to ninety women hitchhikers that summer and approximately half of them had been—approximately half of them said they had either been raped or sexually assaulted.

Q Now, did you teach a class on rape offered by the Community Studies Department at the University of California, Santa Cruz?

A Yes, I did.

Q Now, would you tell us about that?

A That following fall I offered a course which was under supervision of UCSC faculty, it had to be under supervision because I am a graduate student. The class was taken by twenty-five students, men and women, approximately one-third were men. During that quarter which is a ten-week period rapists in prison were interviewed, a forum was held in which policemen and local doctors and lawyers and rape victims participated and talked.

Q And at the present time are you connected with any—in any way with the public defender's office in Santa Cruz?

A At the present time?

Q Or have you been connected with them?

A I was asked by the public defender's office . . . to interview and test Edmunds, Mullins and Kemper who were mass murderers in Santa Cruz County. Mullin dissected a woman to see how she was made and Kemper picked up various hitchhikers and committed a variety of sexual, illegal sexual acts with them.

Q And have you talked on the subject of rape to various groups including University of Santa Cruz faculty?

A Yes, I've been asked to speak on numerous occasions for various groups. I have talked to the faculty at the University of California at Santa Cruz and I have talked on radio shows, radio talk shows which are discussions, question and answer type things. I have also been asked to talk at forums.

. .

Q And all in all how many women would you say you have interviewed in the past few years in connection with your work?

A Approximately three hundred.

. . .

Q Now, would you tell the Court and the jury what you mean by your research and printouts? Would you tell us what you mean by that?

A Yes, I eventually—I interviewed no—pardon me. I interviewed ninety women that were either—that either said they had been raped or that they had been sexually assaulted and each interview was about two hours long, sometimes three or four hours long. Usually I tried to tape interviews, the entire interview. If not, I wrote it down afterward and I used schedule interview forms and I asked the same questions of all the women and after I coded the information so it could be put on a computer and analyzed using the various kinds of statistical tests that are usual for publication in the academic journals. These things here which are rather bulky are called computer printouts and they take each variable and run various kinds of statistical tests to show whether or not it is significant.

Q All right. Now, would you tell the Court and jury just exactly what areas did you interview and what did you do in that connection?

A I was comparing the differences in background and the differences in sexual assault or rape incidents between those that were raped and those that were assaulted but got away.

. . .

Q Would you tell us the kind of evaluation you made of interviewing the persons that you have referred to?

A Of the women that were raped or assaulted?

Q Yes.

A I would prefer a more particular question.

Q Well, for one thing, let me ask you this question. Did you in your work that you did in your investigation arrive at any conclusions as to the number of people—the percentage of persons who would report a sexual assault or rape to the law enforcement bodies?

A Yes, I asked all the women that question.

Q And what responses did you get? What conclusions did you arrive at?

THE WITNESS: Approximately eighty percent of the women did not report either the rape incident or the sexual assault incident to the police.

Q Did you in your studies find out why they didn't?

A Yes, I did.

Q Would you tell us what those reasons are?

A They were usually particular individual highly personal reasons for that particular woman. In general, they were—they came down to not wanting further or any public exposure, wanting to forget the incident as quickly as possible, and a very strong feeling that nothing could be done about it by anybody.

Q Any other reasons?

A As I stated, there each woman had usually a particular very particular way of answering that question.

Q Now, in your studies, did you—were you able to determine what traumatic effects that these different persons that you interviewed had? How it affected them, and over what period of time?

MR. BRAUDRICK: Your Honor, I object to that.

THE COURT: I don't see how that matters. We don't know whether it affected Mrs. Garcia or not, assuming there was a rape. I am afraid that is not material.

MR. GARRY: I have no further questions.

THE COURT: Cross-examination.

CROSS-EXAMINATION

BY MR. BRAUDRICK:

Q Now, you stated that you interviewed ninety women who said they had been raped or sexually assaulted?

A Yes.

Q Where did you get these ninety people?

A I contacted them while in a variety of situations. Some were hitch-hiking, some were washing clothes, in a laundromat, others answered advertisements in the papers, were on the radio, some through friends of friends. I made every effort to contact women from a variety of different backgrounds and locations.

Q So you said you asked friends to find out if they knew anybody had been raped, and you——

A No.

Q You put ads in the paper or what?

A Approximately—well, I realized at the time that it would be very difficult to—that I would have to try a variety of different methods to—I thought in order to get people to come to me. So—because rape is not a topic that people easily discuss with anybody. So, I tried everything that I could. I stood out in front of super markets and talked to women who obviously were buying groceries in the late afternoon. I handed out brochures. I did a mail-out or random mail-out asking people to write in if they have been raped or sexually assaulted, or to tell their friends, to contact me. I put advertisements in local papers such as the Santa Cruz Times—with the Sentinel or Santa Cruz Times, also the San Francisco Chronicle.

Q Now, you state that you did interview ninety women who said they had been raped or sexually assaulted, that's correct, isn't it?

A That's correct.

Q And you said that you interviewed ninety hitch-hikers and half of them had been raped?

A Yes.

Q Is the forty-five within that ninety inside the other ninety women who said they had been raped?

A Some of them, not all of them. A few of them are. That's why I also said that I had contacted approximately three hundred women.

Q Now, you stated that—you say eighty per cent, was it, that didn't report the rapes; is that correct?

A Yes.

Q Now, when you say, "didn't report," you mean didn't report it to the police; isn't that what you mean?

A Correct.

Q You don't mean that they didn't say something about it to somebody else?

A I also asked that question.

Q And what was the percentage there?

A About approximately fifty percent told one person, one confidante. Other than that, they told nobody.

Q Well, a hundred percent told you.

A Yes, I assume they did. I had their stories.

MR. BRAUDRICK: I have nothing further, your Honor.

MR. GARRY: I have one question in connection with one of the questions that was asked.

RE-DIRECT EXAMINATION

BY MR. GARRY:

Q You also contacted, did you not, various women's organizations who are organized for women against rape?

A Yes, I contacted Berkeley and San Francisco Women Against Rape which is also called WAR, and I set up in Santa Cruz the Rape Line which was to give women counseling after the fact, and also to provide liaison to police or other institutions.

MR. GARRY: Thank you. I have no further questions.

. . .

(RT 1051-1061)

SEPTEMBER 24, 1974

The defense's next witness was Father Simon Gagnon, Catholic Chaplain at Soledad Prison. The defense sought through Father

Gagnon's testimony to verify Inez Garcia's remarriage to her husband and what Inez Garcia told him about the shooting incident.

FATHER SIMON ROLAND GAGNON, SWORN
DIRECT EXAMINATION

BY MR. GARRY:

Q You pronounce your name Gagnon?

A Gagnon.

Q All right. Father, I see you are a priest. Are you a Catholic, a Roman Catholic priest?

A Yes, sir.

Q And where are you assigned for your work?

A I am the Chaplain, the Catholic Chaplain in the prison in Soledad.

Q And what are your duties as a chaplain in the prison?

A Many duties.

Q Just generally.

A All kinds, as a priest, I have the ministry of a priest toward the inmates and the staff. There is lots of counseling, listening, phone calls and also visiting with the people in the visiting rooms or whoever I know, whoever wants me there to visit for all kinds of problems like marriage and so on.

. . .

Q And do you know an inmate by the name of Juan Cardenas there?

A Yes, sir.

Q And how long have you known him?

A For at least two and a half years.

Q I see. And do you know Inez Garcia?

A Yes, I know her.

Q And did you perform the marriage or remarriage of the two?

A What we call the solemnization of the marriage.

. . .

Q Well, let me ask you this: How long have you known Inez Garcia?

A Since about two and a half years.

Q I see. And you know they have a child?

A Yes.

Q Eleven or twelve year old child?

A Yes.

Q You have seen the child?

A Often.

Q Now, Inez Garcia has been to confession with you, has she not and I am not asking you what the confession was, but my question is, she has been to confession with you?

A Yes.

Q Now, Father, after March 19, when she was charged in this case for murder, did you have occasion to discuss with her, and I am not talking about the confessional now, did she tell you to pass the information along to her husband?

A Yes, sir.

Q And did that pertain to the fact that she had been raped?

MR. BRAUDRICK: Objection, your Honor.

THE COURT: Sustained.

MR. GARRY: No further questions.

. . .

(RT 1071-1073)

The defense's next witness was Raul Garcia, Inez Garcia's brother in law who she called in Florida on the evening of the shooting incident. As Mr. Garcia did not speak English, an interpreter was sworn to translate Raul Garcia's testimony.

RAUL GARCIA, SWORN

DIRECT EXAMINATION

MR. GARRY: Where do you live, Mr. Garcia?

A In Florida–Miami, Florida.

. . .

BY MR. GARRY:

Q Do you know the defendant Inez Garcia?

A Yes.

Q And how do you happen to know her?

A Because she is married to his brother.

THE COURT: You are not doing that right. I don't think he said to his brother. He said to my brother, did he not?

THE INTERPRETER: I'm sorry.

THE COURT: You are a conduit, madam.

THE INTERPRETER: Yes. Okay.

THE COURT: Just repeat what he says, no more, no less.

THE INTERPRETER: Okay. Sorry.

BY MR. GARRY:

Q And is your brother Juan Cardenas?

A Yes.

Q And did you have a telephone conversation—did Inez Garcia call you on the night of March 19th?

A Yes.

BY MR. GARRY:

Q Mr. Garcia, would you tell us what that conversation was and what her statements—what her attitude was when she talked to you?

THE WITNESS: Inez called me and told me that they had raped her and that they had called her on the telephone and that they were going to kill her and I said that if they kill her, I will kill them.

THE DEFENDANT GARCIA: No, he did not say that. She is doing it wrong. She is translating wrong. She didn't say what he said. She didn't say what he said.

THE INTERPRETER: Okay, I'm sorry. Inez said that before they kill me, I will kill them. I will kill him.

THE COURT: I'm sorry, I missed that last part.

THE INTERPRETER: Before they kill—Inez said before they kill me, I will kill him.

THE COURT: All right.

BY MR. GARRY:

Q And what was her voice like; what did she sound like?

A She was very nervous and very agitated.

Q What do you mean by nervous?

A As if something bad happened to her. She was scared.

Q Did she make any—did you get a chance to reply to her before the conversation ended?

A She hung up on me.

Q I have no further questions.

THE COURT: Cross-examine.

CROSS-EXAMINATION

BY MR. BRAUDERICK:

Q How long have you known Inez Garcia?

A Since she married my brother.

Q How many years is that?

A Twelve years.

Q What time did she call you?

A I was sleeping because the time difference between Florida and here.

Q Do you know what time it was?

A I cannot tell the hour because I was already sleeping. . . .

Q And then Inez started telling you some things?

A Yes, yes, the same things I just said that they had raped her and all that. After that—after they raped her, they called her on the telephone and that they wanted to kill her and she said before they kill me, I will kill them and she hung up the phone. . . .

Q Are you sure that they she told you that she was raped or did she say that they tried to rape her?

A No, that he had raped her.

Q Did you say anything at all?

A No, I didn't say anything.

. . .

(RT 1074-1082)

The defense's next witness was Santos Balli, an aunt of Freddie Medrano's by marriage. The defense sought through her testimony to show that Freddie Medrano looked sick and pale just before March 19, 1974. Her short court appearance set the stage for Freddie Medrano's testimony.

ALFRED MEDRANO, SWORN
DIRECT EXAMINATION

BY MR. WORTHINGTON:

Q Freddie, could you tell the jury how old you are?

A Twenty-five.

Q Where were you born?

A Kennon, Missouri (phonetics.)

Q And you have lived in California for a while, have you not?

A Yes, I have.

Q When did you first come here?

A I believe it was in '65.

Q And did you enlist in the Military Service at some time?

A Yes, in '68.

Q So, did you live in California for three years between '65 and the time you enlisted in the Military?

A No, I was living in Texas and then I came and went to school for six months in Soledad and Gonzales Union High School, then I went back to Texas.

. . .

Q Did you volunteer for the Military Service?

A Yes, I did.

Q Where were you assigned for duty?

A Vietnam.

Q When did you first go there?

A In '68.

Q Now, while you were in Viet Nam, did you earn any kinds of medals?

A Yes, I got a bronze star for valor in combat. . . .

Q Now, your initial tour of duty in Viet Nam was for how long a period of time?

A I spent thirty months.

Q Well, but was that——

A My initial duty was one year.

Q And what did you do at the end of that one year?

A Well, I re-enlisted in Viet Nam, and I asked for security, and I became a military policeman.

Q How long were you a military policeman?

A Until I retired from the service. . . .

Q When did you retire from the military police?

A I didn't retire from it. I became sick while I was on duty and went to the hospital first part of January. Went to the hospital in the Presidio in San Francisco and I was transferred to Fitzsimmons General Hospital in Livermore.

Q In January of what year?

A Of '73.

Q What was your condition diagnosed as?

A Tuberculosis.

. . .

Q When were you discharged?

A In June—around the 14th.

Q Now, were you deemed to be disabled at that time?

A I'm 100 percent disabled.

Q Have you been ever since?

A Yes, I have.

Q Did you begin receiving veterans benefits?

A Yes, I have.

Q How much were you receiving when you first were discharged?

A $524 a month. . . .

Q And how much have you been getting per month since August?

A $618.

. . .

Q When did you find that apartment?*

A January, I think it was January or the first part of February.

Q And at that time, were you living on your Veteran's benefits?

A Yes, I was.

Q Now, did you meet Louis Castillo about that time?

---

* Medrano is referring to the apartment at 1760 Monterey St.

A Yes, I met him when I moved into my apartment.

Q When you moved in?

A Yes.

Q Had you met Miguel Jimenez before that?

A I had just seen him. I knew who he was.

Q You had seen him around town?

A I had seen him around.

Q And how about Inez Garcia, when did you first meet her?

A After I got my apartment sometime in February, I believe, after January. . . .

Q Go ahead. What were the circumstances under which you met her?

A I was with Louie Castillo and I was taking him for a ride to the Motor Lodge.

Q Sometime after that, Inez moved into the apartment with you, did she not?

A Yes, she did.

Q Can you recall about when that was?

A Sometime in March, the first part of March, I believe.

Q What kind of relationship did you have with Inez?

A Room mate.

Q What were your plans?

A See, on the first—I wasn't staying in Soledad. On the first of the month, I was leaving and I was going back to Texas and she needed an apartment to live. She was staying with a friend of hers and it wasn't—you know, it was pretty dirty and everything and I was leaving and it is pretty hard to find a house in Soledad at the time, everybody comes to work, you know, they have a certain period of time, you know, lots of people come to work and they leave, and that was the time I had my apartment and it was pretty hard to find a house or an apartment and she was going to stay in my apartment when I was leaving on the first, but she had agreed also to go half and half on the rent.

Q How much was the rent?

A The rent was $130.00 I believe or $150.00, somewhere along there.

Q Had you gotten to know Inez very well then—before she moved in?

A No, I didn't know too much about her.

Q How many bedrooms does the apartment have?

A Two bedrooms.

Q And what were the sleeping arrangements?

A Well, she slept in one bedroom and I slept in one bedroom, both doors have locks on them.

Q Was there ever sexual relationship between the two of you?

A No, none whatsoever.

Q Was it a romantic in any way?

A None whatsoever.

Q Bringing to your attention to the March 19, 1974, do you recall what you did, let's start early in the afternoon, did you see a person by the name of Bobby Urquidez?

A Yes. . . . We went to the Employment Office in Salinas. . . .

Q What did you do after you got back or after you got done on this excursion with Bobby Urquidez?

A I came back to my house.

Q And what did you do for the rest of the afternoon?

A Well, I smoked marijuana.

Q Now, did a person by the name of Cris Solis come over?

A Yes, he did.

. . .

Q Did he call before coming over to your apartment?

A No.

Q What did he say when he got there?

A Well, he didn't say nothing, he just came in and I was on the phone and I was making a call.

Q Who were you calling?

A I was talking to one of my girlfriends in Texas, this girl I knew.

. . .

Q Okay. Do you remember how many joints you had before Cris came over?

A I couldn't say. I had been smoking almost all day.

Q More than two, more than three?

A Yes.

Q And do you recall how many you had that you shared with Cris?

A Oh, I wouldn't know, maybe three or four or five. He was there quite a long time, you know.

Q Did the two of you smoke the marijuana continuously while he was there?

A Yeah.

. . .

Q Now, did you and Cris Solis go somewhere?

A Yes, to Gonzales. . . .

Q What was the purpose for going to Gonzales?

A He wanted to buy some marijuana.

Q Solis did?

A Yes.

Q And did he say that to you or did you suggest it?

A No, he came up to me and said that is what he had come over for, to buy some marijuana and I told him I didn't have none and he asked me if I knew who had some, and I said, I don't know, I could find out who had some, you know, but we go to Gonzales and I know this guy that had this marijuana and had sold it to me.

Q All right. And did you make any stops when you went to Gonzales?

A No.

Q Did you stop at any places?

A I don't remember stopping no place—yeah, I remember stopping in Gonzales and going in and checking a few houses, you know, for this guy.

Q Were you able to obtain any marijuana?

A No.

. . .

Q Do you recall if you brought anything in with you when you came in to the apartment?

A No, I don't recall that either.

Q Now, was anyone else at your apartment when you got there?

A I believe Inez was there, you know, I am saying I believe because I am not—you know, I am not sure she was there or not. Like I say, you know, I come in and I just go to my room unless I want to eat or watch TV or hear some music, and then I stay out in the living room.

Q Was there anybody else outside?

A I don't remember that either. I remember I just parked my car and I went in.

. . .

Q Do you remember Mike Jimenez calling to Cris, saying hello to him or anything like that?

A No.

Q Now, when you got inside and went into your room, did Cris go in with you?

A Yes.

Q And what if anything did you do in there?

A We smoked some marijuana.

Q And was that marijuana—would you describe it as a different kind of marijuana from what you smoked before?

A Yes, I paid $45 for the lid. It's Colombian red. It is more potent than regular marijuana.

. . .

MR. WORTHINGTON: We're not being facetious about that, and I want you to tell the jury is there—to your knowledge was there something more potent about that marijuana than the average marijuana that a person gets?

A Yes, it's potent—potent.

Q Potent?

A Potent.

Q Stronger?

A Yes, stronger, cause two to three people can get high, and they can get high off a joint.

Q Off of one?

A Off of one.

Q Now, did you share that Colombian red with Solis?

A Yes, I did.

Q And do you recall how many the two of you smoked between you?

A Well, we smoked quite a lot while I was on the phone, and mostly he smoked—a little bit more on the phone. Both were sharing, but I was on the phone, and you know, both more or less, and we went to Gonzales and we smoked and came back and smoked again. But, you know, I didn't keep count. I don't know. We just were smoking.

. . .

Q All right. Did you feel the effects of that marijuana you had been smoking at any time during the day?

A Well, I had felt the effects since I first started smoking it.

. . .

Q Well, did it get you excited, make you feel real good, or did it kind of slow down your system?

A Slowed down my system.

Q And could you tell whether or not Cris Solis was feeling the effects of it? . . .

A Well, I guess. He was stoned, I guess, as much as I was.

Q Now, what happened to end this smoking that you were doing?

A I believe there was a knock on the door, and Inez told me to come and eat or somebody was there. I can't recall.

Q And what did you do after that?

A I walked—I walked out and went to the dining table to sit down and eat. . . .

Q And was there anyone else in the apartment at that time?

A Yes. When I came out, it was Louie Castillo and Mike.

Q Mike Jimenez?

A Mike Jimenez.

Q Solis was still there?

A Yes, Solis was still there. He just went and sat down on the couch. . . .

Q What happened after you started eating?

A Well, when I was eating, I sat down to eat, and they started, you know, telling me that I wasn't shit. That I wasn't a hometown boy. That just because I had money that I thought I was big shit. That I did not belong there. That I was considered as an outsider, and they didn't like that. The home boys stuck together, and they could run me out of town if they wanted to. Then Louie Castillo said, you know Mike Jimenez said—Louie Castillo or Mike Jimenez, I can't remember who, but they said they knifed this guy in Gonzales, and they could, you know, do the same thing to me, and they just, you know, start profane language and all.

Q Back when you had met Louie Castillo, had he ever told you about the person that he had knifed in Gonzales?

A Yeah. This guy named Carnuto (phonetic) I believe.

Q And had he ever pointed him out to you?

A Yes.

Q Where was that?

A That was in Gonzales by the park. At one time we had gone to Gonzales. I was looking for a fender on my car—I mean not a fender, but a door latch for my car, and we go to the junk yard in Gonzales, and I had just gotten my check, you know, and he said, you know, "Maybe we buy a lid," so we were looking, and this guy had some marijuana. And there was another guy with us. I can't recall who he was, and he said, "Well, this guy has some." So, we went to his house, and Louie Castillo didn't want to get out. He said him and this other guy had a quarrel before and they didn't get along together, and he didn't want to get down with us and go buy that lid.

Q And did Louie tell you at that time what if anything he had done?

A Yeah. He said he ripped him off for some money, and the guy was pissed off, and he had jacked him out of the car at the park, and Louie took out a knife and knifed him.

. . .

Q And how did you feel about them attacking you like that?

A Well, you know, at first, you know, I was in a daze. I didn't think it was really happening, you know. I couldn't see it, because like, Louie lived next door to me, and I used to lend him my car, and he always has a key to my apartment. His apartment key fits my apartment, and you know, I more or less gave him my confidence, and then he just—all the way—just turned all, you know, against me all of a sudden. He said—I never had any problems with him.

Q Up until that time, how would you describe the relationship that you had with Louie and Miguel?

A Just an associate, you know. I see them. He lives next door.

Q Was it friendly?

A Yes, it was friendly.

Q And there was, to your knowledge, there was no animosity between you?
A No.
Q No dislike or hatred?
A No, none that I could see. . . .
Q And did you know that Louie had lived in town for a long time?
A Well, I believe, yes.
Q He told you he had been around for a long time?
A He said he lived in Soledad.
Q By hometown boy he meant a person who had either been born there or lived there most of his life, right?
A Yes.
Q He was telling you hometown boys are better than outsiders?
A Yes.
Q Was he saying these things in the earshot of Inez?
A Yes, I believe he was. He was sitting right there in the kitchen in front of Chofero and everybody else that was sitting there.

. . .

Q Did anybody do anything with regard to the food that was on your plate?
A Yeah, I believe Mike put his finger or Louie put his finger in my food.

. . .

BY MR. WORTHINGTON:
Q Was this while they were telling you you weren't a hometown boy and all that?
A Yes, you know, I started getting irritated because like Louie when he was talking to me, he was bringing his hand down like this (indicating) and he said you ain't shit and you ain't this and you ain't that, and he was doing this. He was doing it close to me.
Q Did they say anything about your tuberculosis condition?
A They called me a few names, yes.
Q Tell the jury what they called you?
A They called me a TB patient, you know. . . .
Q So, what did you do after one or the other of them put his finger in your food?
A Well, that is when I got up and I told Louie that I wanted to talk to him outside.
Q Did you go outside?
A Yes, we went outside. . . .
Q What happened when you got outside there?
A Well, when I got out there, you know, I told him, you know, when I first came out, I said why was he doing this for and what did he

have against me and that he lived next door to me and any time he wanted to say anything to me, he could have done it then or afterwards or whatever, but why come to the house and be doing this, you know, and at that time, I had my head down like this (indicating) and the next thing I knew I just felt a blow on my face.

Q And do you know if he hit you with anything?

A I don't know if it was anything, just remember the hand, his fist.

Q And what happened after that?. . .

A I don't think I fell down. I don't know. I don't recall. I just remember getting hit and walking around and then I went back inside. . . .

Q Do you remember what happened after you got inside the apartment?

A I remember when I walked inside the apartment, I was fighting again. I don't remember how it started but I remember I was on the ground with Louie and we were both fighting and then I just started feeling blows up on my head.

Q Do you remember getting up off the floor at any time while you were fighting with Louie?

A No, I don't remember that. I remember getting up afterwards, you know, after I had been hit, you know, on my head and everything, I remember I was bleeding and I remember getting up, yeah.

. . .

Q And what happened after they stopped fighting?

A I remember I got up and I remember I got up and I was bleeding and I had my hand over my nose, and I was bleeding, and I remember seeing the knife, and when I saw the knife, I just ran to my room.

Q Who had the knife?

A Mike.

Q Jimenez?

A Yes.

Q What did you do in your room?

A I don't really remember what I did in my room, I don't know, I just remember running into my room.

Q Did you come out of your room again?

A Yes.

Q Do you know how long you stayed in your room?

A No, I don't know.

Q And do you remember going to the bathroom?

A No.

Q All right. When you came out of your room, what is the next thing you saw?

A When I came out of my room, I started going outside, started going to my car.

Q Did you see who was in the living room when you came back out?

A Nobody was there, I don't think.

Q Did you see Cris Solis?

A Yes.

Q Was he there?

A Yes. Okay. I remember I came out of my room and I started going for my door and I remember Cris was still sitting on the couch.

Q Was he doing anything besides sitting there?

A No, he was just sitting on the couch, and at that time, I asked him where Inez was and he said she was outside talking to Mike and Louie and then I remember I just walked around and the next thing I noticed was my car.

Q Did you see Inez?

A I can be wrong, you know, but I think I saw her when I was going to my car outside the house.

Q And what did she look like when you saw her?

A She was messed up like, you know, she wasn't like she was when I first saw her.

Q Did her hair look different from how it had looked?

A Yes.

Q How did it look?

A Just, you know, not well, it wasn't combed or anything, it was all messed up.

Q And did you notice anything about her clothes?

A I saw a rip in her blouse that was all I noticed.

Q Did she say anything to you that you can remember when you came in?

A I don't remember. No, I don't remember. She could have or she could have not, I don't recall.

. . .

Q And can you describe how she was acting?

A She didn't act, you know, when I saw her, you know, I just got in my car and left.

Q Did she appear to be trying to say anything to you?

A I think she—yeah, she did, but I wasn't paying, you know, I wasn't paying attention to her, you know, I remember her lips moving but I wasn't—you know, I wasn't really paying attention to what she had to tell me or anything.

Q Now, the best you can remember this all happened right after Solis told you that she was outside with Mike and Louie?

A Yes.

Q When you went outside, did you see Mike and Louie?

A No.

Q And at that time, did you form any conclusions as to what had happened to Inez?

A No, I hadn't. I didn't even know anything had happened to her. I don't know.

. . .

BY MR. WORTHINGTON:

Q What did you do when you got to your car?

A I just drove away.

Q Do you recall where you drove?

A I drove down Monterey Street, just driving around town, not town but Monterey Street and the streets around there.

Q Was Inez with you?

A No.

Q Do you recall whether she came out to the car with you or not?

A No. . . .

Q Now, I want to back up for a minute. Freddie, I want to ask you, did you take a shotgun with you in the car?

A No.

Q Did you ever own a shotgun?

A No, I never owned a shotgun, but I had bought a shotgun from a guy but I never saw it again.

Q Well, who did you buy a shotgun from?

A Nick Bunte.

Q That is the person that testified here a couple of weeks ago?

A Yes.

Q And do you recall about when you bought it from him?

A Early March, I believe.

Q What did you do with it after you bought it from him?

A I–nothing, I just kept it. I don't have no shells for it or anything, I just kept it.

Q Did you show it to anybody?

A Louie Castillo was with me when I bought it.

Q He was there when you bought it?

A I think he was there, I don't know if he was there when I bought it, but I remember he saw the shotgun because, you know, he used to come to my room, you know, and he had a key to my house.

Q All right. And after Louie saw it or you showed it to him, did you ever see that shotgun again?

A Well, no, just prior to the 19th, about four or five days we started losing some things from our apartment, you know, tapes and records and the shotgun wasn't there, and a few items, a few clothes.

Q Did Louie Castillo have a key to your apartment at that time?

A Yes, he always did.

Q Do you know if anyone else had a key to your apartment?

A No, not that I know of except maybe for the people that live next door to me where Louie stayed, his uncle.

. . .

Q Okay. Freddie, when you went out to the car, were you still feeling the effects of the marijuana that you had been smoking?

A Yes, I was dazed, you know, everything was happening so fast.

Q Did the blows that you had received from Louie and from Miguel Jimenez—did they seem to be affecting you at that time?

A Yes.

Q Did you feel dizzy?

A I felt dizzy and dazed.

. . .

Q All right. You had smoked marijuana on occasions before, had you not?

A Yes, I have.

Q How long does it usually—do the effects of it usually last for you?

A Oh, about three or four hours.

Q When did you first start smoking marijuana? A In Vietnam.

Q Was there a reason for that? A Well, sometimes—maybe once a month, once every two months, they would take the unit out of combat and they put them in the rear support area for a bunker guard and you stay there about a week to get resupplied and go to the medic and all of this, and then during that time, that week all you do is pull guard duty at night and bunkers and there's really nothing to do and we more or less tended to smoke marijuana to get away from, you know, to try to clear our minds from what we were doing there.

Q When would you smoke marijuana?

A Just around every month.

Q Once a month or so?

A Yes.

Q And then after you got back to the United States, how often would you smoke it?

A About every week.

Q And by March 19, 1974, how frequently were you smoking marijuana?

A When I got out of the hospital, I couldn't find a job and that is what kept me going, I just kept smoking every day.

. . .

Q Do you remember whether there was any phone call that came or didn't come?

A No.

Q Where did you first go when you got in the car?

A Down Monterey Street.

. . .

Q Do you recall what direction you were going?
A Yes, towards town.
Q And what direction were they going?
A Towards town.
Q So, you came up behind them?
A Yes.
Q Do you remember what happened when you came up behind them?
A I don't recall if I was inside the car or I was outside the car, but I remember I was in another fight with Louie.
Q Do you remember whether Inez was in the car or not?
A No, she was not in the car.

BY MR. WORTHINGTON:

Q Did you get out of the car?
A I don't remember if I got out or if I was in the car. I can't recall that.
Q Do you recall having any kind of confrontation with Louie out there on the street?
A I remember I was in another fight. So, I was probably outside the car then. I don't recall, you know, if I was inside my car or outside the car, but I remember I was in another fight with Louie Castillo.
Q You are sure it was Louie and not Mike?
A Yes.
Q All right. Now, what was the next thing that happened that you remember?
A I heard some shots.
Q How long did this fight go on before you heard the shots?
A Not long—not long at all.
Q Well, a matter of seconds or minutes?
A I don't—I couldn't say the time.
Q What did you do when you heard the shots?
A Well, I heard the shots, and I looked back and I saw Inez with the .22 rifle. I jumped right in my car.
Q Can you tell the jury where she was relative to your car when you saw her with the .22 rifle?
A Right by the back of the car a little bit. There was some cars parked on the side. I parked my car just on the right side of the road, and left the engine running, and I left the lights running, and she wasn't too far from where I was at. To the right-hand side by a house.
Q To the right-hand side of the car?
A Yes, to the right-hand side of the car.
Q And do you recall where Mike Jimenez was when she was firing the gun?

A No.

Q Could you tell if she was pointing it at anybody?

A No.

Q Do you recall what happened to Louie Castillo?

A He started running.

Q And did you do anything when you saw her?

A Yes—no. I remember getting in my car. Next thing I remember, she was in my car with me.

Q Did you see the gun that she had?

A Yes, it's a rifle.

. . .

Q . . . Do you remember what kind of a gun that it was she had?

A It's a rifle—.22.

Q And you saw that gun?

A Yes.

Q Is that the only gun you saw her with?

A Yes. . . .

Q Do you recall the testimony of Dima Gallardo to the effect you made a U-turn with your car?

A Yes, I remember she said that.

Q Does that refresh your memory as to whether or not you made a U-turn with the car?

A No.

Q Do you know which direction you went when you left the scene?

A Towards my apartment.

Q That would be the opposite direction from town?

A Yes.

Q And did Inez get into your car?

A Yes.

Q Do you recall when she got into your car?

A No.

Q Did she still have the rifle when she got in your car?

A Yes.

Q Now, do you recall where you went, and I want you to describe the first turn that you made if you remember?

A Alicia's.

. . .

THE WITNESS: I recall going in two houses.

THE COURT: Two houses, all right, proceed.

BY MR. WORTHINGTON:

Q Do you remember who was present at the first house that you went to?

A Alicia was there and that is all I know.
Q Were there any other people there?
A There was some people there, but I don't recall who they were.
Q Do you know where that house was?
A No.
Q Inez was—was Inez still with you when you went to the first house?
A Yes.

. . .

Q Did she go into the house?
A Yes.
Q Do you recall what happened inside the house?
A No.
Q Where did you go after that?
A I remember we were following Alicia and went to another house.
Q And do you recall whose house that was?
A Alicia's.

. . .

Q All right. What did you do after you got into Alicia's house?
A Well, I don't recall but something came up about cigarettes, you know, and I went to the apartment to get some cigarettes.
Q Could you describe how Inez was acting at that time?
A No. I don't know, shocked, I don't know, you know, I really wasn't paying too much attention, you know, I mean, like she was—I remember her just talking to Alicia and you know, they were discussing, you know, some things and I don't know what, but she was talking to Alicia and I was sitting down, and then some cigarettes came up and I remember we went, Alicia and in Alicia's car to go get some cigarettes.
Q How did you feel when you were at Alicia's house?
A I don't know, like, well—I don't know, I never felt that way and I can't explain it. I was just, well, I couldn't think.
Q Were you aware of what was going on when you were at Alicia's house?
A No, I wouldn't say I was aware.
Q And could you remember at that time everything that had occurred in the hour or two hours prior to that?
A No.
Q Where did you go with Alicia?
A I think we were going to the apartment to buy some cigarettes—I mean, to get some cigarettes.
Q Before you left, did you do anything with your car?
A Yeah, I remember moving it. Alicia said to move my car.
Q And did she give you a reason?

A Something about the Jimenez brothers, I don't know, you know, she just told me to move the car so I moved it.

. . .

Q And you were arrested by a policeman, were you not?
A Yes, I was.
Q Did you resist him?
A No, I didn't.
Q And did you tell him where Inez was?
A Alicia did.
Q Alicia did?
A Yes.
Q When you went out of that apartment, did you have any intention to kill anyone?
A No, I didn't.
Q Did you have any intention to kill anyone at any time during that night?
A No.
MR. WORTHINGTON: I have no other questions.
THE COURT: Cross-examine.

CROSS-EXAMINATION

BY MR. BRAUDRICK:
Q We have you starting out with a lid of marijuana in the morning, the morning of the 19th. Is that right?
A Yes.
Q And you said you had some other marijuana?
A You know, I had smoked out of it, that is not what I started out with.
Q Oh, you didn't have a full lid when you started out?
A Yeah, I had a full lid but not on the 19th.
Q When did you get the full lid?
A The day before, the 18th.
Q And at the end of that day you had used the lid all up. Is that right?
A Well, I had smoked it.
Q You didn't have any marijuana left when you got in the fight with Louie and Mike that night?
A Right. I had a little bit of marijuana.
Q So, you went through the lid in two days. Is that right?
A I guess.
Q Now, would you say that was about average?
A I don't know, sir. You know, I just smoke when I want to

smoke, I don't count them.

Q I was trying to find out how much marijuana you were using normally so we can find out what the state of your mind was at the time of the shooting.

A I don't know, one day you can smoke three joints and one day you can smoke a whole lid. How do you determine that?

. . .

Q And, on the 19th when you were in the fight—by the time you got in the fight with Louie and Mike the lid was all gone, isn't that right?

A Well, I had—just prior to that we had about two joints and then it was gone.

Q Now, you testified on direct examination that you were smoking quite a bit of marijuana before March 19th, isn't that right?

A Yes.

Q Would it be fair to say that you smoked marijuana every day during the month of March?

A No, no, it wouldn't be fair to say that. I might have smoked maybe a lid for two or three weeks and then maybe buy another lid and smoke it and sometimes I don't smoke for two weeks and sometimes I let it go for a month.

Q How about during the month of March?

A The month of March, well, I would say about two lids.

Q You only went through two lids in the whole month of March?

A Yes.

Q Well, you went through one lid in two days, the 18th and 19th. Is that right?

A Right.

Q So, you are telling us that you had only used one lid of marijuana from the 1st of March up to the 18th of March?

A Well, sir, you know, it is not habit forming.

Q Would you answer the question, please?

. . .

THE WITNESS: When I—well, I finished it way before the 18th of March if that is what he wants to know.

Q Well, what kind of arrangement did you make with her* as far as the apartment is concerned?

A Well, sir, I was leaving on the 1st and at that time it was very hard to find a house, you know, in Soledad and with the migrant people coming and they occupy a lot of the houses in town and everything, and it is very hard to find an apartment so when I met her we were going to

* Medrano is referring to Inez Garcia.

be roommates for that month and she knew I was leaving on the 1st and I was leaving on the 1st back to Texas so we decided to share the apartment and the expenses half and then she would stay with the apartment when I left.

Q Okay.

A I had already, you know, we had already—I had already talked to the landlady about that and she agreed.

Q The landlady lived right across from you?

A Right across from me, yes, sir.

Q Well, did you make any arrangements as far as who was going to cook and who was going to clean house and so on?

A No, sir. You know, everything was done, the food and everything.

Q You cooked some meals and she cooked some meals?

A I can't cook. She wouldn't cook all the time for me, she would cook for me, you know, when she had time, but, you know, I didn't expect her to cook for me every day, you know. I mean she could do her thing and I did my thing. She had her key to the apartment and I had my key to the apartment. I didn't, you know, like I said, I found out more about her here than when I first met her.

Q She also kept the house clean, didn't she?

A Yes, sir.

Q Who did the laundry?

A Who did the laundry? Well, sometimes I would take it to my sister to do it and sometimes she got there and she offered to do it but I would pay for the laundromat and stuff.

Q Sometimes Inez would take the laundry out and sometimes you would take it out?

A My own, not hers.

Q When had you first met Inez?

A Sometime in January, I believe. January or February.

Q Had you ever seen her before that?

A No, I had never met her before.

. . .

Q Where did you meet her?

A I met her in the motor lodge.

Q Why were you at the motor lodge?

A I had taken Louie to visit his aunt. He wanted a ride. He has got an aunt who lives in the motor lodge.

Q And Louie was a friend of yours at that time, wasn't he?

A No, he wasn't my friend. He asked me if I could take him down there, you know. Sir, you keep insinuating he was my friend. He wasn't my friend. I choose my own friends.

Q He had a key to your apartment and you let him drive your car.

A Let me explain. It is a duplex apartment and the key to his apartment fits my apartment.

Q And you lived there for three or four months, didn't you and didn't get the lock changed?

A Well, like I said, I didn't figure for him to go in my apartment or anything like that.

Q You let him drive your car?

A Yes, I lent him my car, yes.

Q Well, more than once as a matter of fact?

A Two or three times, not out of town, you know, it is a small town, just in town, to ride to the store and liquor store.

Q You let him drive it around town?

A Right.

Q Would you loan him your car so he could go cruising it around town?

A Not out of town, no, sir.

. . .

(RT 1091-1166)

SEPTEMBER 25, 1974—10:00 A.M.

Resumption of cross-examination of Alfred Medrano by Mr. Braudrick.

BY MR. BRAUDRICK:

Q How old are you?

A I'm twenty-five.

Q How old is Louie Castillo?

A I don't know.

Q Seventeen, isn't he?

A Well, if he says he's seventeen. I don't know.

Q Bobby Urquidez is seventeen, isn't he?

A I don't know.

Q Had you used any heroin on March 19.

MR. WORTHINGTON: I object, now. That calls for speculation—it's argumentative kind of question, Your Honor, and it calls for testimony that would be highly prejudicial and completely irrelevant. Counsel has no right to go into a matter like that. It's never come out on—nothing like that has come out.

THE COURT: I don't agree with your objection in whole, but it would be prejudicial unless you have some basis for asking the question.

MR. BRAUDRICK: Well, Your Honor, he stated that——

MR. WORTHINGTON: No offers of proof in the presence of the jury will just compound the problem. I ask the court to take this offer of proof, if we even need one, Your Honor, out of the presence of the jury.

MR. BRAUDRICK: I'm trying to find out his state of mind on that particular day, and I think I have a right to go into what drugs, what alcohol he used, and so on and so forth.

THE COURT: Objection overruled. Continue.

THE WITNESS: No.

MR. WORTHINGTON: Could the jury be admonished again the question does not constitute evidence.

THE COURT: That is correct. Merely the answer. Question was asked of him and he said no. Question of course with a negative answer is not to be considered as evidence.

BY MR. BRAUDRICK:

Q Do you know what heroin is, don't you?

A Yes, I do.

Q Have you ever used heroin?

A No.

MR. WORTHINGTON: Object. That is irrelevant.

MR. BRAUDRICK: It is not, Your Honor, we went into the thing about motive.

MR. WORTHINGTON: I am going to assign misconduct if counsel tries to keep getting these little comments in in the presence of the jury. He knows better. We are trying this man for his freedom, Your Honor. It does not involve heroin.

MR. BRAUDRICK: He is now doing what he just accused me of doing.

MR. WORTHINGTON: You may be correct. I'm sorry. Thank you. I do object to the question, Your Honor. I think it's irrelevant.

. . .

BY MR. BRAUDRICK:

Q Now, you stated on direct examination that you purchased a shotgun from Nick Bunte; is that correct?

A Yes, I did.

Q And this you stated also, I believe, that you had purchased the shotgun some time in March, 1974; is that correct?

A Yes.

Q How much did you pay for the shotgun?

A Well, it was supposed to be $60.00 but I gave him $30.00.

Q You gave him $30 in American money?

A Yes.

Q Did you give him anything else? . . .

BY MR. BRAUDRICK:

Q You are sure that you gave him money and not some other item in exchange for the shotgun. Is that correct?

A Sir, I am positive I gave him money.

Q And how much money did you give him?

A $30.
Q $30?
A Yes, sir.
Q And this was for a twelve gauge pump shotgun?
A Well, sir, see–yes, it was a shotgun. I really–you know, I really didn't even look at it, you know, he just took it out and, you know, I looked at it but I didn't mess around with it or anything. He said, look, I need money but if I have the money sometime next week, would you return the shotgun? And I said all right. So, it was more like a loan and he gave me something in collateral to hold in case he didn't pay me back then I kept the shotgun.
Q Well, isn't it true that you showed the shotgun off to some friends of yours?
A I don't know, sir. I know Louie Castillo saw my shotgun, yes.

. . .

Q I'd like you to take a good look at this case and tell me whether or not it was a .22 rifle that was in the case?
A Sir, I already told you I don't know. You know, when I bought the shotgun, it was in a case. I just grabbed it–I didn't pay too much attention to it. I just put it in my closet, you know. I never took it out. I never went hunting. I never had any use for it, really.
Q How about the .22 rifle, did you ever have any contact with that?
A That was Inez' .22 rifle. I never asked her anything about that.
Q You never used that?
A No.

. . .

Q And you don't recall whether or not you have ever touched it or handled it?
A I never handled it.
Q I show you People's Thirteen which is a plastic case containing numerous rounds of .22 ammunition. Have you ever seen that?
A Yes, I believe I have.
Q Where have you seen it?
A When–with the .22 when it came in.
Q In where?
A When she brought in the .22.
Q What did she do with that, do you know?
A I don't know.
Q I'd like you to take a good look at People's Thirty-one. This is a picture which shows a little letter opener, and it shows a picture of your bedroom; is that correct?
A Yes.

Q Now, take a real good look at the picture. You can see the picture of yourself in there?

A Uh huh. . . .

Q You can also see this box of .22 caliber ammunition on the headboard, can't you?

A Yes, sir.

. . .

Q Had you ever seen this package of .22 ammunition in your bedroom?

A Never in my bedroom.

Q Somebody must have put it there?

A Somebody must have.

Q Who do you think that could have been?

A You tell me, sir. I wasn't there that night.

. . .

Q Now, when you made the phone call to Texas, did you charge that on your own phone?

A No, I believe I had a credit card number. . . .

BY MR. BRAUDRICK:

Q Where did you get the credit card?

A Friends.

Q Who gave it to you?

A Don't recall, but you can ask Louie. He gave it to me.

Q Louie gave you the credit card?

A Yes.

. . .

BY MR. BRAUDRICK:

Q Did you ever give the number of Inez?

A No.

Q Now, after you and Mr. Solis smoked the marijuana, you stated yesterday that there was still a little bit left. Is that right?

A Yes, but what I meant a little bit left, there was one joint left, one or two joints but they were rolled.

Q What did you do with what was left from each cigarette after you smoked it?

A What did we do?

Q Yes.

A Put it in the ash tray.

Q What did you do with the one joint that was left after you and Solis finished it?

A Well, we smoked it all.

Q There was nothing left?

A No, there was nothing left.

Q Well, you just——

A —I meant—what I meant when I told—you told me there was a little bit of grass left, I mean after me and Solis, you know, smoked—well, you know, we smoked and we went to Gonzales and we came back and smoked again and we smoked again and finished it all before I went to eat and then I didn't know which time you said.

Q Okay. On page 1149, question: You didn't have any marijuana left when you got in the fight with Louie and Mike that night? Answer: Right. I had a little bit of marijuana.

Now doesn't that mean that you had a little bit of marijuana left?

A Well, that is what it says, then, I must have. I don't remember. I don't recall. I thought I smoked it all. I knew there was a little bit left, one joint or two joints in a roll. They were rolled, but I don't know where they were at.

Q So, you have forgotten between yesterday and today as to how much was left.

A Well, I knew there was some left, but I thought we smoked it all.

Q Well, if there was some left, what happened to it; did you take it with you?

A No, it must have stayed in the apartment. I don't know.

Q So, if the police searched your apartment, they would have found it?

THE WITNESS: Solis could have took it too.

BY MR. BRAUDRICK:

Q You are speculating on that, aren't you?

A I don't know. He could have took it, I mean, he was smoking with me.

Q Did you have any discussions that night at all with Louie and Mike regarding drugs?

A No, I don't remember having any discussions involving drugs.

Q Is your answer no you didn't or you don't remember?

A No, I didn't. I will just say no, I didn't. It wasn't anything about drugs.

Q Was there the argument that you had with them, did it have anything to do with your dealing heroin? . . .

A I didn't even have an argument with Mike Jimenez, it was mainly with Louie. Mike Jimenez was the one that was pounding down on me. There were no words said to him.

Q Didn't he threaten you with a knife?

A He came at—I saw a knife. Now, I don't remember whether he said to me or anything, you know, I saw a knife that he took out on me and that is when I went to my bedroom.

. . .

Q Have you ever sold heroin?

A No, and I don't even use it.

Q Well, isn't it true that you did not buy the shotgun for $30.00 in American money but that you gave two balloons of heroin for the shotgun?

MR. WORTHINGTON: I object, Your Honor, that is highly prejudicial. I told counsel I would assign that as misconduct if he went into something like that and he has no basis for asking a question like that.

MR. BRAUDRICK: I certainly do, Your Honor.

MR. WORTHINGTON: That is a bold face attempt to prove this crime by slandering him with other irrelevant stuff that is not proven and I assign that as misconduct.

THE COURT: Objection overruled. you may pursue it.

THE WITNESS: No, it was not true.

. . .

Q Your recollection is better of the events—your recollection is better back in March than it is now, isn't it?

A They were still fuzzy to me and everything, you know, I couldn't really—it was spotty like it is now.

Q But, you did tell Sergeant Perez that you kicked Mike?

A That's what they say from the statement*

Q Do you want to look at the statement?

A I already looked at it.

Q "Question: You remember when Mike took the knife out? Answer: After I kicked him." Is that correct?

A After the fight, yeah.

. . .

Q Can you recall the statement that you gave to Sergeant Perez that—"Question: What hand did he have the knife in? Answer: In his right hand. Question: What events happened next? Answer: He came at me with the knife. He said I'll kill you. He had the knife. I ran to my room. When I came out, Chofero was just sitting on the couch."

. . .

Q "I asked him where Inez was. He said that she was outside talking to Mike and Louis. I went to the door and looked outside. Inez wasn't there. I started up to the door. That's when she, Inez, came in. I saw her. She was beat up. Her top was torn."

Is that correct?

A If that's what I said, yes, sir.

---

* Mr. Braudrick is referring to the police report of questioning made by Sergeant Perez.

Q Mike did say something. He said, "I'll kill you," when he came at you with the knife.

A I think. I recall it now.

Q But you recalled it then back in March?

A Well, yes.

. . .

Q All right. You came out of the bedroom and you don't know how much time elapsed between the time you ran into the bedroom and after Mike pulled the knife on you and who was present in the house then?

A Well now, sir, I don't recall, but there in the statement you just read to me you said Chofo was the only one there, so——

Q So, Chofo was sitting on the couch when you came out?

A Well, that is what I said in the statement, yes.

Q So, he would be sitting right here?

A Yes, sir.

Q Okay. Now, were Mike and Louie in the house?

A Was Mike and Louie in the house?

Q Yes.

A I don't remember.

Q Was Inez in the house?

A Sir, I just told you I don't know. You know, you have asked me and I can't even recall Chofo in the statement says that I said so, so I am sticking to what I said on the statement. I must have talked to–but I don't recall now, but I did not see Inez or Mike or Louie.

Q Okay. What did you do then after you came out?

A I remember going to my car.

Q Did you go directly to your car?

A Yes, I remember going to my car.

. . .

Q Now, why did you go out and get in your car and drive away?

A Well, sir, it is, you know, ever–I don't know, I can't even recall that, why I did that.

Q Can you recall telling Officer Perez that you jumped in your car and went after them?

A I could have, yeah. I could have said that.

Q And your memory was better in March when you gave the statement to Officer Perez than it is now. Is that right?

A Well, it was still fuzzy then but now wouldn't be anything compared to that.

Q All right. So, you told Officer Perez what happened after you saw Inez beat up that at that time I jumped in my car and went after them. Is that correct?

A That could be correct, sir.

Q Now, can you recall saying to Officer Perez's question, they had already left?

A Yes, apparently they had already left.

Q Where did you go?

A I went looking for them.

Q What happened next?

A I caught up to them down in front of the park.

Q Did you give that statement to Officer Perez?

A If that is my signature there then that is what I said, sir, that is what I said.

Q That is what happened, isn't it?

A Well, what I believed, yes.

Q Do you know how long it took you to find Louie and Mike?

A No.

Q Do you know where you went to try to find Louie and Mike?

A No, sir, I just remember driving around.

Q Okay.

A Until I saw them.

Q In the statement that you gave to Sergeant Perez: "Question: How long did it take you to find Mike and Louie? Answer: About some time, I didn't find them right off, I went two or three times. Question: Around where? Answer: Down Monterey and back."

Is that correct?

A I went to a couple of streets, sir.

Q And when you told Officer Perez that you went down Monterey Street and back, is that correct?

A Yes, I must have gone down Monterey and back.

Q So, would it be fair to say that when you gave the statement to Officer Perez that you did remember what street you were driving on?

A Well, no, not really.

Q Did you lie?

A I mean like he was—which streets and which is that and this and that, you know, trying to make me pinpoint everything, you know, so Monterey Street, you know, is the street from my house down to the park.

. . .

BY MR. BRAUDRICK:

Q After you had driven up and down Monterey Street, did you see Inez at any time?

A No, I didn't.

Q When was the next time you saw Inez after—after you left the house?

A When I heard the shots.

Q You did not see her before then?
A No, sir.
Q And did Louie or Mike come over to where you were?
A That is what I can't understand. I can't recall. I don't understand if I was inside my car or out. No, I was in another fight and I remember it was Louie.
Q Well, do you recall whether or not the car door was open?
A No.
Q Do you recall if Louie hit you with his fist?
A I recall we were in a fight.
Q Can you recall if he hit you with his fist?
A I just remember we were fighting.
Q Did you get struck at all during that fight?
A Yeah, I believe I did.
Q Whereabouts did you get struck?
A I don't know.
Q Can you recall if you ever fell to the ground?
A Yeah, I remember I was on the ground.

. . .

Q Can you remember being asked a question by Sergeant Perez back in March and this would be on page four, Q What happened when you found Mike and Louis? A I left my car running and got out. I left it on the street. Q What happened next? A I yelled at them. I told them what they had done to Inez and it was never answered. Louis came at me.

Now is that what you told Sergeant Perez back in March?
A Yes, sir.
Q So then, in fact, you were out of the car when the fight started between you and Louis?
A I must have been, yes, sir.
Q Okay. Now, did Mike get involved in the fight?
A I don't remember, you know, about him, you know, I was with Louie.
Q Did Mike intervene in the fight at all?
A No, sir, like I say, I didn't know—I don't even know about Mike.
Q You don't remember anything about Mike?
A I think I saw him with a knife, but I don't remember if he ever got to me or anything, with Louie, you know, I wouldn't say that because I don't remember.
Q And you think you saw him with a knife?
A Yeah, I think I saw him with a knife.
Q Did he pull the knife out on you?
A I don't know. I don't know. I don't know if I even saw him, you know, I think I did.

. . .

Q Can you recall being asked by Sergeant Perez in March—"Question: What happened next? Answer: We were fighting on the ground. Mike was on me again, hitting me again." Can you recall that?

A If that's what I said, yes, sir. I remember. I remember it was Louie from what I remember, not Mike.

Q The statement seems to imply that Mike intervened in the fight. Can you recall, now, if he intervened in the fight at all?

A No.

Q He didn't?

A I can't recall, sir.

Q Okay. When was the first time you saw Inez after you left the house?

A When I heard the shots.

Q Where were you when you heard the shots?

A On the ground. I was fighting with Louie.

Q Did you see her then?

A Well, that's when I remember he—you know, the fight all of a sudden—he just ran, and when I turned around, I saw Inez.

Q Okay. Where was she?

A Farther back from me.

Q Was she out in the street?

A I don't recall being out in the street.

Q Was she on the sidewalk?

A I believe she was. I'm not sure exactly where, if it was the sidewalk. I just knew she was in back of me.

Q She was in back of you?

A Yes—not—well, say again from about where—here to where that chair is when I turned around and I heard the shots, and then I turned around. That's when I saw her. About then.

. . .

Q So, she would have been very close to the front of the car?

A She could have been, yeah.

Q What was she doing when you saw her?

A Well, I don't recall. I just—I just remember I heard the shots. After I heard the shots—well, during the shots, Louie started running. I turned around and I saw Inez and she had a .22 rifle.

. . .

BY MR. BRAUDRICK:

Q Who told you to or what did you decide to go to do after you got to Alicia's house and she wasn't home?

A I don't know, sir, I just remember Inez was—well, I knew that I wasn't myself, you know, and I don't know, I—it was just like flashes, you know, like I just wanted to get her with somebody that she knew because, you know, I was pretty shook up myself.

(RT 1168-1206)

Upon the conclusion of Mr. Braudrick's cross-examination of Freddie Medrano, the prosecution played the following interview with Medrano taped the morning following the shooting. The prosecution sought through the interview to underscore contradictions and inconsistencies in Medrano's account of the incident.

(Whereupon the taped interview of Alfred Medrano was played.)

ROBERT S. RUSSELL: As I identified myself to you last night, I'm Bob Russell, I'm an investigator with the District Attorney's Office. This interview is taking place in the Monterey County Jail, and the time now is 11:20 a.m., date being March 20, 1974, and your full name is Alfred Medrano? M-E-D-R-A-N-O. Is that right? I can't hear you if you're just nodding your head. . . .

ROBERT S. RUSSELL: Now, Alfredo, you have been charged with murder. You told me last night that you didn't do this, that you didn't have anything to do with it and yet you're willing to talk to me about it, but you don't want to put it down in a statement form, you don't want to put it on a recording. You've been advised of your constitutional rights and I'll advise you of your constitutional rights again. 1. You have the right to remain silent, and anything you say can and will be used against you in a court of law, that you have the right to have an attorney present during the interview. If you can't afford to hire one, one will be appointed to represent you. Keeping these rights in mind, would you like to talk to me at this time about what happened down there? Give me some idea of eactly the sequence and time of events that everything took place. Cause man I know you want to lay on out and don't understand the, why you want to tell me without putting it in a statement form or putting it on a recorder. Because if you're telling me the truth, then you want it recorded so that it can't be altered. That's up to you. But I have to go from memory from what you told me. Okay. Do you want to talk to me? Yes or no? You're shaking your head no. You do not want to give me a statement? You want to let it go at the statement you told me last night. Do you think this is going to help Inez? Really, Al, do you think this is going to help Inez? Man you were there, you saw what happened, she ain't got no one else to say what happened, what took place, you were there and you're not saying nothing.

ALFREDO MEDRANO: I could start, you know.

ROBERT S. RUSSELL: Okay. You went; what you told me last night is that you went on over to the house and when you, as you were getting there, you saw Jimenez and Louie walking away from the house, from the apartment, is that right? You're shaking your head yes?

ALFREDO MEDRANO: Yes.

ROBERT S. RUSSELL: You went on up to the apartment and when you went in there you saw that her sweater was torn and she's telling you about what these guys had done. What did she say they had done to her? Did she say they had pushed her around?

ALFREDO MEDRANO: She had a black eye and her thing was torn.

ROBERT S. RUSSELL: Her sweater was torn.

ALFREDO MEDRANO: I just can't (inaudible) . . .

ROBERT S. RUSSELL: Okay. And she was telling you who it was who had done it? What happened then? Did you see those guys again? Did they come back? Did you call the police?

ALFREDO MEDRANO: I started to call the police.

ROBERT S. RUSSELL: You started to call the police, but what happened?

ALFREDO MEDRANO: Well, I had found out what they had done and they started beating up on her.

ROBERT S. RUSSELL: Well how did you try to find out what they had done, did you go out and find them? Outside the house?

ALFREDO MEDRANO: No, I talked to her and she told me.

ROBERT S. RUSSELL: Okay, Inez told you what they had done, then what happened?

ALFREDO MEDRANO: I don't remember that, exactly. . . .

ROBERT S. RUSSELL: Okay then, let me ask you this question, did they come back over to the house while you were there?

ALFREDO MEDRANO: Yes.

ROBERT S. RUSSELL: Is that yes . . . You're going to have to speak louder Al. What happened when they came back to the house then? Did you try to talk to them? Or did you get upset with them and try to throw them out of the house because of what they had done?

ALFREDO MEDRANO: Told them to leave.

ROBERT S. RUSSELL: You told them to leave. What happened?

ALFREDO MEDRANO: Took out a knife and started beating up on me.

ROBERT S. RUSSELL: The big guy, Jimenez, took out a knife and he started beating up on you. Which hand did he hold the knife in?

ALFREDO MEDRANO: It was his right, his right I think.

ROBERT S. RUSSELL: And then he started hitting you with his left hand?

ALFREDO MEDRANO: It was him and Louie both that were hitting me.

ROBERT S. RUSSELL: Louie hit you too?

ALFREDO MEDRANO: Both of them.

ROBERT S. RUSSELL: Did they put marks on your face?

ALFREDO MEDRANO: Yeh right here.

ROBERT S. RUSSELL: Is that those marks that I see up at the bridge of your nose?

ALFREDO MEDRANO: Yeh, and a bump right here.

ROBERT S. RUSSELL: And bump on the right temple area or the left temple area.

(Medrano asks Mr. Russell to feel area of bump, and he complies.)

ROBERT S. RUSSELL: Okay, by God there is a lump there, and okay you had a little fight with them up there at the house what happened then, did they leave? Or did you leave?

ALFREDO MEDRANO: I took off, I wanted to see if I could find some friends.

ROBERT S. RUSSELL: You took off to see if you could find some friends. What were they doing when you took off, where were they?

ALFREDO MEDRANO: In my living room.

ROBERT S. RUSSELL: They were still in the living room of the apartment? And where did you go to look for friends?

ALFREDO MEDRANO: I didn't know where, you know, it was late at night and I went down there to Lisa's house.

ROBERT S. RUSSELL: That's your girlfriend Lisa?

ALFREDO MEDRANO: Yeh. Told her what had happened.

ROBERT S. RUSSELL: You told her what had happened?

ALFREDO MEDRANO: Yeh I told her, you know and I had blood and everything and told her I had been beat up, and to go to the house because Inez was there, you know.

ROBERT S. RUSSELL: You told her that Inez was still at the house and for her to go over there. Were you bleeding from the nose?

ALFREDO MEDRANO: Yeh, but I had a towel, then.

ROBERT S. RUSSELL: You had a towel then? Did Lisa go over to the house?

ALFREDO MEDRANO: She started going with me.

ROBERT S. RUSSELL: She went with you. What happened when you started over to the house then, with Lisa?

ALFREDO MEDRANO: We saw Inez.

ROBERT S. RUSSELL: You saw Inez. Where was she?

ALFREDO MEDRANO: She was by the house.

ROBERT S. RUSSELL: She was by the house.

ALFREDO MEDRANO: She was walking, and I picked her up, and I knew she had the gun.

ROBERT S. RUSSELL: Okay, she was walking and you picked her up and she had the gun and you and Lisa picked her up.

ALFREDO MEDRANO: I picked her up. I did.

ROBERT S. RUSSELL: Yeh but Lisa was in the car.

ALFREDO MEDRANO: Yeh, she was at the house, No she was at the house, I had gone out first to try and find some friends of mine (inaudible . . .)

but then you know, I knew what I had done, he beat me up and I had left my own house you know, she was there . . .

ROBERT S. RUSSELL: By herself, and you were kind of embarrassed about it.

ALFREDO MEDRANO: Yeh, well it was my own house, you know, and . . .

ROBERT S. RUSSELL: So you got in your car . . .

ALFREDO MEDRANO: Everything happened so fast, you know, and . . .

ROBERT S. RUSSELL: So you headed back there in your car with Lisa, to try to get back to help Inez.

ALFREDO MEDRANO: Yeh!

ROBERT S. RUSSELL: And, you saw Inez she was walking down the street and she had the rifle, did you see the guys?

ALFREDO MEDRANO: (Inaudible) . . .

ROBERT S. RUSSELL: Not yet. You're shaking your head no . . .

ALFREDO MEDRANO: No.

ROBERT S. RUSSELL: Okay. Then you picked her up, then what happened, did you go riding, looking for the guy?

ALFREDO MEDRANO: No. Took her down to Lisa's house.

ROBERT S. RUSSELL: You took her down to Lisa's house. What happened after that?

ALFREDO MEDRANO: I got in my car to go down to my house, then the cops arrested me.

ROBERT S. RUSSELL: Well, the police arrested you after you took her down to Lisa's house, wasn't there some kind of a shooting that took place from the time you first saw her and picked her up, you left that part out. Now last night you told me you saw the shooting.

ALFREDO MEDRANO: Well you know, I just, I didn't actually see it clearly, you know, I just know that she was firing, you know, and she was . . .

ROBERT S. RUSSELL: Okay, you were driving down the street and you saw her, what was she doing? With the rifle?

ALFREDO MEDRANO: She was carrying it.

ROBERT S. RUSSELL: Okay. When did you see the shooting.

ALFREDO MEDRANO: I don't even know when, or what time or anything. It was just so fast, you know, and then afterwards I saw her, you know . . .

ROBERT S. RUSSELL: Okay, cause this is what's got me a little confused, cause first of all in the witnesses say the first shot was fired out of your car. There's a cartridge, you know a spent cartridge, you've been in the service, you know what that means. It was in the passenger side of your car so she fired the first time from your car. Is that right?

ALFREDO MEDRANO: No. I really don't know. I got inside the car and I just remember that.

ROBERT S. RUSSELL: Okay, is this when you saw the guys?

ALFREDO MEDRANO: Yeh.

ROBERT S. RUSSELL: Okay she was in the car with the rifle, you saw the guys and then what happened?

ALFREDO MEDRANO: You're bring it all back now.

ROBERT S. RUSSELL: I know I'm bringing it back to you, I want you to try and remember it. I'm gonna ask you a question right out. Cause I don't understand why you're hesitant to some answers. Do you feel that you helped her in anyway.

ALFREDO MEDRANO: No. I know I didn't, help her.

ROBERT S. RUSSELL: Okay. When you picked her up with the rifle, she was mad, right?

ALFREDO MEDRANO: Yes.

ROBERT S. RUSSELL: That's correct. So when you were going down the street, you were driving Lisa was what, sitting in the middle?, and Inez is sitting on the passenger side, did she start shooting before you knew it?

ALFREDO MEDRANO: What do mean did she start shooting before I knew it?

ROBERT S. RUSSELL: I mean in other words, by surprise she starting pulling the trigger? Man you were there, you can tell us what happened.

ALFREDO MEDRANO: (Sigh)

ROBERT S. RUSSELL: Did these guys beat you up any other place but at the house?

ALFREDO MEDRANO: (inaudible) . . . I stop, I saw, I went up to talk to them, and they started beating me up again, and this is when she started firing.

ROBERT S. RUSSELL: Okay, now, you got beat up at the house, you ran on over to look for help, your coming back and in the car, and you stop cause you see them again, but first you stopped and picked up Inez. You stop and you start talking to these guys and they start beating you up again?

ALFREDO MEDRANO: (inaudible) . . .

ROBERT S. RUSSELL: And Inez started shooting from the car or had she gotten out of the car?

ALFREDO MEDRANO: Gotten out of the car.

ROBERT S. RUSSELL: She had gotten out of the car.

ALFREDO MEDRANO: (inaudible) . . .

ROBERT S. RUSSELL: Okay. Were you guys out there riding around looking for them?

ALFREDO MEDRANO: No.

ROBERT S. RUSSELL: Let me get the thing straight from the beginning. 1. You went on over to the house that evening, you saw Miguel and Louie leaving. You go on up to your house and Inez has been beat up or has been hit a couple of times and her sweater torn and she tells you what happened. Right? If you'll please answer me. A yes or no.

ALFREDO MEDRANO: I don't want you to be putting any words in my mouth.

ROBERT S. RUSSELL: That's why I'm asking you . . . tell me what happened . . .

ALFREDO MEDRANO: I know one thing, Mike did have a knife and he did take it out.

ROBERT S. RUSSELL: Okay.

ALFREDO MEDRANO: . . . I got beat up . . .

ROBERT S. RUSSELL: . . . okay . . .

ALFREDO MEDRANO: . . . before I knew it this had happened, you know it was just, you know so fucking fast, you know, like boom, boom, boom, just like that, the next thing I know . . . she's in my car, you know, and I want to take her to the police station and she says well take me to the police station, you know, . . . At first I thought may she, you know, I don't know she had gone lu-lu or something, it was too fast you know, I never . . . I don't know.

ROBERT S. RUSSELL: Okay but you could help . . . and yourself in regards to the sequence of events because of what the other people tell us I want to be able to see how truthful you're being. 1. Is the fact that the shooting started from inside your car. Is that true or not true?

ALFREDO MEDRANO: I don't think it did.

ROBERT S. RUSSELL: You don't think it did? Had you picked up Inez before the shooting started?

ALFREDO MEDRANO: I don't think I did.

ROBERT S. RUSSELL: You don't think you had. Were you heading back to her house in the car? Did you get out of the car?

ALFREDO MEDRANO: I didn't get out of the car, I was all . . . you know I saw her on the street, you know, and I opened my door and I said get in, get in, what's wrong, get it.

ROBERT S. RUSSELL: You told her to get in, this was after the shooting?

ALFREDO MEDRANO: Yeh.

ROBERT S. RUSSELL: Had you seen the shooting? Like last night you told me you saw her standing across the street from the guys, just shooting away.

ALFREDO MEDRANO: (inaudible) . . . You know there was, I just saw her carrying the gun, she must have been shooting at something, you know and . . .

ROBERT S. RUSSELL: At the time she started shooting, just before the shooting, where these guys beating you up? Up on the street? (long pause) Let me ask you, how many times did those guys beat you up last night?

ALFREDO MEDRANO: Up at the house and then I had seen them and I wanted to talk to them and they started beating up on me, the next thing I knew Inez was there, that's after the guy took a knife out on me.

ROBERT S. RUSSELL: How did you get out of the way when she started shooting?

ALFREDO MEDRANO: Cause I saw it was the weapon and started running towards, you know, say what's wrong, you know, what did you touch the gun for, she said just get out, she just . . .

ROBERT S. RUSSELL: . . . She told you to get out of the way and she started shooting?

ALFREDO MEDRANO: Well the guy had a knife, you know, he . . .

ROBERT S. RUSSELL: How close was he to her?

ALFREDO MEDRANO: Twice as this, I think.

ROBERT S. RUSSELL: Okay, twice the size of this room. Let me walk this off here and see how wide it is . . . Okay this is six feet wide . . .

ALFREDO MEDRANO: I mean this way . . .

ROBERT S. RUSSELL: . . . Oh the longer way, okay so let me walk this. Okay it's, this is 10 foot, so she was about 20 feet away when she started shooting, that's twice the length of this. Is that about right, something like that?

ALFREDO MEDRANO: Uh-um.

ROBERT S. RUSSELL: Yes?

ALFREDO MEDRANO: Yes.

ROBERT S. RUSSELL: And it all happened pretty fast? What did you do when she told you to get out of the way and she started shooting? Did you tell her to stop? Did you try to get the gun away? You're shaking your head yes, what did you do?

ALFREDO MEDRANO: I was just shouting at her "Don't," next thing I knew Louie was running, I just . . .

ROBERT S. RUSSELL: Louie was running? What's Louie's last name?

ALFREDO MEDRANO: Castillo.

ROBERT S. RUSSELL: Louie Castillo? Did uh, how long from the time you was at the apartment till the time of the shooting, how much time had passed? An hour? Two hours?

ALFREDO MEDRANO: I couldn't say.

ROBERT S. RUSSELL: Was it more than an hour?

ALFREDO MEDRANO: I really couldn't say, sir, I just lost track, you know, I don't know.

ROBERT S. RUSSELL: Did you know __________ had the rifle in the house?

ALFREDO MEDRANO: She had it now, she also had a shotgun, you know, she has a sawed off shotgun, they're legal, they're hers. And that weapon's her son's, it's a .22, it's her son's.

ROBERT S. RUSSELL: And where does she keep the .22 in the house?

ALFREDO MEDRANO: In the house.

ROBERT S. RUSSELL: In her bedroom?

ALFREDO MEDRANO: In the closet.

ROBERT S. RUSSELL: Is it kept loaded?

ALFREDO MEDRANO: No, I don't think it was.

ROBERT S. RUSSELL: Where are the bullets kept?

ALFREDO MEDRANO: She had a plastic thing, you know, that the bullets come in, and they were there too, someplace. In a drawer, I think . . .

ROBERT S. RUSSELL: In your bedroom or her bedroom?

ALFREDO MEDRANO: My bedroom.

ROBERT S. RUSSELL: Did you know that . . .

ALFREDO MEDRANO: No. In the drawer in the kitchen, where you pull out the knives and stuff. (inaudible) . . .

ROBERT S. RUSSELL: Okay, so after you left the apartment you went on over to your girlfriends, Lisa's house, you were driving on back, you saw the guys and you got out and you talked to them and you got in an argument with them, then you saw Inez coming down the street with the gun and you went over there and tried to stop her. She told you to get out of the way and she started shooting. Is that correct?

ALFREDO MEDRANO: The guy hit me, you know, he hit me again.

ROBERT S. RUSSELL: He hit you again? Which guy?

ALFREDO MEDRANO: Mike.

ROBERT S. RUSSELL: Mike hit you.

ALFREDO MEDRANO: Took out the knife on me again. That's when it happened.

ROBERT S. RUSSELL: Okay. That's when it happened. After you left, with Inez, where did you go?

ALFREDO MEDRANO: Lisa's house.

ROBERT S. RUSSELL: How long before the police?

ALFREDO MEDRANO: Oh, not too long after.

ROBERT S. RUSSELL: Where were you going when you left?

ALFREDO MEDRANO: I was going to my house.

ROBERT S. RUSSELL: What were you going to do at your house?

ALFREDO MEDRANO: You know it had been left opened, and sec Louie has the key to my house also.

ROBERT S. RUSSELL: Louie has the key to your house also.

ALFREDO MEDRANO: He lives next door.

ROBERT S. RUSSELL: What were you going to do, lock up your house, or get some stuff or what?

ALFREDO MEDRANO: No I was just going to lock up the house, and call the police after, or Lisa was supposed to call the police.

ROBERT S. RUSSELL: Okay. Was Lisa with you when the shooting took place? Did she help in showing what happened? You shake you head no.

ALFREDO MEDRANO: No, she wasn't with me.

ROBERT S. RUSSELL: What if she says now that she was? Would she be telling the truth? These are the things I gotta straightened out. You're hesitating.

ALFREDO MEDRANO: (inaudible) . . . she wasn't with me.

ROBERT S. RUSSELL: Okay. Would you want to go over one straight story as to what happened?

ALFREDO MEDRANO: Sir, I know one thing, I shouldn't be in here, and I don't want to be in here, you know. I just don't.

ROBERT S. RUSSELL: Okay. I'll take this tape recording back to the District Attorney and I'll let them hear it and he'll attempt to make a decision on it. We're still waiting for all the reports to come up from Soledad, so he can review them. I thank you for talking with me, and I'm going to turn the recording off. Oh before I do that, has any promises been made to you or anything else to talk to me?

ALFREDO MEDRANO: She just told me, you know, and she knew I didn't do it or anything but it's still your saying that and I'm still in jail, you know.

ROBERT S. RUSSELL: I told you that I knew that you did not do it, shoot those guys. Did you shoot em?

ALFREDO MEDRANO: No I didn't shoot 'em.

ROBERT S. RUSSELL: Okay so, from what you tell me and from what other people tell me, I know you didn't shoot him. End of this recording.

. . .

(RT 1316-32)

RE-DIRECT EXAMINATION

BY MR. WORTHINGTON:

Q Freddie, now that conversation that the jury just heard, the stipulation was that it was given on March 20, the day after the shooting, at 11:20 in the morning; is that about as close as you can remember about when it was?

A Yes.

Q All right. Now, the questions I want to ask you are going to be referring to another statement that you gave to the police on about March 26, 1974. All right. Before I go through that, could you try to describe to the jury if you can how you felt on the 20th about twelve hours after this had all occurred?

THE WITNESS: Well, when I finally got to the County Jail, it was about 12:00, 1:00 o'clock–something like that before I got to the police station in Salinas in the County Jail. I was still confused and dazed. I didn't sleep all night. It came in the morning–the district attorney investigator came in the morning. He said they would get me out. They just need some information. Then they came back two or three hours later, and that's when they came with the recording. I hadn't slept. I couldn't remember then. I don't remember saying all that from now.

Q Did things seem clear to you at that time when you were talking to the District Attorney?

A No, not really, I just wanted to cooperate with him, you know, so like–you know, they told me even before they took me to Salinas that I was going to be a State's witness for this and then all of a sudden it just turned, you know, and they were trying–well, I kept up, you know, but–well, see, the time I got arrested to the time I got released, the next day––

Q All right. Then, between the 20th and the 26th, did you try to reconstruct in your mind what had happened?

A I was trying to.

Q Now, when you talked to the police on the 26th,* did things seem more clear to you or less clear, or the same?

A Some things were clearer, but a lot of things were spotty.

. . .

MR. GARRY: I have just one question.

BY MR. GARRY:

Q Mr. Medrano, I believe you stated that Inez started living at the apartment about three or four days before the 19th; is that right?

A Yes, sir, about.

Q Now, did Inez ever see the shotgun that you say you bought from Mr. Bunte at any time?

A No, sir, she never saw that shotgun.

. . .

(RT 1335-1343)

The defense's last witness was Inez Garcia.

---

* The statement on March 26, 1974 was the one given to Officer Perez which Mr. Braudrick used in his cross-examination.

INEZ GARCIA, SWORN
DIRECT EXAMINATION

BY MR. GARRY: Mrs. Garcia, I believe you said you wanted to say something to the Judge before we started?
A Yes.
THE COURT: I'm sorry, but I do not wish to hear from Mrs. Garcia except by question and answer.
MR. GARRY: She only wants to apologize to the court.
THE COURT: That's all right. No apologies are necessary.
MR. GARRY: That's the only thing she wants to say.
THE COURT: Okay. Proceed.
BY MR. GARRY: Mrs. Garcia, you are the defendant in this action, aren't you?
A Yes, I am.
Q You are charged with murder here?
A Yes, I am.
Q And could you tell us how old are you?
A I'm thirty years old.

. . .

Q And how old is your son?
A Eleven years old.
Q And your husband is in where?
A Prison.
Q And how long have you been living in Soledad?
A Two and a half years.
Q And in the two and a half years, where have you been living?
A Soledad.
Q At what address, what areas? Would you briefly run over the areas that you lived in?
A I was living at Soledad Motor Lodge Motel which they rent rooms, and they rent apartments, and they rent overnight rents, too. And they rent them by the week, and they rent them by the day, and they rent them by the month.
Q And where had you been living, say, in the last six months? Before March 19th?
A Six months? I was at Soledad. Soledad Motor Lodge.
Q And did you live there by yourself?
A Yes, I did, with my two sons–I mean, my nephew and my son.
Q Your nephew is your——
A Like my son.
Q Your sister's son.
A Yes.

Q And your son at the present time is here?
A He is right here right now, but he was in Florida a few days ago.
Q And your son goes to school in Florida now, is that right?
A That's true.
Q Now, Mrs. Garcia, did you kill Mike Jimenez?
A Yes, I did.
Q Why did you kill him?
A Why did I kill him? Because he helped Louie rape me.
Q Now, was there any other reasons why you killed him?
A That's only reason why I kill him.
Q Was there any threats made against your life?
A Yes, there was.
Q Would you tell us about that?
A Well, after they raped me, they called to prove to the other hometown boys that they had done this action, that they had beaten up Fred and that they had raped me and that they had done this with their friends and they called me and told me that they wanted me out of town and if I didn't get out of town worse was going to happen to me, and that they were going to kill me and before me, somebody else. Besides that, I feel that anybody that rapes anybody or commits any violent act like that has a right to defense theirself.
Q Now, Mrs. Garcia, where were you raped?
A I was raped behind the apartment house.
Q And would you tell the jury how they did it?
A Well, the whole thing started—first, they came into the house and Alicia was there, her sister was there, and they came in and they asked for Fred and Fred wasn't there. They stayed there and they bought some liquor and I don't know what kind of liquor it was, but they came inside the house and they were drinking already. They wanted us to have a drink with them and they was acting out of hand. Alicia decided to leave and I stayed there by myself and after a while Freddie got home with Chofero and they went in the room. Then, I went in there and told Freddie to come out because those people was waiting for him outside, so when he came out, I started putting his food—I was fixing his food so he could set down and eat.
Q And then what happened?
A Then they started the whole thing again because they had been harassing me before Freddie was there, you know, before he got there.
Q How were they harassing you?
A Harassing me, touching me, pulling me, all over and you know, being nasty. I can't put it into words.
Q Was there an argument?
A Yes, there was an argument with Freddie about hometown boys and he wasn't a hometown boy and they was going to—they did not

want him there and they wanted us out of town.

Q Was there anything ever said in any of that argument about drugs?

A No, there was nothing about drugs in that argument.

Q Now, I show you this rifle here, is this your rifle?

A Yes, that is my rifle.

Q Now, where was this rifle on the 19th?

A It was in my closet.

Q And was it by itself like this or did it have a cover?

A It had a case on it.

Q And did the case—what did the case look like?

A Like that one right there. He went into the house and I told him it was mine, I forgot his name, Perez or whatever, he went to the house with me down there to check it.

Q When you say he went with you, you are talking about Sergeant Perez?

A The officer whatever.

Q Sergeant Perez?

A Right.

Q Went with you after you were arrested?

A Right.

Q And you went to the house?

A Right.

Q And you said you showed this case?

A That's right.

Q This was in the house?

A Right.

Q You said it was on the what?

A It was on the green chair.

Q All right. Now, you used to own a shotgun, did you not?

A Yes, I did.

Q And did you sell that shotgun?

A Yes, I did.

Q Who did you sell it to?

A Officer Armstrong.

Q The man who testified here in court?

A Yes.

Q And how much did you sell it for?

A $40.00 and he cheated me out of it, too.

Q And when you sold it to him for $40.00, did you sell him the case?

A No, I did not.

Q And what did you use the case for after that?

A To keep my .22 in.

Q And calling your attention then to—let me ask you this: When did you get your .22?

A Oh, I got that here in Soledad.

Q No, I mean when did you get the gun, after the events that happened?

A I bought that when I was living at the Motor Lodge.

Q I see.

A It must have been a year back, I think.

Q Now——

A They keep a record of all that anyway when you buy guns.

MR. GARRY: I have two pictures, can I have them for identification on both of those, and they can both be the same number, A and B, is Your Honor please?

THE COURT: All right.

THE CLERK: Garcia Six.

THE COURT: Garcia Six-A and B.

BY MR. GARRY:

Q I show you Garcia Six-A and B and ask you if you would look at that and tell me what you recognize that representing?

A That is where I got raped and that is where I got raped.

Q And you notice that there are some things on the ground there, but was anything on the ground at the time?

A No, there was nothing on the ground then.

Q And is this—where is this in relation to the apartment?

A That is behind the house where we live, the apartment.

Q And the demonstration of the picture in here showing how wide it is, does that demonstrate how wide that area is?

A Yes, I guess so.

Q I want to offer this into evidence.

MR. BRAUDRICK: No objection, Your Honor.

THE COURT: All right. Received in evidence as next in order, 6-A and 6-B, for Garcia.

MR. GARRY: May I pass that to the jury, Your Honor?

THE COURT: Yes.

BY MR. GARRY:

Q Mrs. Garcia, you said you received a telephone call after you were raped. Is that right?

A That's true.

Q And was it after you were raped that you got the rifle?

A Yes.

Q And what was said in the telephone call that caused you to get your rifle?

A It was said that they wanted me out of town, that what had happened to me was nothing, that it was going to happen to me and if I didn't get out of town, they was going to kill me.

Q And that's why you got your gun; is that right?

A Yes, I got my gun to defend myself.

Q What did you do when you got your gun?

A I loaded it and I went out looking for them.

Q And how did you—did you use your car to go for them or how did you go?

A I walked. I went on foot.

MR. GARRY: May I have that folder for identification, please? I think this is it. I'm going to open up Garcia Number Three for identification, if Your Honor please?

THE COURT: All right.

BY MR. GARRY:

Q I show you Garcia Number Three for identification. Would you tell the court and jury if you recognize that?

A Yes, those are my shoes. Those are the shoes I had on the night I did the shooting.

Q And you walked out in the street with these on?

A That's right.

MR. GARRY: May we offer these into evidence if Your Honor please?

THE COURT: They may be marked Defendant's Garcia in evidence.

BY MR. GARRY:

Q Do you know how far you walked?

A I don't—I really don't know.

Q Were you frightened when you were walking?

A I don't know. I don't think so.

Q You were scared?

A Well, I was scared when this was happening to me. That's why I gave in and let them rape me.

Q By the way, Mrs. Garcia, the police talked to you at 11:30 that night, did they not?

A Yeah.

Q Chief Jimenez and some other police officers were there?

A Yes.

Q Now, did you come right out and tell them that you were raped?

A No, not exactly.

Q Why not?

A Because you just don't—I just didn't. That's all. I was ashamed to talk about it. That's all.

Q Why are you able to talk about it now?

A 'Cause I have talked—I have spoken to other people that have been raped and I see that there's a lot of womens that is raped, and they keep quiet just the same way I was doing, and they don't come forward because of the same reasons I have—most of them, and I think it's about time somebody did something about it and came forward. And not only me, even kids get raped and nobody does anything about it.

MR. GARRY: You may cross-examine.

CROSS-EXAMINATION

BY MR. BRAUDRICK:

Q Mrs. Garcia,—

A Uh huh.

Q When did you move in with Freddie Medrano on Monterey Street?

A I really—I don't know anything about dates, but I was living at Minga's. I stayed in the Jimenez Camp two weeks. I move out of Soledad Motor Lodge, because they were going to throw me out of there because I had Minga and her kids living with me there, and there was too many people staying at my house, and the man at the Motor Lodge—it wasn't because of me that he wanted me to move out. He wanted me to throw out this lady with her kids and I couldn't do that. So, I decided to rent a place and move in with her instead of paying the rent where I was staying at, and I stayed two weeks at Minga's and after that, I started moving out to Fred's house.

Q Who was the person you were living with at the Motor Lodge?

A At the Motor Lodge? I was living there by myself first, and then Minga was living, I think, in Fresno and she lost her home or whatever. She has four kids and she didn't have a place to stay. So, I let her stay at my house. That's Chofero's girlfriend or wife, or whatever. She didn't have a place to stay, so I let her stay at my house. So, the owner of the Motor Lodge, or the manager, decided that he didn't want them there. So, I had to get out of the Motor Lodge or else throw her out so I couldn't throw her out, so I had to move out.

Q Was Chofero there at that time?

A No, Chofero was not there.

Q Did you ever live with Minga when she lived at the Jimenez Camp?

A That's what I'm talking about. That's when we rent at the Jimenez, because when she couldn't stay there with me—they did not want her at the Motor Lodge.

Q So, you moved from the Motor Lodge to the Jimenez Camp?

A Yes, I left the Motor Lodge, because of the reason, because they wanted me to throw her out, and I can't throw out people with four kids out in the streets.

Q Who was living with you at the Jimenez Camp?

A Me, Minga and her four kids.

Q How long did you live there?

A I stayed there two weeks, and I gave her $120.00—what they pay at the Jimenez Camp for staying there.

Q Okay. And that's when you moved in with Freddie?

A With Freddie. I started moving in, because half of my things are still in Minga's and Chofero's* house, which I think I told Perez, and I told the Chief of Police that I had to get my things and my things out of there when I got arrested. I think you remember that, don't you? I was supposed to go and get the things out of there, but I went to jail and they told me to call back and somebody would pick them up, ain't it true?

Q You still have things with Chofero?

A Yes, over there at the house, because I didn't finish moving into Freddie's.

Q Now, you stated earlier you have one son who is eleven years old? Is that correct?

A Yes, I do have a son. He's eleven years old.

Q And you had a nephew living with you also?

A Yes, that's right.

Q Were they living with you when you moved in with Freddie?

A No. My son had gone back home.

Q When did he go back home?

A He went back home after—I had an argument with a girl named Pauline.

Q And—well, can you remember what month he went back to Florida? That's where he went, didn't he?

A I don't remember about dates, but I do remember I sent him back home, because this little one was trying to sell drugs to my kids, and I do not mess with drugs.

Q And was that in December?

A I don't really know. Ask them. They—I mean, he should know. He's a policeman from Soledad. He knows me from over there.

Q Did you have your children with you when you lived at the Soledad Motor Lodge.

A Yes, I did.

Q But you didn't have them with you when you lived with Minga?

A No, they was already gone home.

Q How long did your nephew live with you?

A My nephew?

Q Yes.

A Two years and a half. The same thing I was here.

* "Chofero" is Chris Solis' nickname. At the time of the shooting he lived with Minga and her children.

Q And you were supporting him during that time?

A Yes, and how you say, when I didn't work sometimes, the Welfare would pass me money and sometimes my parents would sent me money, but most of the time I would try to work to support myself.

Q Now, when your nephew—is he?

A Uh huh.

Q —Is he the son of a man who testified here?

A That's right.

Q And did he go back to Florida at the same time your son went back to Florida?

A That's right. I send them both back home.

Q Now, you stated earlier that you purchased this rifle from a store in the City of Soledad? . . .

A I bought it for me and my gun—I mean, for me and my son, most of all for my son. My son is underage to use it yet.

Q And had you shot a rifle before you bought it?

A Yes, I used to have a shotgun.

Q That is a shotgun that you sold to Officer Armstrong?

A That's right.

Q What kind of a shotgun was that?

A A twelve range or whatever you call it.

Q And it had a shorter barrel than normal, didn't it?

A Yes, they call it a sawed-off, but it is in the law, it is in the law, I mean, right there.

Q So, it is a sawed-off shotgun, but it is legal, right?

A Yes, it is legal.

Q And how many barrels did it have?

A Two.

Q Okay. When did you get that shotgun?

A I got that around four years ago, around there.

Q When did you sell it to Officer Armstrong?

A One day I needed money, I don't remember that day.

Q It was a couple of weeks before you killed Mike Jimenez, wasn't it?

A No, no, it was a couple of months before even I thought if anything like that would happen to me. I sold it to him around six months or seven months or maybe even more, because I was in jail four months and I sold around a year.

Q Okay. Now, you stated that you sold him the shotgun?

A Uh huh.

Q But you kept the case that the shotgun came in?

A Uh huh.

Q Now, would you take a look at this case, People's Number Twelve, is this the case?

A That is the çase I identified as mine.

. . .

Q And did you always keep the shotgun with you?

A Yes, I always kept it with me. I had an M-2 but that is in Florida.

Q Okay. You knew how to shoot those guns, too, didn't you?

A Oh, yes, I mean—I don't know how to shoot very well, but I like guns.

Q Did you target practice with the .22 that you bought for your son?

A Not exactly. I would go out and sometimes my son would shoot it.

Q Did you ever shoot it?

A Yeah.

Q Okay. Whereabouts would you go to shoot it?

A Up in the mountains like going towards Fresno, they have a place where you can go and a lot of people go there and they shoot, you know, blanks and stuff like that, you know, just anything.

Q Now, you state that after you bought or after you sold the shotgun to Officer Armstrong,——

A Uh huh.

Q —that you kept the case?

A That's right.

Q I think you stated also that you stored your rifle in that case. Is that correct?

A Yes.

Q And how long did you then keep the rifle in that case?

A Since I have it.

Q So, that would be about six months or so before you killed Mike Jimenez?

A I don't know, I bought it. I bought the gun a long time before this whole thing ever happened and that is very easy to find out because they keep records of those things. I don't keep records because I can't read.

Q Okay. What I am trying to find out is how long you stored the .22 rifle in the case?

A I store it every time I can.

. . .

Q Where did you—did you keep the .22 rifle in the case in your bedroom?

A Yes, I did.

Q And did Freddie ever have it?

A Not that I know of.

Q Was it ever kept in his bedroom?

A Never. It was kept in my closet with my things, even when he went over there and Yvonne and the other man went over there, my things were still packed there and everything because I haven't quite finished moving in there and everything that I took over there, I kept in that room.

Q That would be your own room?

A Yes, the room that I was supposed to occupy or whatever they call it, you know, the one that I was going to be staying in.

Q Did you keep the .22 rifle in the case in the closet in the room?

A Yes, I did.

Q And did you keep it loaded or unloaded?

A Unloaded. I never keep my guns loaded.

Q I show you People's Thirteen, a plastic case that has numerous rounds of .22 caliber ammunition.

A Yes, I know, that's mine.

Q That is yours?

A Sure.

Q Where did you keep this?

A I kept it in the room. I had a purse which we couldn't find that day to which I keep more than that, it is more ammunition, more bullets in there and shotgun shells, which we couldn't find that day or that night when we went there to check. It was like a wallet where I keep all the bullets and things in it. They used to belong to my guns, like the one I sold to Armstrong and this too, this one that was missing, too, and we looked for it in there because I told them about it, and I told the other policeman, too.

Q Did you ever store this in Freddie's bedroom?

A No, I never did. I left that in the parlor with the case when I loaded the gun.

Q I show you a picture, People's Thirty-one, that is a picture of part of Freddie's bedroom, isn't it?

A Yeah, that is where they found the things, the bullets, that I remember because I told him that I didn't leave it there, it was supposed to be on the green chair where they found the case.

Q And those bullets in that picture, and is that the same case?

A I know because I went in the room with him.

Q Now, when you had—had you slept at the apartment on Monterey Street?

A On Freddie's house, yes, I stayed there.

Q And how many nights had you slept there?

A I don't know, one time or two times, it all depends, one day I would stay—one day I would stay at my friend's house and come back and stay there, and I really stay there on and off.

Q Did you have any living arrangements with Freddie as far as doing cooking or anything?

A We had an arrangement made, we were going to be room mates and we were going to share rent half and half, and everything, but I was still moving in so I would either stay at Mr. Hyers which he wanted me to move back into the Motor Lodge, but I decided to move in with Freddie because he wanted me; you know, I didn't want to stay at Minga's place because I didn't like the way what was going on there, so I decided to move out. But, I would either stay in Freddie or I would stay in Hyers or somebody else's house and I would stay sometimes at Minga's and I was still moving out.

Q This was all during the time after you and Freddie made the arrangement?

A That's right because I have a lot of things and I haven't finished moving out, I just had half of my stuff almost over at Freddie's and all the kids in Soledad and people helped me. Chofero helped me move and Minga and all the kids.

Q They are the ones that moved you into the house?

A They were helping me take the stuff over to Fred's house.

Q And you were good friends with Chofero Solis?

A I was good friends with Minga, and Chofero and that is why I don't understand when that thing happened that day he just stood there and watched the whole thing and didn't do anything. I still don't understand it, and he said right here he just sat right through the whole thing and didn't say anything either, and that is another thing, and Alicia, too, denies knowing me and she knows me for three years and people will testify to that.

Q You had known Alicia for three years?

A I know Alicia since I got to Soledad almost and all the police there knows that I do know her since I got there, and they stood on this stand and lied and said she didn't know me.

Q You first met her three years ago?

A . . . She knows me since I came down from Florida.

Q Had she always been living out on Metz Road across from the school?

A No, she used to live at the Motor Lodge when I first came, she used to live at the Motor Lodge and that is where I met her at.

Q Okay. Then, later she moved out?

A Then she moved out to the little street there was a shack and then she moved out of there to another house that used to belong to a girl they used to call Fat Maria and I don't know her last name, next to the school, you know, where the school is now because my kids used to go to school there and they just traded houses or something or another. I don't know, I know Alicia for a long time and I even loaned her—I had an old TV that somebody gave me and she needed it for her kids and I loaned it to her and she sat here and said she didn't know me.

Q Did you know her sister, Rosa?

A Oh, Rosa, I only know her around a month. That is, I really don't know that much.

Q How about Rosa's husband, Willie Bracamonte?

A I really don't know him, either, I heard a lot of rumors about him but I don't like him. He's a person who doesn't work. He doesn't even support his childs.

Q So you considered at least on March 19—you considered Alicia a good friend of yours?

A Yes, I did up until the other day. Really, I don't know why she sat over here and lied.

Q Now, what you said that you slept at the house, that you and Freddie Medrano lived together?

A Uh huh.

Q The night before the shooting; is that right?

A No. The night before the shooting, I been staying there. I was staying there, be there two days already staying there, and I was fixing some of my things. I was taking out of boxes, because I had some more things to bring over, and I wanted to get some of the things already in place, so I could bring the rest of the things over to the house. 'Cause everything was just piling up, and I was just bringing boxes in and things, clothes and stuff. So, I decided to stay those days to start fixing up there and putting my things in places, and I say this—they just happened to happen. But, I was cleaning the house at the same time then, but I just had moved into that house, and I haven't even finished moving in and they know because they went there, and they saw my things how they was when they went to check the house.

Q Is your answer to the question then that you didn't sleep there the night before?

A I did. I been sleeping there for two nights. It would have been a third night if this thing wouldn't have happened.

. . .

Q Okay. What did you do when you got up that morning?. . .

A Alicia was there. She came over and so does her sister came over. They came over.

Q About what time did they come over?

A I don't remember. I know she was eating, you know, they came over to eat. Usually come over, and they keep me company and we cook for them and, you know, they eat there with me.

Q Would that have been for dinner or lunch?

A Well, really, to tell you the truth, they would come for lunch, dinner, or whatever, 'cause I like to cook. I couldn't—I mean—no, it's not funny really. You know, this is a thing that went on in Soledad. I did this because this is what I felt like doing.

Q Well, how about on March 19, the day of the shooting, did they come over for lunch that day?

A Yeah, they was there. She was there when Jimenez and Louie got there, and she took off, because when after this thing happened to me that I got raped, I went to her house, you know. I went to her sister, and I told her, and she said nobody would believe me that I got raped. Then we went to her house, and she told me that the reason she left my house that night because everything was getting out of hand. It was true, but she left me there by myself.

Q So, they were there at dinner time?

A Yeah, she was there at dinner time. Then she left. She left me alone with them, and after a while, Freddie came home. He came home with whats' his name, Chofero. They went in the room, and I went in there and told him those people were waiting for him outside because they were acting all——

Q Were you at the house when Chofero first came?

A Yes, and I knocked on the room and I told Freddie that Chofero wanted him, and he told me to send him in, and I did. I sent him in.

Q When Chofero got there, who was at the house?

A Who was at the house? Alicia.

Q Who else?

A Her kids, and her sister, and her daughter and another little daughter that she got. A little girl. She's still walking, you know, she doesn't walk very well. She's learning how to walk.

. . .

Q Now, can you recall Licia coming over to your house and bringing her children over?

A Yes.

Q When you had a visitor from Florida or a relative visiting you?

A That's a lie. I don't lie to my family. My brother-in-law was here. My husband was here. You should have asked them. When I move in with somebody, I tell them.

Q So, she didn't——

A I don't have anything to—how you say—hide from them 'cause if I go out, I tell them I go out. If I live some place when they come from Florida, they go where I'm at.

Q So, she didn't come over to the house with her children and make like she lived there, and you were just staying with her and Freddie?

A No, sir.

Q That never happened?

A No. That never happened.

Q Did you ever have any of your relatives visit you?

A My family always comes from Florida to visit.

Q Which members of your family visited you at the house?

A At which house?

Q The apartment on Monterey Street?

A They never got nobody to visit me there because when my brother-in-law came, he went to the Jimenez Camp, and then Minga told him I was moving in with Freddie Medrano and she took him over there to, how you say, Fred's house, and from there we went back to Minga's house. So, it wasn't no reason for me to lie to them.

Q Okay. Now, after Freddie and Chofero left, they left you, Alicia, Rosa and some other people who were dropping in and out of the house?

A Yeah.

Q When did Louie and Mike Jimenez come to the house?

A I don't know. I was cooking, I think. No, I have finished cooking and the kids have finished eating, and Alicia had finished eating. Me and her, we was together and her sister. And all of a sudden, they dropped in, and they asked for Fred, and we told them he wasn't there, but they decided to wait anyway. They like that. So, his other friend decided to leave and they were just, you know, acting terrible.

Q Who's the other friend that decided to leave?

A I don't know. Some guy that brought them, I think, over there.

Q Dejuetta (phonetics)? Could that be it?

A I don't know, and he kept grabbing me and saying I was his girl, pulling on me and saying a lot of things, you know. I don't know these people for them to be pulling on me and grabbing me all over.

Q Okay. Had you met Mike before that night?

A I had seen them. I have seen them.

Q How about Mike? You have seen him before?

A I have seen them all, in Soledad is a small town. You know everybody and everybody knows you and everybody knows your business and everything you do. There is no secrets there, and that's the truth. He could tell you himself. That man right there (indicating).

Q Had you known—had Mike or Miguel Jimenez ever been to your house before?

A Well, he came to the house. Not to my house. To see Fred, maybe. I don't know. I know Louie has. He been there. He knocks—he comes and he talks to Freddie. That I know.

. . .

Q Now, how long did licia—Alicia and Rosa stay after Louie and Mike got there to your apartment?

A Well, she stayed a while and then all of a sudden she decided to leave, and that I remember. That's all. She just decided to leave, period.

Q Did she leave—did Alicia leave with Rosa? They left together at the same time?

A Yes, I think they did.
Q And the children too?
A Yeah.
Q So, that left you at the house alone?
A Alone with both of them.
Q How much longer after they came did Chofero——
A Chofero? Five minutes after—while I was alone with them, they was hustling me there. They got on my case and they were getting nasty with me and stuff like that and then when they came, I don't know if Freddie realized they was there or not, but he went straight to the room with Chofero. So then, I went in there and I knocked on the door and told them they was waiting for him outside. Then I started fixing his food to eat. And like that.
Q Did they hit you or harm you at all before Freddie got back?
A No. They was just getting nasty.
Q They had been drinking, hadn't they?
A They was drinking, yes.
Q They were drinking at your house, too?
A That's where they brought the bottle to, to the house.
Q Had you had anything to drink?
A I had to.
Q You had to?
A Yes. I had to—I had to go along with everything they did. I was there with them around five minutes by myself with them.
Q And so you drank during that five minutes?
A Uh huh.
Q What did—what did Louie do when Freddie came back home?
A He started—he got on his case when Freddie came out of the room. He got on his case. He started telling him all these things about hometown boy. That he wasn't a hometown boy and that something other—he was too big, or something or another, and then he was—he has to have somebody and something or other. It was a big mess. I can't remember very well what they were saying then. They told me that I thought I was too good for the mens in Soledad, and that they was going to show me what a hometown boy was.

. . .

Q Now, how long did Freddie stay inside of his bedroom when Chofero—when they got back from wherever they had gone to?
A I don't know because I called him and I told him that these people was waiting for him because I thought that Freddie had seen them, but he just went straight into the room with Chofero and left me out there with them and they were still, you know, acting kind of—they was acting up so I just went in there and told him so he came out and that is when the whole thing started, you know, they started, you

know, harassing and all this bullshit, excuse the expression, but that is what it was, so they decided to get on——

. . .

Q Okay. After you warmed up his dinner, then you went to the room where he and Chofero were and told him—

A No, no, no, I went in and I called him while he was sitting at the table talking to Louie and Mike because they was behind him and, you know, they was on his case and I decided by, you know, giving him his food, maybe those people—I was just trying to calm things down and I was trying to go along with them to see if they would calm down and they wouldn't, and they just kept on and on and on and on and then they decided to beat up on Freddie.

Q Can you remember what they were saying?

A They were talking about hometown, that he wasn't a hometown guy from there and he wasn't a hometown boy and I wasn't a hometown girl.

Q Is that what they were saying to you before Freddie came in?

A Before Freddie walked in and they started on him, too, and they was going to show me how a hometown boy was.

Q Who was saying all of this, was Louie and Mike?

A Both of them.

Q Both of them?

A Both of them was saying this, they was both saying this and Mike was bragging about how bad he was and what he would do to people when he doesn't like people, and about that he has a lot of pull in Soledad because he is a hometown boy, and he has a lot of pull there or he has a lot of influence or whatever you call it.

Q And was he saying this when he was talking to Freddie at the table in the kitchen?

A That's right.

Q Okay. And then you brought Freddie his dinner?

A Yes, and he put his hand right in it, you saw—I think you saw it on—and the other policeman saw it, too, the dinner, I put back there and his finger was still marked because it was beans and things and when it dries out, you see the finger print on it.

Q Mike is the one who did that?

A Yes.

. . .

Q And it was Louie talking about the hometown boys and so on and so forth?

A No, and Fred—Jimenez was, too. Jimenez was saying that he had a lot of pull there and that if he wanted, he could have us killed and he could have us—he could have anything done to us because the hometown boys listened to him because he has a lot of pull.

Q Okay. Why was he saying that?

A I don't know. Don't ask me.

Q Well, did you hear any mention of drugs or heroin or anything like that?

A There was no mention of drugs or no heroin.

Q Okay. Have you—had you ever seen any heroin or any drugs in the house?

A I never did. I don't mess with drugs. I don't smoke—I don't do none of that. The only cigarettes I smoke is Winstons and that is all I smoke.

Q Did you ever see any marijuana in that house?

A I never did.

Q Did you know whether or not Freddie smoked marijuana in your house?

A Well, if they did, that is their problem, I don't do that.

Q But, do you know if he did?

A I never saw it.

Q Okay. Now, Louie was having an argument with Freddie and Mike is there and he puts his finger in the food, and what did Freddie do after Mike put his finger in his food?

A I think he got up finally and went out with, what's his name, Louie, and they started—I think he hit him outside and he came back in and they started to fight. All I know was that they took over the house. In other words, like they owned the house, they was the one that owned the house and in different words, I was nobody at the house and he was nobody at the house, and they took over the house. They took over the whole house.

Q What did they do when they took over the house?

A What they did, they started pushing things around, and you couldn't tell them anything. He threw everything and did anything they felt like.

Q Now, you saw Louie and Freddie go outside the house, didn't you?

A Yes, I did.

Q Do you know how long they stayed outside?

A I really don't know.

Q Did you see Louie come back in the house?

A Yes, he came back in bragging about how he beat up Freddie and then Fred came in and they beat him up again, they threw him against the couch and Chofero was right there sitting on the couch and Chofero didn't even lift a hand to help him and they were beating up on him and then if he rushed back out or he rushed in his room, I don't know where, but I thought he rushed right out, and how you say it, I think when I went out with them, when they told me to come outside and they grabbed me and took me outside and he told me he was going to show me what a hometown boy was, and he did show me what a hometown boy was.

. . .

Q When it first started, wasn't it just Louie and Freddie?

A Louie and Freddie, yeah, and Louie hit him, but Mike got in it because Mike wanted to hit Freddie and had been dying to do it all day, you know, I think this whole thing was planned and everything and Chofero knew that it was going to happen to us and that is the way I see it. I think he knew this whole thing was going to happen to us because he just sat there and watched it.

Q So, after Louie and Freddie started fighting, Mike comes in and he starts hitting Freddie, too, is that right?

A Uh huh. No, I don't know if he came in, he was already in there.

Q But, he came into the fight?

A Oh, yes, he came into the fight.

Q All right.

A But, he was in the house.

Q Now, was Mike and Louie, were they pretty drunk?

A I really don't know if they were drunk or not, but I know they brought a bottle of liquor inside the house.

Q And that is the liquor you drank from?

A Yes, I said that is what I drank from, which I only had, I think one, because they made a test on my blood to see if I was drunk, too, and I think what is his name could testify to that, or either the records will show that, too.

Q Okay. What happened to Freddie after Mike beat him up and threw him against the couch?

A What happened to Freddie, I know they made him leave, he was bleeding all over.

. . .

Q Okay. Did you do anything to get involved?

A I was trying to stop the fight and they wouldn't stop.

Q Okay. What were you doing to try to stop the fight?

A I was screaming their names telling them to stop it and stop it, and they wouldn't.

Q Okay. Did you try to get in between them or twist them away or anything like that?

A Are you crazy, if I got in between them, I would have got beat up myself.

Q So, you were standing back away——

THE COURT: Ladies and gentlemen, I will remind you again this is no show and if you must laugh, leave the room. The next one who laughs I am going to have the Bailiff pick you up and take you outside. Proceed.

THE WITNESS: What was the question?

BY MR. BRAUDRICK:

Q Okay. You never got in any physical contact with Louie or Mike then?

A No.

Q Before?

A No.

Q Before Freddie was bleeding?

A No.

Q After Freddie was bleeding, is that when he went into his bedroom?

A I think so, I thought he had gone outside.

Q He had gone where?

A I thought he had gone out. That was the second fight that they had and I thought he had gone out and had left me alone, and that is when I went out with them and that is when they raped me and then when I came back in the house, I saw him or I thought I saw him, but Chofero was still there and then he left again because at this time to me, Freddie just kept going and coming and that is the way I saw it.

Q So, you are saying after you were raped that you came back in the house and Freddie was there?

A Yeah, and they they called and told me these things over the phone and I called my family and I told my family what I was going to do and I went out and I did it, and that's it.

Q So, you are not sure where Freddie went after the fight and he was bleeding, you don't know whether he went in the bedroom or outside?

A I think he went in the bathroom to clean his nose because there was blood all over the floor which I think you was the one that picked it up with a little thing, what they call it, a Q-stick or something and they picked it up for the lab, wasn't that true, Mr. Perez, that is your name, no?

THE COURT: You are not in a position to ask questions, ma'am.

THE WITNESS: Well, I am trying——

THE COURT: The questions will be asked of you.

THE WITNESS: I'm sorry but I am trying because I can't read or write and I got to make sure.

THE COURT: Please just a moment–you have counsel and he will ask you questions if necessary to straighten out your testimony. Go ahead.

THE WITNESS: Well, anyway, that is what they did. There was blood all over.

THE COURT: I believe you answered the question. Next question, please.

BY MR. BRAUDRICK:

Q Okay. You saw Freddie come out holding something to his nose?

A I guess so.

Q But, you don't know whether it was the bathroom or the bedroom he came out of?

A I really don't know.

Q Was Chofero still sitting on the couch?

A That's right.

Q And when Freddie came out, Louie and Mike were still there, weren't they?

A When he came out?

Q Yes, holding the towel to his nose?

A When he was holding a towel to his nose, I don't know.

Q Well, was that before you were raped? Or after you were raped?

A I think it was after I was raped.

Q So, Louie and Mike went outside before you saw Freddie come out with the thing on his nose?

A Uh huh.

Q Is that right, you have to answer so——

A —I said yes.

Q What did Louie—where did Louie and Mike go after Freddie went into his room?

A I really don't know if Freddie went into the room.

Q Well, after Freddie left the living room?

A I know Freddie left me alone, and to me, I thought he had left me alone with these people, to me I thought he had, you know, rushed out and I went out with his people outside because they wanted me to go out with them and if I put up a force, I don't know what would have happened to me, so I decided to give in anything they did to me or anything they wanted to do to me was all right with me as long as I was still alive and that is all that counts to me then.

Q So, after Freddie left the room and Louie and Mike went outside. Is that right?

A After he ran out, then I went out with his people and then they raped me and after they raped me, I went back in the house and they called me and told me all this beautiful things and then I went out and shot them.

Q Did they make you go outside the house?

A No, I went out because I felt like it.

Q Are you trying to be funny or telling me the truth?

A No, I already told you they forced me to go outside.

Q They forced, what did they do to force you to go outside?

A They pulled me and they told me come on, I want to show you what a hometown boy is.

Q Who pulled on you?

A Both of them.

Q Whereabouts did they pull on you?

A Around my blouse.

Q Okay. Was that when your blouse was ripped?

A No, my blouse was ripped in the back when they hit me and they started hitting me and they told me, bitch, take your clothes off.

Q Now, so they grabbed you around your neck and by your blouse and this would be Mike and Louie?

A And Louie.

Q And they take you outside?

A Right, and Chofero was right there.

Q And took you out into near where Fred's car was parked?

A I don't know where Fred's car was parked there because I had my car there, too, you see, I had a car, too, I had a Volkswagen.

Q Now, did you say anything at that time when they were taking you out of the house?

A I was trying to calm them down and be nice to them and anything they wanted.

THE COURT: The question is, did you say anything or not?

THE WITNESS: Did I say anything to what?

THE COURT: Read the question back, please.

(Reporter reading question.)

THE WITNESS: Nothing, I agreed with everything they said. I said that I didn't think I was too good for the hometown boys, it was just that was my way——

THE COURT: You have answered the question. Next question, please?

THE WITNESS: That is the question.

THE COURT: You say, I didn't say anything, that seems to be an adequate answer. If more is desired, your counsel will develop it. Next question, please?

BY MR. BRAUDRICK:

Q When you were going out, when they were dragging you outside and Chofero was sitting right there, did you ever say anything to him to ask him to help you?

A He didn't want to help. He knew we needed help. He didn't want to do anything.

THE COURT: Strike the answer. Read the question back to her.

(Reporter reading the question.)

THE WITNESS: We both did and he just set there and watched the whole thing.

BY MR. BRAUDRICK:

Q He didn't watch them attack you outside, did he?

A Oh, no, he stayed inside, I guess he couldn't take watching them maybe outside, it is a miracle he didn't go outside to watch it, too, because he stood there and watched the rest of the things.

Q Okay. Did they take you—they took you around to the back of the house. Is that right?

A That's right.

Q Did they drag you or did you walk along freely?

A I walked freely after it.

Q Okay. You knew that there were people living next door to you, didn't you?

A Yes, I know there is people living next door to me.

Q And you knew that there were people living in this yellow house, right?

A Yes, I know there was people living there.

Q You knew people were living on this side or the south side of your house, too?

A Yes, I knew there was people living all along there.

Q Do you remember if it was dark or daylight?

A It was dark.

Q And there were lights on in the houses, too, weren't there?

A I don't know if there was lights on in the houses, I was too nervous to realize, and I was too scared to realize if there was any lights or not.

Q Now, which—what side of the apartment did you go around, did you go around the street side here?

A No, they have like a little thing, I guess, if this is the house the way you have it there, we went right around here and there is a thing there, you have a picture right here, and this is it right there.

Q But, they took you then out the front door out toward Monterey Street and around the back of the house?

A They did not take me out to Monterey Street.

BY MR. BRAUDRICK:

Q Now, where was Louie and Mike as they were taking you back there? Did you walk in front of them or did they carry you?

A Right beside me.

Q Did they have ahold of you?

A Yes.

Q Did Mike have ahold of you?

A They both did.

Q One on each arm?

A One on each side. Not arms. On each side.

Q Where were they holding onto you?

A They wasn't holding onto me. They was talking and telling me what they was going to do to me.

Q What were they saying to you as they walked you around to the back of the house?

A They telling me I think I was too good for the hometown boys, and they was going to show me what a hometown boy was, and that I was just another bitch, and in different words because I gave in and I tried to agree with them, and I tried to tell them I wasn't the way they thought I was. It was just that was my way and I tried to agree on everything they said. They still wouldn't reason with me.

Q Then, they took you around back of the house; is that right?

A Yes.

Q Now, this G-6?

A I don't know anything about G-6.

Q That's the picture of the back of the house?

A Yeah, that's the picture of the back of the house. That's where I got raped.

Q Now, this picture shows a mattress?

A Which wasn't there at that time.

Q And boxes. Were they there?

A That wasn't there then, (indicating.)

Q Can you see these utility meters, boxes there?

A Yeah, that was there. That was there, but this wasn't there, and that wasn't there at the time (indicating.)

Q How far down this little alley did they take you?

A It was right–okay. It was right–okay. I want to mark it for you so you don't have to ask me twice. Could I?

Q Go ahead. I don't think that works.

A Well, it was right along this thing. I can't–it's between these two things right here. That's where it happened. (indicating.)

. . .

BY MR. BRAUDRICK:

Q Okay. Now, what did–what did they do to you when they took you around the back there?

A I have–I have to go and tell you what they did to me?

Q I'm not asking you to show me. I'm asking you to tell me what they did to you as they took you around the back?

A Well, he hit me.

Q Who hit you?

A Louie hit me, and he grabbed my blouse.

Q Where did Louie hit you?

A My face.

Q Whereabouts on your face?

A I don't remember at this time, but he hit me and he ripped my blouse and I told him he didn't have to do that, and I took off my clothes.

Q Now, did Mike hit you at all?

A Mike stood there and just so I wouldn't, you know, get out of the alley.

Q Mike didn't touch you?

A No.

Q But Louie hit you?

A Yes.

Q Did he hit you with his fist?

A Uh huh.

Q Right in the face?

A Uh huh.

Q Were you hit in any other place?

A I don't know. I don't remember. I was too nervous, and I was scared. All I knew is I didn't want to get beat up, and I didn't want to get killed. Anything they did to me was fine with me at that moment.

Q Okay. Now, it was Louie that ripped your sweater; is that right?

A That's right.

Q And––

A I told him he didn't have to hit me. He didn't have to do that. I'll take off my clothes, and I did.

. . .

BY MR. BRAUDRICK:

Q I show you People's Fourteen, this blouse–sweater. Is this what you were wearing that night?

A Yes.

Q Okay. And Louie grabbed it and ripped it?

A He didn't grab it like that. He grabbed me. He grabbed like that and ripped it (indicating.)

Q And did he rip it as far as it is ripped right here?

A Yes, he did.

Q All the way down to there?

A He ripped it. I don't know how long, but he ripped it.

Q Well, is it ripped this more–more now than it was after he ripped it?

A I don't know. I was ripped. That's all I know.

Q Was it ripped any more that night?

A I really don't know. I don't remember being ripped after that.

Q You don't remember what?

A I don't remember being ripped after that. It was ripped like that.

Q Now, was Miguel–was he standing on the street end of that alley way? Do you know what I mean?

A He was standing in the alley so I wouldn't get out.

Q So, Jimenez was between you and the street?

A Yes.

. . .

BY MR. BRAUDRICK:

Q After you say that Louie ripped your blouse—your sweater rather—you then said that you had just taken your clothes off yourself?

A Yes, I did. I gave in. I took them off.

Q And what was the first thing you took off? Can you remember?

A I don't know. I don't remember if it was my pants or my blouse. I think it was. And then I took off my pants.

Q Were you wearing a brassiere?

A No, I don't wear brassieres.

Q These are the pants you were wearing?

A That's right.

Q So you took off your blouse. You took off your jeans?

A Uh huh.

Q And——

A I don't know if I took off my blouse but I think I took off my jeans. I don't remember, but I know I took off my clothes.

Q And did you take off your panties, too?

A Yes, I did.

Q Okay. And where did you put the clothes?

A Where did I put my clothes?

Q Yes.

A They was right there on the ground.

Q You threw them down on the ground?

A They was right there, right by where they were raping me.

Q Okay. What—you took off your clothes?

A Uh huh.

Q And Louie was standing right there and Miguel was still standing where you indicated on this photograph?

Q Okay. Then what happened after that?

A You want me to tell you what happened after that?

Q Yes.

A He fucked me. What else do you want me to tell you?

Q Now, was Miguel holding you down at all during this time?

A No. He was being nice. He was very nice. He was saying, "don't do it."

MR. BRAUDRICK: Your Honor, could you instruct her not to—she's just playing around.

THE COURT: I can't——

MR. BRAUDRICK: She's just playing around, your Honor. She's not answering the questions.

THE COURT: Well——

MR. BRAUDRICK: I'm not trying to be sarcastic, but she's giving me sarcastic answers.

THE COURT: I couldn't hear her. Please speak into the microphone and answer the questions as best you can.

MR. BRAUDRICK: What was Miguel doing while Louie, you say, was having sexual intercourse with you?

A He was watching me having sex with this creep, and he was enjoying watching the other creep have sex with me.

Q Have you ever said that Miguel was holding you down?

A Yes, he was.

Q He was holding you down?

A Yes—not holding me down, but holding me there.

Q Was he holding you down physically or not?

A Holding me there. In different words, so I wouldn't move out of that alley. He was right there in between the things while this other creep was having sex with me.

Q Could you go out the other end of the alley?

A Yes, you could go out at the other end of the alley, but at that time, I wasn't thinking there was another side—another alley, 'cause when something like that is happening to you, you do not think of another alley or anything like that. After it happened, you think all the things you probably could have done, but at that moment, you don't find anything to do. Just to give in. That's all, as long as you stay alive.

Q At any time when you were back in that alley did Miguel put a hand on you?

A He—aw—they both say, "they was all alike." That's all and they laughed and they laughed and then they call up their friends to reassure that they did this act.

MR. BRAUDRICK: Your Honor, could you——

THE WITNESS: I know. Could he read the question.

MR. BRAUDRICK: The answer is nonresponsive.

THE COURT: Read the question back. Strike the answer. The jury is admonished to disregard it. Read the question back.

(Question read by the reporter.)

THE WITNESS: Did he put a hand on me? I already answered that twice. He held me there.

THE COURT: Madam, it's a simple yes to answer the question, or no.

THE WITNESS: Yes, he put a hand on me. That means he did it, yes.

THE COURT: He did put a hand on you. All right.

BY MR. BRAUDRICK:

Q Now, did he hold you while Louie was having sexual intercourse with you?

A He held me there. Holding me there.

Q Okay. Did he strike you at all?

A Did he strike me?

Q While Louie was having sexual intercourse with you?

A No, he didn't strike me. The one who striked me was Louie, but he held me there.

Q He held you down?

A He held me there. He held me. In different words, he had me there.

Q Did he hold you down?

A Not down. He held me there. You want me to show you how he did it to me? Would you like me to show it to you?

THE COURT: Just a minute, now. You just give the Judge a chance to talk, too. I think if you would describe as to whether it's physically or perhaps emotional, or mentally holding them there. I think there may be some difficulty with some words here.

BY MR. BRAUDRICK:

Q Did he physically hold you there?

A He physically—I don't know what physically is, but he hold me there.

THE COURT: By the use of his hands or feet or any part of his body touching yours, did he keep you there?

THE WITNESS: Yes, he threw me in there, and Louie grabbed me, and the other grabbed me, and that's the way they went. So, and he hold me there. He held me there because he was putting his hand over here and over here, and he was cracking up while the other guy was raping me.

Q Okay. What did Louie do after he finished having sexual intercourse with you?

A He said we were all alike and decided to call and made sure all his friends knew all about it, and tell me to get out of town.

Q What did he do after he had sexual intercourse with you?

A What did he do?

Q Yes.

A I don't know what he did. He just said that and left. I put on my clothes, and I went back in the house.

Q Did you put your clothes on back of your apartment?

A I put the clothes on. I put on my pants. I think I had on my blouse. I'm not quite sure, and I went in there, and I just was—I don't know what I said or what I did. I went in there. Then I got a phone call, and then these people told me—this guy called himself named Tiger, claiming he was Tiger or something or other, asking me all kinds of things and was cracking up and laughing and all this, and you have all that in your report yourself because you know that that's the truth.

Q Okay. Did you see where Louie and Mike went afterwards?

A No, I did not.

Q Okay. Then after you—Louie had sexual intercourse with you, then you got up, put your clothes on and went back into your house; is that right?

A That's right.

Q When you got back in the house, was Chofero still there?

A Yes, he was.

Q And you stated earlier that he was still there; is that right?

A I think he was there when I went in.

Q What did you do when you got back in the house?

A When I got back in the house?

Q Yes.

A I don't remember what I did. I think I went—the phone rang. I answer it. These people started saying things over the phone, because I guess they went over there to prove to the hometown boys that they have done this thing, and they call and they was all laughing about it. It was a big joke to them, they wanted me out of town, and if I didn't get out of town, worse was going to happen to me or else they was going to kill me and before me, that.

Q What did you do before you got the phone call after you got in the house?

A After I got that, I call home and told my parents.

Q What did you do before the phone call from Tiger?

A What did I do before that?

Q After you got in the house?

A I don't know. I was just—I couldn't believe this thing had happened to me. I was—I still—I couldn't believe it. I couldn't believe it, and then I thought of all the things I could have done that I didn't do.

Q And did you talk to Chofero when you got back in the house?

A I don't remember. I don't know, but I knew that I got raped, and I think he knew the whole thing was going to happen.

Q Did you talk to Freddie at all when you got back in the house?

A I believe I did. I'm not sure but I know that—well, anyway.

Q And did you recognize the voice on the phone?

A I don't recognize nobody's voice, because I don't know those people.

Q Okay. Do you know whether or not Louie was talking on the phone?

A I really don't know. I know they was laughing and carrying on, and they was joking about what had happened to me, and what had happened to Freddie, and they were saying all kinds of things on the phone.

Q Was there more than one person that talked to—on the phone to you?

A There was a couple of them. They got on there.

Q Were they talking at the same time? Can you remember?

A I don't remember, but I know all they were saying was nasty things, and they was cracking up and they was laughing. It was a big joke to them what had happened.

Q What did you say to them over the phone?

A I didn't say anything.

Q Do you know how long that they talked to you?

A I didn't say anything to them.

Q Do you know how long they talked to you?

A I don't keep up with time.

Q Do you have any estimate?

A No.

Q Then, after that phone call, what did you do?

A I called my parents and my brother-in-law answered the phone and I told him what I was going through and I went and did it.

Q You called them in Florida?

A That's right.

Q Now, you didn't call your brother-in-law collect, did you?

A No, I used a credit card.

Q Okay. Where did you get the credit card from?

A It belongs to my lawyer and I have another one that belongs to my family.

Q Okay. Now, that didn't belong to Mr. Garry, did it?

A No, sir, it belongs to another lawyer; it is my family's lawyer.

Q Can you remember how long you talked to your brother-in-law?

A I don't remember.

Q Can you remember what you said to him?

A I remember that I told him that I was going to go out and kill these people.

Q Did you say why?

A Yes.

Q What did you say?

A I think I did—I don't remember what I said exactly, but I recall what he said here yesterday, but I don't remember if I told him that exactly, really, but I—all I remember was that I did tell him that I was going out and kill them.

Q Now, was Freddie still in the house when you called your family in Florida?

A I don't know, he had left in the car, I think.

Q Okay. Did he leave in the car after the other phone call?

A I really don't know, I really don't know.

Q Did he leave during the other phone call?

A I don't know. I know when I left, I left by myself and I walked and I killed a guy and I missed Louie but I meant to kill him, too.

Q What did you do then after you called you family in Florida? . . .

A I took my gun, I loaded it and I went after them and if I would have had to walk to Jimenez Camp, I would have, and another thing I want to say, I am not sorry that I did it and the only thing I am sorry is that I missed Louie.

Q Okay. Now, you got this .22 rifle, People's Eleven?

A That's right, it's mine, that is the one that I killed the guy with and that's it.

Q And you went into your bedroom and got it out of your bedroom?

A Yes, I got it out of my bedroom and I answered that twice and I don't want to answer no more.

Q You got it out of this case?

A That's right, I would say.

Q This is after the call to Florida?

A Yes, that is the case. I don't have anything to say to you no more. I don't have anything. I shot him and killed him and if I had to do it again, I would do it again. That's all.

THE COURT: You haven't been excused from the witness stand.

THE WITNESS: I'm sorry, I don't have any more to answer.

THE COURT: Mr. Bailiff, place the young lady back on the witness stand.

THE WITNESS: I am not going to get on the stand. Don't lay your hands on me.

(Defendant Garcia exits courtroom).

MR. BRAUDRICK: I would ask that we take the afternoon recess.

. . .

(RT 1352-1402)

SEPTEMBER 30, 1974 – 10:00 A.M.

. . .

On this thirteenth and last day of testimony in the trial, Inez Garcia resumed the witness stand and Mr. Braudrick concluded his cross-examination.

Q Now, after you loaded—when you were loading the .22 rifle, was Freddie Medrano in the house?

A I don't remember.

Q Did you talk to him at all about going out and looking for Mike and Louie?

A No, I never did.

Q Did you ever at any time say to Freddie that you would do that—you would kill them because you could get out on bail?

A I never did.

Q Did you ever at any time that evening discuss killing Mike and Louie with Freddie Medrano?

A I never did.

Q Did you talk to Freddie at all about the phone call that you got from this person called Tiger?

A I didn't discuss that with him. I am not quite sure if he was there or not, but I got—when they called, they called to threaten me, telling me all kind of things and they threatened my life through the phone. They told me that they wanted me out of town.

Q Did Freddie ever get on the extension phone during that conversation?

A I don't remember because everything happened so fast that I really don't remember that.

Q Okay. And it was after the phone call from Tiger that you then went into your bedroom and got the rifle and loaded it. Is that correct?

A That's correct.

. . .

THE WITNESS: No, when they called to the house and they started threatening me, that is when I went and got my rifle and loaded it; and before that, I hadn't got the gun out or anything and I wasn't thinking about the gun then.

BY MR. BRAUDRICK:

Q You weren't thinking about going and killing Mike and Louie before the phone call?

A I was not. I was just—I can't explain it. I was just thinking what happened and all the things I could have done at that moment that I didn't do.

Q How much time was there between the time that you stopped talking to Tiger and stopped talking to your relatives in Florida, do you know?

A I really don't know. All I know is when this happened to me, I was scared at the moment and that's it.

Q Okay. After you hung up the phone on the call to Florida, is that when you picked up your rifle and walked out the door to go look for Mike and Louie?

A Yes, I think it is.

Q Freddie was not in the house at that time. Is that your testimony?

A I think so. I think he wasn't. I don't know. I think that I saw him there but I am not sure or he had gone, I am not sure.

Q You are not sure whether Freddie was in the house at the time you left with the rifle?

A I am not sure. I don't think he was there.

Q After you go outside of your apartment, you are carrying the rifle?

A Uh-huh.

Q And then you are looking for Mike and Louie?

A That's right.

Q You decided to walk and go find them. Is that correct?

A That's true.

Q You went out to Monterey Street?

A I walked to Monterey, I guess that is Monterey Street.

. . .

Q You were going toward town?

A I was going toward town until I saw them and then I crossed over, and I didn't get over. I was like in the middle of the street and the car was right here, Freddie's car, and I was like toward behind it, like close to the car.

Q Okay. Now——

A —That is when——

Q You stated earlier—excuse me. You stated earlier that you had a Volkswagen car. Is that right?

A That's true.

Q Why didn't you take your car to look for Mike and Louie?

A I don't know. I don't know. It just didn't cross my mind. Like I said, everything happened so fast that I don't even think that I remember I had a car then or what. I really don't know.

Q And you were going to look for them even if you had to go all the way to the Jimenez Camp, weren't you?

A I guess so. I don't know.

Q And the Jimenez Camp is located a mile or two miles north of town?

A Yeah, it is out of town, it is a little bit out of town.

Q Now, after you shot Mike Jimenez, then you got into Freddie's car. Is that correct?

A Yes, that was the only time I was in Freddie's car.

Q And whereabouts did you go after you got in Freddie's car? . . .

A We went over to Rosa's house and then we went to Alicia's house.

Q Did you stop—did you go to Alicia's house and stop by Alicia's house before you went to Rosa's house?

A We stopped, I think we went to Alicia's house and I think she wasn't there and then we went to Rosa's house, I am not quite sure.

Q You didn't stop any place else?

A No.

. . .

Q What did you do when you got in Rosa's house?
A Well, I went in there and I told them what had happened to me.
Q What did you say to them?
A That I got raped.
Q You told them all that you were raped?
A I told them that I got raped.
Q Was your blouse ripped at all while you were in Rosa's house?
A Yes, it was when I went there.
Q The blouse was ripped when you got to the house?
A Yes.
Q Was it ripped any more while you were in the house?
A No, I don't remember they ripped my blouse.
Q You don't remember if they ripped your blouse?
A I don't remember that, I don't recall that. I don't remember it. I don't remember them ripping my blouse.
Q Was your blouse ripped as far down when you got to the house as it was when you left the house?
A I don't know, my blouse was ripped when I got to the house.
Q And you don't remember it being ripped any more?
A I don't remember it being ripped any more.
Q And was that at Rosa's house that Juan hit you with his fist, isn't that true?
A I don't remember when Juan hit me with his fist, I mean——
Q You don't remember?
A I don't remember.
Q Can you remember what you did inside the house?
A Nothing, I talked and she told me they wouldn't believe me that I have got raped and that we should go to her house because she didn't want the police to come back to her sister's house and she was supposed to call the police.
Q Now, before today, you hadn't told the police or anybody that you had gone to Rosa's house that night, did you?
A I don't know. I don't remember.
Q And you are positive when you got into that house you told them that you had been raped?
A I did tell them I was raped.
Q And can you recall going into the kitchen in that house?
A No, she just pulled me over to the side and said we should go over to her house.
Q So, you were just in the house for a second then?
A For a second and left right away.

. . .

Q Can you recall Freddie Medrano ever calling you Querida or Carida, or lover in Spanish?

A Calling me that?

Q Yes.

A Querida, I don't remember that.

. . .

Q You gave Chief Jimenez the rifle?

A Yes, I did, and I never put that gun down, I had it on the side, I had it right near me and I never let it out of my hand.

Q And you said that you told Chief Jimenez that you had killed Mike Jimenez?

A No, I didn't tell him I have killed Mike Jimenez, he told me Mike was there—I told him that I was the one that had shot him and I gave him the rifle.

Q Then, you were taken to the police station. Is that right?

A That's right.

Q And you saw Yvonne Restani?

A Yes, I saw Yvonne.

Q And she was—at no time did you tell Chief Jimenez or Yvonne or Bob Russell of the District Attorney's office that you had been raped, isn't that correct?

A Well, I didn't tell them I got raped, I told them that they tried to rape me and that they was getting fresh with me.

Q And you told that to Chief Jimenez, and you told that to Yvonne and you told that to Bob Russell?

A I don't know Bob Russell.

Q He is the investigator from the District Attorneys' office that took a tape statement from you?

A I guess so.

MR. BRAUDRICK: I have nothing further at this time, your Honor.

THE COURT: Re-direct.

RE-DIRECT EXAMINATION

BY MR. GARRY:

Q I just have that one question. When you got on bail after being in jail for four months, you moved in with Pat Richards,* did you not?

A Yes.

Q And stayed there two or three weeks?

A Yes, I did.

Q Why did you move in there?

---

* Pat Richards is Mr. Garry's legal assistant.

A I didn't have no money and I didn't have no place to go and she was nice enough to keep me at her house.

MR. GARRY: No further questions.

THE COURT: Mr. Worthington, any questions?

MR. WORTHINGTON: No questions, your Honor.

THE COURT: That's all, madam.

THE COURT: Next witness.

MR. GARRY: If your Honor please, at this time, defendant Inez Garcia rests.

MR. WORTHINGTON: The defendant Alfred Medrano rests, your Honor.

. . .

(RT 1404-1416)

Upon the conclusion of the case for the defense, each side is entitled to call rebuttal witnesses. The prosecution's first rebuttal witness was Soledad Police Officer, Richard Perez, who was asked again whether he found evidence of marijuana in his search of Freddie Medrano's house.

RICHARD PEREZ, SWORN
RE-DIRECT EXAMINATION

BY MR. BRAUDRICK:

Q Sergeant Perez, late the night of March 19 or early morning of March 20, you searched the house or apartment of Freddie Medrano and Inez Garcia on Monterey Street, did you not?

A Yes, sir.

Q And did you search that house thoroughly?

A I believe we did.

. . .

BY MR. BRAUDRICK:

Q Did you find any marijuana in the house when you searched it?

A No, sir, we did not.

Q Thank you.

. . .

(RT 1417)

The prosecution's second rebuttal witness was Officer Yvonne Moranda.

YVONNE MORANDA, SWORN
RE-DIRECT EXAMINATION

BY MR. BRAUDRICK:

Q Mrs. Moranda, late on March 19 or early on the morning of March 20, did you have contact with Inez Garcia?

A Yes, I did.

Q And did you examine her for any superficial wounds such as bruises or cuts and that sort of thing?

A Yes, sir.

Q Did you find any?

A Yes, I did. It was on the side of her face. It was a red mark on the side of her face.

Q I show you People's 16 which is a picture. Was that picture taken to show that bruise?

A Yes, it was.

Q Did you examine the upper part of her body?

A Yes, sir.

Q Were there any bruises around her breasts or anything?

A No.

MR. BRAUDRICK: Thank you. I have nothing further.

RE-CROSS EXAMINATION

BY MR. GARRY:

Q Mrs. Moranda, did you, Officer Moranda, did you examine her lower extremities?

A No, sir.

Q So, you don't know whether there was any bruises in her thighs or legs?

A No, sir.

MR. GARRY: All right. Thank you. I have no further questions.

. . .

(RT 1432-1433)

Following Ms. Moranda's testimony, the defense re-called Inez Garcia to the stand as a rebuttal witness.

INEZ GARCIA, SWORN
RE-DIRECT EXAMINATION

BY MR. GARRY:

Q Mrs. Garcia, would you tell us if there were any bruises in the lower extremities of your body?

A Yes, after I got in jail, I had bruises on my legs over here, but I didn't know I even had them that night and Yvonne, I don't think she knew I had them.
Q You are indicating––
A –you know––
Q –in your thighs?
A Yeah.
Q In these?
A Yeah.
Q Is that right?
A Around there.
Q Would you describe these bruises to us?
A Well, I don't know. It was like black and blue marks and I think some–I don't know, maybe some of the matrons saw it when I was there.
Q But you definitely saw it yourself?
A Yes.
MR. GARRY: I have no further questions.
THE COURT: Any questions?
MR. BRAUDRICK: No questions–oh, wait.

RE-CROSS EXAMINATION

BY MR. BRAUDRICK:
Q I have one question. Didn't you take off your clothes or your Levis in the presence of Mrs. Moranda who was just here?
A At the house, yes.
Q And you gave her your Levis at that time?
A Yes, I put on another pair of pants.
Q She was present when you did that?
A Yes, but I don't know–I don't know–I don't think she saw them because she would have said so if she did.
Q Was she standing right in front of you when you took off your pants?
A Yes, she was.
Q Okay. Thank you.

RE-DIRECT EXAMINATION

BY MR. GARRY:
Q Did you have your back turned to her when you were taking your–did you have your back to her when you took your trousers off?
A I don't know. I was–I don't recall too much of it. No, we were

talking, me and her. She is a very nice person anyway. Can I get off?

MR. GARRY: That's it. Thank you.

. . .

(RT 1433-1435)

The prosecution's last rebuttal witness was Dr. Roy Clausen, Jr., a court-appointed psychiatrist who at the request of the prosecution was appointed to interview both Inez Garcia and Freddie Medrano to rebut the findings of the defense's two psychiatrists who testified earlier. Dr. Clausen was in private practice after retiring as a medical officer with the U.S. Army.

ROY L. CLAUSEN, JR., M.C., SWORN
DIRECT EXAMINATION

BY MR. BRAUDRICK:

Q Dr. Clausen, now what's your occupation?

A I'm a neurologist and psychiatrist and practice in Monterey, California.

. . .

Q Now, did you examine Inez Garcia?

A I did.

Q What exactly did she tell you about her history?

A Well, I was particularly interested in her recounting the history of the crime involved and just prior to the commission of the alleged offense and her behavior and actions during that time. During her history, she indicated that she had been attacked in the house in which she was living by Mr. Jimenez and Mr. Castillo, and that they in fact did rape her. A large part of my questioning her was concerning the history and concerned the matters that at the time of her apprehension following the alleged offense she did not in so many words complain either to the arresting police officer or to the investigator from the office of the district attorney that she had in fact been raped. We went into some of the reasons for this and she said that at times she was so angry, frightened and ashamed of the situation that she couldn't bring herself to tell the investigator or the arresting officer that this had in fact took place but couched it in the terms of "they tried to rape me" but she insisted that she had in fact been raped. In fact, she stated the following day she asked for a medical examination which was taken to County Hospital on Natividad Medical Center in Salinas and was not in fact examined at that . . .

Q And what was your decision about the medical records that you examined, the ones in both Bellevue and in Florida?

A Well, I felt that the assessment at Bellevue which took place when she was approximately 14 years of age, I believe had a correct assessment of what the problem was. That is Mrs. Garcia suffered from emotionally unstable personality, and the other record I had from Jackson had given a provisional diagnosis to Mrs. Garcia of schizophrenic reaction undifferentiated type. However, I did not feel that that was well sustained by the medical records. In fact, Mrs. Garcia was hospitalized in that particular facility only two days after which she signed herself out and the main upshot of the situation is that there certainly is no question of Mrs. Garcia being insane. As a matter of fact, she insists that the two previous episodes that she had had nothing to do with the present case and that she in fact knew what she was doing all the time. I tend to agree with that, but with a certain amount of reservation in that I feel that Mrs. Garcia does have a tendency to be impulsive, particularly when angry, which with circumstances somewhat similar to the situation in which she was hospitalized on the two other occasions of which I have knowledge and that this anger could indeed perhaps interfere with the critical judgment under certain circumstances should the stimulus be powerful enough.

Q Doctor, do you believe that she had—could form an intent to kill on the night of March 19th?

A I do.

Q And do you believe that she could deliberate and premeditate on that night?

A I do.

Q Now, how can you reconcile that with your evaluation of her as being an unfavorable personality, emotionally unstable personality?

A Well, she had—in the case of the hospitalization at Bellevue where she had entered into an altercation with her family, apparently, concerning some support payments of her father, at which time she threatened to throw herself off of the roof, and I believe—off a roof—and was hospitalized for a period of time following this. There was noted that she is capable of, and did at that time in fact retain an angry demeanor for quite some time after she was in the hospital. It's a matter of time, really. I think that given sufficient facial separation between the alleged assailant, Mrs. Garcia, herself, that she might well have cooled off during the period of time reflecting on the possible consequences of her act. But as I reconstruct the situation itself that it's very likely that I feel that Mrs. Garcia was so angry that at that particular time she would have proceeded to commit an offense even reflecting upon the possible consequences of it. This is because of her basic emotional stability. This is why I think that her—or came to the conclusion that this basic condition tends to impair Mrs. Garcia's judgment from time to time.

Q Do you feel that she has any impaired consciousness on March 19th?

A No.

. . .

CROSS EXAMINATION

BY MR. GARRY:

Q Dr. Clausen, you were asked to ask what history you obtained from Mrs. Garcia, and I believe you didn't answer that. You limited it to a certain area. But she did give you a history about the events that evening, did she not?

A Yes, that's correct.

Q And did she tell you at the time of the shooting she saw that Freddie Medrano was being attacked?

A Yes.

Q And she also told you she saw a shiny object in the air?

A That's correct.

Q That she assumed to be a knife?

A Yes. As a matter of fact, she cited two attacks, one upon Mr. Medrano at the house which culminated in the attack on her and then allegedly an attack took place in the street later on where Mr. Medrano was again being attacked.

Q And she at that time fired and shot the man?

A That's correct. She told me she specifically as far as the details of the matter was concerned that Mr. Jimenez was once again advancing upon her in a threatening manner and that this led her to shoot at him.

. . .

Q Did you notice during the discussion when she talked about certain aspects of this event that she got emotional?

A Yes, she became quite emotional. As a matter of fact, when discussing the events of assault and the alleged crime itself and although I did not cite this in my report, she exhibited religious concerns about the possible implications of her attack on Mr. Jimenez that this may be an unforgivable sin and the thing she would have to bear for the rest of her life.

Q And she also told you that she was normally nonviolent, didn't she?

A Yes.

Q And she told you that she was very ashamed about what had happened to her?

A That is correct.

Q And you also stated, did you not, in your report that it is difficult to completely assess the affect that her demonstrated emotional unstable personality may have exercised on her critical judgment at the time?

A That's correct.

Q Would you amplify on that?

A Well, it is sort of a quantitative thing. An individual can be emotionally unstable, for example, to a point of breaking down and crying under relative stress or getting angry and a matter of concern as is Mrs. Garcia is so emotional and unstable I think she does have an emotional instability in her personality so emotional unstable that given such stimulants that she would actually, deliberately, with intent go out and kill someone even knowing at the time that this was going to result in probably her apprehension and imprisonment. It is conceivable given sufficient stress an individual would do that. In fact, they do fairly frequently, but I don't think that people who do this sort of thing engage in sober reflection on either the consequences or even the nature of the act at the time even though they may intellectually realize all these things at a later date or even prior to the event.

Q That is why you mentioned the fact that it is difficult to assess the difficulty that she has under these circumstances?

A Exactly.

Q And tremendous trauma like rape to her would be something that would trigger off this, wouldn't it?

A It very well could.

CROSS-EXAMINATION

BY MR. WORTHINGTON:

Q So, as far as you know, judging his* demeanor and everything you could see about him, he seemed to be telling the truth?

A As far as I could judge, yes.

Q All right. Did it seem to you that his memory on the subject of the events of March 19 was rather spotty?

A Yes, I felt it was spotty . . .

Q Now, there is a possibility then in your opinion that Mr. Medrano's lack of memory was partially the result of lapse of time, would that be a fair statement?

A Either that or his head injury, or both.

Q Okay. That was what I was going to ask you. Could be the head injury, also?

A Yes.

Q That can cause——

---

* Mr. Worthington is referring to Freddie Medrano.

A —(interrupting) It could.
Q And it could also be the effect of the marijuana, assuming that it was strong enough to induce such effects?
A That's correct.

. . .

Q And is it possible to be unaware of what is happening around you and still be able to walk and perform other routine motor activities?
A Under certain circumstances, yes.
Q What kind of circumstances?
A Well, under the circumstances of head injury, for example, or intoxication with alcohol, drugs or other agents.
Q So in either one of those cases, it would be possible if a person who had suffered either the head injury or the intoxication from marijuana would be completely unaware of what was happening around him, yet be able to do such routine things as drive an automobile?
A That is true.

. . .

Q Well, just to be sure that we have your answer clearly, you are saying that it would be consistent with a person's inability to account for four minutes of time after being struck in the face, it would be consistent with the theory that he had suffered a concussion and some degree of unconsciousness. Is that correct?
A Impairment of consciousness. I have to emphasize he doesn't have to be unconscious, an impairment would be sufficient.

. . .

Q Then if the person who had allegedly suffered a concussion and had been under the influence of marijuana gave a statement within about twelve hours to the—to an investigator for the district attorney's office at the Monterey County Jail, and that statement in general terms was self-contradictory, confusing, and basically muddled, would that tend to reinforce your opinion that he had suffered a concussion and was unaware of what had happened?
A Yes, I am aware of that statement, and it confused me, too. Yes, under certain circumstances it would, unless the events are such that the individual concerned was for one reason or another trying to evolve a different story, which is also a possibility, and that was the judgment I could not make.

. . .

(RT 1436-1473)

Mr. Worthington's cross-examination of Dr. Clausen concluded the presentation of witnesses and testimony phase of the trial for both the prosecution and the defense. The stage was now set for the closing statements by each side and the judge's instructions to the jury as the trial neared its dramatic conclusion.

QUESTIONS FOR STUDY AND ANALYSIS
THE DEFENSE'S CASE

DR. OLDDEN'S TESTIMONY
(pgs. 161-183)

1. Does Judge Lawson show proper respect for Dr. Oldden by referring to her as "madam witness" on p. 162? Is the Judge just old-fashioned or is he being hostile and sexist?

2. What is the importance of Inez Garcia's early social and psychomedical history to the diagnosis of impaired consciousness and capacity?

3. Is Dr. Oldden's conclusion that Inez Garcia suffers a "psychoneurosis of a hysterical type" (p. 169) consistent with the evidence presented in the trial at this stage? Does this conclusion reveal the strategy of the defense?

4. What are the various functions of Dr. Oldden's testimony? Does Dr. Oldden fully explore the issue of rape and what it means to the victim?

5. Does Dr. Oldden's testimony portray Inez Garcia's actions in a way that justifies the shooting as a reasonable response after the rape, the threats to her life, the knife incident with Mike Jimenez, and the authorities' refusal to take the rape or attempted rape seriously?

6. Is Dr. Oldden's testimony designed primarily to get a verdict of manslaughter rather than homicide? See the definitions of murder and manslaughter in the jury instructions p. 336 *Supra.*

7. What is Mr. Braudrick's attitude toward Dr. Oldden's testimony? To the rape issue?

8. Does Mr. Braudrick succeed in shaking Dr. Oldden's psychological analysis and diagnosis? Does he succeed in attacking Inez Garcia's credibility through Dr. Oldden?

9. What is the significance of Dr. Oldden's statement that Inez Garcia admitted to her that she left the apartment with an intention to kill? Does this admission hurt the defense? Is it consistent with her analysis and diagnosis?
10. What is the strategy of Mr. Garry's re-direct examination? Why does he attempt to qualify Dr. Oldden to testify as an expert on the

number of women who are raped and report it to the police?

11. Why does Inez Garcia interrupt the proceedings and address her outburst at Judge Lawson? Is her action part of the defense strategy? Does she help or hinder her cause?

STEPHEN'S TESTIMONY
(pgs. 184-186)

1. What is the function of Mr. Stephen's testimony to the defense case?

2. Why does Mr. Garry ask whether the tests show Inez Garcia to be retarded? Does the psychologists conclusions help or hurt Inez Garcia's image in front of the jury?

FATHER BOYLE'S TESTIMONY
(pgs. 186-189)

1. Does Mr. Braudrick succeed in limiting the effect of Father Boyle's testimony?

TESTIMONY OF CHARACTER WITNESSES FOR INEZ GARCIA
(pgs. 189-196)

1. Do the defense attorneys succeed in establishing a consistent reputation for truth, honesty and chastity for Inez Garcia in Soledad?

2. Do the four character witnesses represent a cross-section of the opinion of a town like Soledad with a population of approximately 5,000?

3. What is the importance of Inez Garcia's reputation for chastity to the defense's case?

4. What is the significance of Officer Moranda's testimony to the defense strategy?

OFFICER PEREZ' TESTIMONY
(pgs. 197-198)

1. What point is the defense trying to make through officer Perez' testimony?

DR. ELLIS' TESTIMONY
(pgs. 198-203)

1. What is Mr. Worthington's strategy in examining Dr. Ellis? Is he anticipating the introduction of the police interview tape? (p. 242 *Supra)*

CARDENAS' TESTIMONY
(pgs. 203-206)

1. Is the defense successful in conveying the relationship between husband and wife even though most of the questions are objected to?

SMITH'S TESTIMONY
(pgs. 206-210)

1. Is Mr. Garry effective in bringing out through Ms. Smith's direct testimony the attitude and response of women to incidents of rape?

2. Would Mr. Braudrick have accomplished more by not cross-examining Ms. Cameron Smith at all?

RAUL GARCIA'S TESTIMONY

1. Why does Inez Garcia interrupt the interpreter? (p. 213) Is the difference in translation that Inez Garcia points out significant to the defense's case? Does it help or hinder the defense?

MEDRANO'S TESTIMONY

1. What is the significance of the fact that Medrano receives a substantial Veteran's pension check each month?

2. What was the basis of the relationship between Louie Castillo and Freddie Medrano that emerges from Medrano's testimony? Does Medrano supply a motive as to why Castillo picked the fight and turned against him?

3. Is Mr. Braudrick's question whether Medrano used heroin on March 19th or ever sold heroin reasonable in light of Medrano's admission that he was using marijuana? Is such a line of questioning highly prejudicial and irrelevant as argued by Mr. Worthington? (p. 232) What is the effect of the suggestion by Mr. Braudrick that Medrano gave Nick Bunte two balloons of heroin plus $30.00 for the shotgun?

4. Does Mr. Braudrick succeed in impeaching Medrano's testimony about what happened after the fight in the apartment on cross-examination? Is Medrano's fuzzy and spotty memory credible in light of the blows to his head and his heavy use of marijuana before the shooting as suggested by Medrano's psychiatrist?

5. What is the effect of the introduction of the taped interview between Inspector Russell and Medrano? (p. 242) Is the statement consistent with Medrano's testimony in court? Does Inspector Russell try to put words in Medrano's mouth as Freddie suggests in the tape?

INEZ GARCIA'S TESTIMONY

1. Why does Mr. Garry immediately direct his line of questioning to the circumstances surrounding the rape? Is this strategy consistent with his opening statement? (see p. 7-10)

2. Why does Mr. Garry terminate his direct examination of Inez Garcia after only a few minutes of testimony? Does his abrupt conclusion of his direct examination indicate a difference of opinion on the strategy of the defense at this critical point between attorney and client?

3. Does Inez Garcia supply a motive for why Chris Solis and Alicia Alcaraz might be hostile to Inez and Freddie on cross-examination?

4. Does Inez Garcia's testimony regarding why Mike and Louie "got on my case" and "was going to show me what a hometown boy was" (p. 266) supply a motive for the rape? Does it supply a reason for the attack on Medrano?

5. Why does Inez Garcia respond sarcastically to Mr. Braudrick's questions about the events leading up to the alleged rape? (p. 269) Does Ms. Garcia's attitude help or hurt her case?

6. Why does Judge Lawson interrupt Ms. Garcia's testimony at page 270? Is Ms. Garcia responding to the prosecutor's questions or trying to give self-serving, non-responsive answers?

7. What is the strategy behind Mr. Braudrick's questioning about the alleged rape? Are the details necessary? Does the prosecutor's questions and attitude toward the alleged rape support Cameron Smith's conclusion as to why women victims are reluctant to report rapes to the police? Does Mr. Braudrick try to humiliate Ms. Garcia on the rape issue in front of the jury?

8. Why does Mr. Braudrick insist on asking whether Mike held Inez Garcia down? (p. 277) Is the prosecutor deliberately trying to frustrate Ms. Garcia?

9. What is the effect of Ms. Garcia's statement that she told her brother-in-law "that I was going to go out and kill these people"? (p. 280) Is her statement consistent with Dr. Oldden's conclusion that she would not have been able to premediate a killing? That she was operating under a "diminished capacity" or "impaired consciousness"?

10. Does Ms. Garcia hurt her case when she states "I am not sorry that I did it and the only thing I am sorry is that I missed Louie" and "I shot him and killed him and if I had to do it again, I would do it again"? What is the effect of her abrupt termination of her testimony? (p. 281)

REBUTTAL TESTIMONY

1. Does Ms. Garcia's testimony about the existence of bruise marks on her thighs help or hurt her case? Compare Mr. Braudrick's and Mr. Garry's interpretation of this testimony in their closing arguments.

2. Is Dr. Clausen's testimony consistent with the basic conclusions of the two defense psychiatrists?

THE CLOSING ARGUMENT FOR THE PROSECUTION

OCTOBER 1, 1974

. . .

Argument of Mr. Braudrick to the jury.

MR. BRAUDRICK: Ladies and gentlemen: Now is the opportunity for myself and for the two defendants to argue to you. Now, our arguments are not evidence in this case, they are merely our interpretation of the evidence. If anything we say or they say about the facts in this case disagrees with what you believe, you can ask for the reporter to read it back. I am sure that any mistake that either of us makes about the facts are going to be inadvertent. We have had a lot of testimony and it is easy to make mistakes about small little facts.

Now, I will have two opportunities to argue to you. I open the argument and the reason why I open the argument is because the People have the burden of proof in a criminal case. They will have an opportunity to argue, Mr. Worthington and Mr. Garry, and then I will have a chance for my rebuttal argument, rebuttal because the People do have the burden of proof.

Now, both defendants are charged with murder, and one thing that you are going to find perhaps a little bit peculiar is that although they are both charged with murder, at the end of the argument when the Judge reads the instructions to you and gives you the law, you are going to have the opportunity to find them guilty of many different kinds other than first degree murder. He will read you instructions on first degree murder, second degree murder, voluntary manslaughter, involuntary manslaughter. Now, why is that? Well, first degree murder requires certain mental states for a person to be guilty of it. They must deliberate, premeditate, it is a killing with malice aforethought and that is murder of the first degree. If an individual kills somebody and has the intent to kill but they don't deliberate, and they may be found of second degree murder, if you find that they acted with malice. If you find that—if you find that—His Honor, as he will instruct you on heat of passion, in other words, if a person is involved in a fight and kills as a result of his passion involved in that fight, you may find him guilty of voluntary manslaughter. In this particular case, there is also going to be an instruction and argument concerning diminished capacity. His Honor will read you the instructions concerning diminished capacity and if you find that the defendants were unable to deliberate, or premeditate because of a diminished mental capacity brought on by a mental illness or mental defect or intoxication, then you may find him guilty of second degree murder. If you find that in fact they, because of a mental disease, defect or diminished capacity were unable to even form the normal intent to kill, you can find them guilty of involuntary manslaughter. . . .

There are a lot of options open to you in terms of what you find the defendants guilty of. How do you determine which applies or what law applies, well, the way you determine that is the facts of the case, the testimony of the experts and the experts including the psychiatrist, Dr. Titus, Dr. Bowden.

. . .

Now, this is going to be difficult for you to do because you have had three psychiatrists testify, all of whom went into detail as to what the defendants told them in their office but you can't consider that as evidence in this case, you can only consider in terms of whether or not their diagnosis, their conclusion is reasonable and this is something that you as the jury can decide. You don't have to accept what a psychiatrist or what an expert says just because he is an expert or just because he is a psychiatrist. You can examine what they say and use your common sense and form your own conclusions about their testimony. You can throw it away completely and you don't even have—you can look at it and consider it and say, well, we don't think it applies here or we think he is incorrect.

. . .

When you took your oath as jurors and during voir dire examination, you all promised that you would follow the law, whether you agreed with the law or not and that you wouldn't be making your decision based on sympathy or passion or anything else, but you would follow the law and you would interpret the facts and make your decision and that is your job as jurors.

Now, the evidence in this case is, I would say, in some areas we have had the same facts or same story given from both sides, both the prosecution and the defense, and then there are some other facts which have come out a little differently. The evidence has shown that Louie Castillo went over to see Mr. Medrano at his house and when he got there, there were some other people in the house and that he went into a bedroom. The evidence has shown that it was Inez Garcia's bedroom, that is the bedroom where the telephone was, and that Freddie Medrano was talking on the phone making a phone call to *Florida* in which he used a credit card given to him by Louie Castillo; that Solis and Medrano smoked marijuana cigarettes while they were in the room and they decided to go to Gonzales to try to get more marijuana and they went to Gonzales and couldn't find any more marijuana and came home to Medrano's apartment. Mr Medrano—rather Solis said that at that time it was about 8:30 and they went into the bedroom and Solis says that he saw some other people in the house at that point and they went into the bedroom and smoked marijuana. The evidence is uncontroverted that Solis states when they got back to the house that Louie Castillo and Mike Jimenez were inside the apartment and Solis and Medrano were in the bedroom. Medrano comes out and goes to his—goes out to eat his dinner and at that time gets involved in an argument with Miguel Jimenez and Louie Castillo and Medrano says basically the argument was with Castillo. Solis said that there is an argument, they got into an argument and they went and that Louie Castillo and Medrano went outside and both Louie Castillo and Medrano say that Louie Castillo hit Medrano, punched him once in the face. Louie Castillo went back inside the house and Medrano stayed outside for a while and then went back inside the house. He got back inside the house and there is another fight, a fight between Medrano and Louie Castillo, two people who up until this point had been good friends. Castillo had a key to Medrano's apartment and he let Medrano use a credit card. Medrano let Castillo use the car to drive around town. At this point, arguments, and Castillo and Solis say it is about heroin, it is about the fact of heroin traffic in the small town of Soledad, and they want Medrano to get out of town. In fact, after the second fight, Miguel Jimenez takes a knife and he tells him that he has got to get out of town and that he will be doing no more dealing in this town and no more dealing with heroin. Take a look at who the witnesses have been in this case so far, Castillo is a self-confessed user of heroin, in common parlance he would be called a doper, a good friend with Medrano and he uses his car. Solis, Solis states that he was using marijuana that night and seemed to have used it frequently before. Medrano states he used marijuana, but never had anything to do with heroin, yet why is he hanging around Castillo and Jimenez. Jimenez used heroin according to the testimony of Castillo. Alicia Alcaraz stated that Mike was a nice guy and they were all part of the same group. Louie Castillo and Miguel Jimenez don't appear as saints in this case and neither do the people that they hung around with, Inez Garcia and Freddie Medrano. It doesn't make any difference in the eyes of the law whether you are a good person or a bad person, you still have the right to live and that is what we are talking about here. Miguel Jimenez was somebody who used heroin and maybe Louie Castillo, seventeen years old, who has been using heroin since he was fifteen, but they have the right to live. After Freddie Medrano comes into the house, he and Louie Castillo get involved in another fight. The testimony by Solis who is sitting on the couch is that they both went down on the ground and that is what Louie Castillo and I believe Medrano also testified. At that point, Miguel Jimenez got involved in the fight and picked up Freddie Medrano and hit him, and according to some of the testimony threw him against the couch. In one of these photographs which unfortunately doesn't show much, there is even some spots of blood shown on the floor and if you look carefully, perhaps with a magnifying glass, you might see it. There is no doubt there was a fight and there is no doubt that Miguel Jimenez beat up Freddie Medrano and that is not in issue here at all. After the fight, Solis testified that they stayed in the house and they stayed there and acted like they owned the house according to what Solis testified. They are not acting like nice people, they just have been involved in a brawl and they have beaten somebody up, and we have a fight going on because of heroin traffic, and this isn't the nice pleasant experience for anybody, it is not the kind of experience that you will ever experience either. It is at this point that the testimony changes. Solis states that Castillo and Jimenez leave and Inez goes to the doorway, just outside the doorway talking to him and he doesn't know what they are saying. Castillo says that they go outside and that Inez comes out and that she talks to Mike and he doesn't know what she says. Solis says that Inez came back in the house and that when she came back in the house, he also said that he didn't lose sight of her, that she was at the doorway, just outside the doorway, and when she came back in the house, her blouse wasn't ripped and it didn't appear to be anything amiss at all.

Now, here is where we get big diversions in the testimony. Medrano states that he doesn't really remember much of what is going on. Inez says she thinks Medrano is still in the house when she comes back in the house. Medrano states when she came back in the house, her blouse was torn and that she was messed up. Solis states her blouse wasn't torn. Solis all this time is sitting on the couch and he gets up during the fight and he goes back down and sits on the couch. He sates that when they leave, Freddie says, I want to kill these guys and there is a phone call, a phone call that Solis says that Inez talked on the phone on. The phone call was from a person called Tiger. Castillo states the phone call was from Joe Mendoza, and Miguel Jimenez, and that he and Miguel Jimenez left the house which is Medrano's apartment which is right here and walked all the way to right here, which is Joe Mendoza's house. They got there and Mendoza calls and uses the name of Tiger, and we are not quite sure what is said on the telephone. Inez talked on the telephone and Solis is sitting there. After the telephone call, Solis states Freddie is talking about Mike and Louie, and he wants to get them. He stated that Inez made a phone call to her relatives or lawyer in Florida and that is uncontroverted. Inez said she made the phone call, in fact, they even brought a man from Florida, her brother-in-law, to testify that he received the phone call. Solis states that Inez said, no, don't you do it, let me do the shooting, let me kill them because I can get out on bail. At that point, they go into the bedroom and Inez loads the .22 rifle and to load the rifle, she has to pull out the slide and she had to drop in the shells. We can tell from the testimony that she put in at least ten shells because of the number of casings that are found, the number of bullets that are found. She has to put this back inside and this is after talking to Freddie and talking on the phone to Tiger and after making a phone call to Florida, and after telling Freddie that she will do it because she can get out of jail. She loaded the rifle. Solis testifies that Freddie loaded the shotgun and that Inez got the shotgun shells out of her bedroom. Of course now, the question is, where is the shotgun? Freddie loaded the shotgun, in fact, Solis testifies that they took two guns out with them when they went into the car, when they went out the door, they took a .22 rifle and they took a shotgun. Well, we have Nick Bunte testify that he sold a shotgun to Freddie Medrano in the early part of March before the killing, and he said it was a twelve-gauge Remington pump shotgun and that when he sold it to him, he stated that it was in a case and he also stated this looked to him to be exactly like the same case he gave him. He said that this is the case. We have had other testimony that stated that no, this isn't the case, this is the case I kept the .22 in, but I used to keep a sawed-off shotgun, a shotgun is what Inez says, a shotgun was just over a legal barrel, the length of eighteen and a half inches in this case, a double-barrel shotgun and not a single-barrel shotgun. She had had it for some time. Now, what is the truth about the story about the shotgun case? Well, take a look at the inside of the case, take a look at where the wear is in the case, right in this area here. Take a look at the end of the case which you will be able to do in the jury room and you see a small impression in there, a circle for the placement of a barrel. Look at the size of the barrel. Look at the marks that is made around that, is that the barrel marked of a single one-barrel shotgun or is it the mark of a .22 rifle? Was the .22 rifle stored in there, look at the .22 rifle, that didn't sit in there and make these marks down here. Check the barrel against the hole in here for the barrel to set into and see if that was made by the .22 rifle, it wasn't, and obviously it wasn't made by a double-barrel shotgun, a double-barrel shotgun wouldn't fit in there and sit up there, would it? It was a single-barrel shotgun stored in this case.

This is the case that Nick Bunte had. This is the case that he sold that contained the shotgun that he sold Freddie Medrano, the shotgun that Medrano took with him into the car. Medrano states that he got into that car and went by himself and nobody was with him, and he went out looking for them. Inez states that she was taken behind the apartment and she was raped, and she went into the house and called her family, loaded the rifle, and they went out looking for the men that she said raped her. Now, let's take a look at the whole situation as far as the rape is concerned. She testified that there was a house right across from their apartment, right here in this photograph, her apartment being right here, and that she was taken bodily out of the house around the house and to the back and that there Miguel Jimenez held her down and Louie Castillo hit her, ripped her blouse and then she said, all right, that's enough, I will give in. Is that a reasonable story? Does that seem like a reasonable story to you that this woman here was raped that night? Where did she get—Now, afterwards, she is seen by Yvonne Restani or Yvonne Miranda who came here and testified as a character witness for her. She stated that there were no bruises except for one. There were no bruises on her face except for one on the side of her head which is rather poorly shown in this photograph. There were no bruises on the upper part of her body or on her breasts, no bruises at all, no bruises on her arms where a 300-pound Miguel Jimenez supposedly took her out of the house with Castillo hanging onto her and also taking her into the back of the apartment. Where did these come from that is on her face, the only bruise that she had on her, it was the bruise that Juan gave her at Rosa's house after the shooting, after Miguel Jimenez was killed and that is the only bruise and that is when Juan, who was probably—well, I think you would all say he was somewhat of an amazing person, the oldest seventeen year old boy in the country, but he stated that his aunt Alicia told him to hit her, hit Inez and so he just drew back and he hit her, he hit her in the side of the head and gave her the only bruise that she received that night. Of course, as soon as Yvonne got off the stand, Inez got up there and says I have bruises all over my thighs, my legs, but she also said that Yvonne took these pants from her. She also said that she took those pants off and Yvonne was standing right there, and Yvonne testified the only bruise that she saw was the one on the side of her head. Do you think Inez Garcia was telling you the truth that the only bruises were the ones that she says that she has on her thighs or is she suddenly saying, wait a second, wait a second, I had some bruises and I have got to get up and show she is not telling the complete truth. Inez Garcia didn't say she was raped, but after the rape she said occurred, she doesn't tell anybody about it. She says that she told Mr. Cardenas in Florida and everybody else testifies that she said they tried to rape me or they got fresh with me, or something like that, think about the whole situation for a second. How often does somebody have as good a situation as to have a good friend of theirs present when they are arrested, somebody they can bring in as a character witness? Why couldn't she tell Yvonne if she was concerned about not telling anybody because she was ashamed of it or something? She certainly wasn't ashamed to kill somebody. This whole thing is a story, a story made up afterwards. The police were never informed about any rape and there is no evidence of a rape. There was evidence of a fight, of what might even be termed a drunken brawl in the living room of her house, evidence in which Freddie Medrano was told to get out of town, to get out of town and stop your dealing, evidence that after the fight, those two men took over the house and the people don't contend that Louie Castillo and Miguel Jimenez were the nicest people in the world, but they were friends of Freddie Medrano and Inez Garcia. Now, Medrano states that he is in the car and drives the car up and down Monterey Street and he drives it around and he is not sure where. He sees Louie Castillo and Miguel Jimenez and pulls his car over and stops his car and gets out on the passenger side of the car to go and talk to them, and that he gets in another fight with Louie Castillo and the next thing he knows, there is shooting and he gets back in his car and Inez gets in the car and drives away.

Inez states that after she loaded her rifle, she walked down the street looking—in her own testimony—looking for Miguel Jimenez and Louie Castillo to kill them. She is walking on this side, what would be the west side of the street and she sees them across the street and shoots them, shoots at them with a .22 rifle according to her and that she walked all the way there. Now, what does the other witnesses testify? Well, we have two witnesses, two high school kids, Dima and David, who were right here on this diagram sitting on the porch or standing on the porch talking. They are not connected with this group, the group made up of Freddie Medrano, Inez Garcia, Alicia, Rosa, Louie Castillo, they are standing there and they see the car that they know is Medrano's car coming down the street like it is going to turn on First Street and then continues on and slows down and pulls over and they thought David—they thought they were going to be giving Louie and Mike a ride because they had just seen Louie and Mike come across the street from Joe Mendoza's house, walking down the sidewalk, and they said hello to them. They were walking this way and they lost sight of them at the camper-truck. Less than a minute, less than thirty seconds after they walked by here, the car pulls up and David and Dima are telling the truth when they say to you, they saw Freddie Medrano's car driving up, they are telling you the truth when they say, when asked, they say a man was driving and there was a woman who was a passenger, but they can't identify who those people were, but they do know this, that in fact one of them testifies that the girl gets out of the car before the car is completely stopped and had a rifle and started shooting. The next thing they saw was Louie running across the street, they both testified that it was a girl who got out of the car. David said the next time he saw the car, it was headed in the other direction and he heard the girl say, give me the shotgun to the guy who is in the car. Why did she say, give me the shotgun, well, the rifle had jammed on her and she couldn't shoot it any more. The man riding in the car said, no, let's go. The girl gets in the car and they testified the car goes and turns up First Street. Elmer Moran testified at this point the only thing he could really testify to was when that car left, it had its lights off. The lights were on when the car came down. I believe David Ferrel said the lights were on and when the car left, its lights were off. Louie Castillo says that the person driving the car was Freddie Medrano, and the person doing the shooting was Inez Garcia. Freddie Medrano doesn't deny driving the car that night. Inez Garcia doesn't deny doing the shooting, but they deny doing it together, they deny being together in this at all. Inez Garcia shot a total of eight casings that were found in this area here, eight shots.

Dr. Titus testified that Miguel Jimenez was shot three times, the fatal one was a shot in the eye. He testified that after someone received a shot like that in the eye, it went into the brain which killed him and that he might be able to take a step or two and that he would fall. He testified that this isn't pretty, he also testified that when he did the autopsy on Miguel Jimenez, there was a grazing wound in his opinion, and he is a forensic pathologist, and he testified to his expertise a wound caused by a grazing bullet on the side. He testified that there was a wound here on the stomach that went in and then went out and then a wound also here on the stomach which went from this direction and out. What does that indicate? It indicates that the first shot, two of the shots came at him from the side, came in here and out here, and one shot grazed his thigh as he was walking along the street and turns like this when the car pulls up and was shot here and has one bullet graze the thigh and he turned around and is shot in the eye and falls down. After he falls down, he is shot again because the only way he could receive this wound here would be if he were lying on the ground because it enters up here and exits down here. Miguel Jimenez fell down right here where it is shown on the diagram. The ambulance came and picked him up and he died, he died from a bullet shot from that rifle shot by Inez Garcia. David testified that the police were called and people were wandering around and people were kept away from the area. The police came and Louie Castillo finally came back and a knife was found next to Miguel Jimenez. There is no evidence about that knife. The only evidence before you is that Inez Garcia left the house with the intent to kill him and to kill Louie Castillo, in fact, after she shot Miguel Jimenez, she started to go this way to shoot Louie Castillo, in fact she shot at him but missed him. The next testimony is that they go—Freddie says they go by Alicia's house, and Inez says they go by Alicia's house and also Alicia's house is located up here and also on this picture here, across from the school and nobody was home so they went over to Rosa's house. Freddie parked the car and they went in the house. The testimony of the people who were in the house, Rosa, Alicia, and Juan, is that they came there about a half an hour or so, fifteen or twenty minutes or half an hour or so after the shooting, and how did they know that? Well, we know that because Sergeant Perez who went to the scene where the body of Miguel Jimenez was, was at Rosa's house because she was having a fight—well, actually, I guess it was Juan and Willie having a fight, and Rosa's husband and much later they came by, and I believe Alicia said up to a half an hour came to Rosa's house. Well, we don't know what happened in that period. That is more time than it would take to drive from here to the scene of the shooting up First Street to Rosa's house. We just don't know what happened. We know that—we know a shotgun in that car was never recovered and nobody has been able to account for that time. They can account for the time after they get to Rosa's house. They get to Rosa's house and Rosa says that her blouse was ripped when Inez first came in the house but it was only ripped about an inch and a half or two inches and that when she left the house, her blouse was ripped like this, all the way down. Nobody seems to know who tore the blouse the rest of the way, Juan said he didn't, Alicia said she doesn't know, and Rosa said she didn't know, but she knew this blouse was ripped more before Juan hit her and that the blouse was ripped between the time she came in their house and before Juan hit her, and that Juan gave her a coat to cover herself while she was in the house before he hit her. Some of the people who were in the house don't really know what the conversation was. Rosa said Inez said, well, shouldn't I get hit so it would look like I was raped, and Freddie refused to hit her, in fact, Juan testified that Freddie called Inez his querida or lover, and Freddie refused to hit her, and Willie wouldn't hit her, and then Juan hit her. Juan hit her. He hit her so hard that she had to be caught to be kept from falling to the ground and Inez doesn't remember that. She doesn't remember being hit. She remembers who the people are in the house and she remembers Alicia was there and Rosa was there and another man and that Juan was there, but she doesn't remember being hit in the house, but she testified to it. Freddie doesn't remember anybody hitting Inez in the house. He doesn't remember anybody ripping her blouse, but he does remember where people are standing in the house and where he is sitting on the couch and where Willie and another man is sitting on the couch and he remembers who was in the house. He remembers everything that goes on except conversations and the fact that Inez was hit. He remembers everything that is not going to hurt him as far as this trial is concerned and so does Inez. Alicia then gets concerned and wants to take Inez, her friend, a friend that she had brought her children over to her house so that she would have a good appearance for her relatives, so her relatives wouldn't think she was living with Freddie by herself, takes her friend Inez and Freddie Medrano to her house, and the car is eventually moved to the side of the house so it can't be seen. Inez brings a rifle in. The police arrest Freddie and goes to the house and arrests Inez. Inez says that she shot him and Chief Jimenez gets the rifle. So, basically we have sort of two stories, one story being that Inez is by herself and she is the one that does the shooting. The other story being that the two are together in the car and the two plan the shooting and took two weapons with them and that they went out and hunted together and shot—Inez shot and killed Miguel Jimenez; that Freddie Medrano then gets Inez back in the car and turns off his lights and leaves the scene and they go to a friend's house after an interval of twenty minutes to a half an hour and then starts to manufacture evidence. She gets her blouse ripped.

It is interesting to note that Freddie is involved in the fight and there is no question about that and that there is no question about that and there is even a picture that is in evidence which tries to show some of the bruises but there is no question that he bled on the floor, and it is interesting to note that a couple of witnesses stated they had seen scratches on his face, finger nail scratches. Where did he get those finger nail scratches from? He got them from Inez at the same time they were getting rid of the shotgun and at the same time her blouse was getting ripped the first time.

They went to Alicia's house and this is testimony that the cars were moved to the side of the house; that Medrano and Alicia go to get some cigarettes for Inez and Juan is there at the house and they are arrested. The car is stopped and Chief of Police arrests Inez and gets this rifle.

. . .

When he got the gun, it was jammed with the last bullet that had been fired and there was still one live round. What significance does that have other than the fact that she couldn't shoot the last shot at Louie Castillo because the gun was jammed. Sergeant Perez testified that he searched Louie Castillo's car, this blue Chevrolet and that in the car when he searched it that night, he found one live round of ammunition, . . . Now, what does that mean, this live round is sitting there and she loaded the gun when she was at the house and she went like that to flip a live round so it would be ready to fire and she was in the car and as the car pulled up or sometime when she was getting ready to shoot, she went like that again to cock it, forgetting she had cocked it before. Now, if you have a live round of ammunition in there and you go like that, the live round is ejected and a new live round goes in. Now, the live round that is found in the car could not have gotten there afterwards because the gun was jammed and there is testimony that this rifle wasn't in that car before.

Freddie Medrano didn't help her move, the testimony is Solis helped her move so we have corroboration. We also have Rosa who testifies she does not know who it was that got in the car but she saw two people getting into Freddie Medrano's car that night and drive away. There are two people in the car when it pulls up past where Dima and David are. Castillo says there are two people in the car and that Medrano is driving. Dima and David said Inez got out of that car, or a woman got out of the car and started shooting, got out of the passenger side, corroboration of eye witness testimony. The eye witness testimony of the shotgun being in the car, where is that corroborated? Davis says he heard somebody say to the guy—the girl say, get me the shotgun. The live round is in the car and two people are in the car as testified to by Rosa. Why have they made up this story, they made up the story because Inez Garcia is trying to protect Freddie Medrano and because Inez Garcia believes that given the sympathy of the jury, that she would be acquitted because she can say that she was raped. It is your job as jurors not to decide this case on sympathy or passion, but on the facts. Look at the facts and don't decide the case based upon which attorney argues best because that doesn't mean anything either, and what counts is the facts. When you decide this case, you look at the evidence, look at the evidence carefully and you will have a lot of time in that jury room, and look at it carefully and you will decide the facts are that they conspired to kill Mike and Louie, and they only failed in one respect, in that they only killed Mike. Thank you.

. . .

(RTA 1445-1468)

THE CLOSING ARGUMENTS FOR THE DEFENSE

Argument of Mr. Worthington to the jury

BY MR. WORTHINGTON:

Now the evidence on the subject of what Freddie did, if anything is ambiguous, it is conflicting, and the prosecution's witnesses tell stories that go in all kinds of different directions. We don't know whether to believe Louie Castillo and Cris Solis or not. You are the people who are going to have to decide whether to believe them. The next thing that I wrote up there is, can you believe those two people? You heard them testify and you heard them change their stories several times. You heard them come up with a—at the very last minute with this baloney about this argument being over drugs. You heard that they are junkies. You heard that they don't like Freddie because he is an outsider and they don't like Inez because she is an outsider and they don't like Inez because she didn't want to have too much to do with them because they are nothing but a bunch of useless junkies. You heard them testify to those things. You heard them change their stories again and again and again and again. We heard Solis admit that he lied to you people under oath; that he lied to the Grand Jury under oath; that he lied to the police; that he lied to the defense investigator and defense attorney and then after he got done telling all his lies, the prosecution asked him a little bit to explain why he had lied, and he lied some more and said he hadn't lied. That is what Solis is all about. How about this guy, Castillo, can you believe anything that he says? Didn't it seem just a little bit remarkable to you how much Castillo knows about this case? Didn't it seem a little bit remarkable that he thought it was funny when Mr. Garry asked him if he raped Inez and that he laughed at that? Do you believe a man who has been accused by Inez of being a brutal rapist and who has admitted to being a junkie for two of his seventeen years of life, do you tend to believe that kind of man? Do you tend to belive a man who said that he made a positive identification of Freddie in that car out on the street, positive, just as positive as he could be in the dark in a 1941 Chevrolet with high sides and very poor visibility, a positive identification while he is running in the opposite direction for dear life in a hail of bullets? Do you believe that kind of testimony? Do you believe that a man who says things like he had seen the shotgun that Nick Bunte sold to Freddie, that he had seen that shotgun very shortly after Freddie got it, who admitted he had a key to Freddie's apartment, and a person who, as Freddie said, saw the shotgun and then the shotgun disappeared, a person who had contacts with Nick Bunte and with the police about halfway through this trial and very conveniently informed the police all about that shotgun?

Now, first of all, let's get these irrelevancies out of the way and all that baloney about Freddie Medrano dealing drugs. Ladies and gentlemen, you recall when the Judge allowed the District Attorney to bring in that evidence, he said it would be limited to motive in some obscure way the allegation that Freddie dealt drugs to these people was supposed to be motive for which he later participated in another rather obscure way in killing of one of these people. Well, I want to ask you, did the District Attorney do his job, did he tie that in in any way? Go ahead and assume for a minute that it was true that Freddie had dealt some drugs to those people, how does that establish a motive, it has nothing to do with it, you see, it doesn't matter what they were fighting over. We have admitted all along there was a fight in that apartment and that Freddie got beaten up by these guys. What difference does it make what they were fighting over? The reason that that came in is to try to muddy the waters and to dirty things up a little bit because all you have to do when you are talking to a dozen average citizens like yourself and like myself, for that matter, is mention heroin and we all see red, it is one of these red flags you wave and that is exactly what the theory of the prosecution had to be since there could be no other reason for introducing that kind of testimony. They knew that they had been told by Inez that these guys had gotten fresh and that they had attacked her in some way and they knew that all along, and they knew that that was a pretty plausible story given what they knew about Mike Jimenez and Louie Castillo. They figured since that was a very good motive for the killing, if they want to get Freddie into this at all, they better come up with a different motive for Freddie and that is what they came up with, with the help of your dear friend, Louie Castillo, on August 23 after we had already voir dired all of you people, after we started this case, that is what they came up with. Ladies and gentlemen, I submit that is a cheap shot, it is a bold faced attempt to get you to convict to some degree of homicide on utterly irrelevant evidence.

. . .

So, we know that is a fact that that is what happened to Freddie.* Now, how did he respond after that, he ran away, he ran into his room, does that sound like a man who's forming an intention to kill somebody? He came out of his room again and came out unarmed. There has been testimony that there is a rifle in that house, at the very least there was a rifle—at the very least, there was ammunition for the rifle, at the very least, there was a dagger on the headboard of Freddie's bed, and is there any evidence that Freddie came out with any of those weapons, no, there is none, in fact the evidence shows that he did not come out armed. He came out unarmed and as best he could, in a conciliatory frame of mind, and tried to tell Louie and Mike that they shouldn't have done it and that they didn't have any reason to do it. Now, Freddie didn't remember it, it's true, that other witnesses testified that he went back into the bathroom then to try to clean up his face some more and then after that, he came out again and what did he see after he had been in the bathroom about five minutes, again leaving Inez unprotected, what he did see, he came out and said to Castillo—I'm sorry—he said to Chofero, where is Inez and Mike and Louie, and Chofero is sitting there in a stupor as he had been sitting there all evening, said I guess they are outside, and just about that moment, Inez came back through the door as he recalls and she seemed to be trying to say something, but she never really got anything out that he can remember. She was beaten up. She was bruised. Her hair was disheveled. Her blouse was torn and he noticed those things. Freddie has never claimed that he saw Inez get raped, never. He has never tried to say that

* Mr. Worthington has referred to the first and second fight and beating by Castillo and Jimenez.

she did get raped because he was not—in fact, he doesn't in fact know. The District Attorney implied that Freddie's memory is convenient and that he only remembers the things that can help him. Ladies and gentlemen, if he were trying to do that, would he not have, if he were making up a story that sounded good, would he not say that he saw Inez get raped so there wouldn't be any question about it? He could have easily done that and why not, if he is going to make up the rest of the story, why not make up that? He did not do any such thing, he admits that he didn't see her get raped and all he can say is what he saw after she came in and what happened in his mind at that time.

. . .

Now, ladies and gentlemen, you have a man out there, Freddie Medrano, who is in another fight being attacked by Louie and Mike and this is a man who knew Mike had a knife and physical incident shows that Mike did have a knife; that they were attacking him again and that it wasn't enough to beat him up in his own apartment but they were attacking him again and that Inez came along at that very time and started firing. Ladies and gentlemen, I will submit to you that if Inez hasn't come along at that time, this would have been a lot shorter trial because Freddie Medrano would have been dead and those guys would have killed him the second time. The first time they beat him up pretty good and they pointed a knife at him and they told him that he could get the same thing that that guy in Gonzales got that they could knife him and they had a knife out there. I submit to you that they were ready to kill him and they would have killed him if it hadn't been for Inez saving his life.

. . .

Solis testified that the guns did not come out until after the telephone call was received. Solis also testified that the contents of the telephone call as related by Inez Garcia that the call, he used the word, tip, that it was some kind of a tip and somebody was coming over right then to do something. Now, Solis wasn't clear and of course he didn't hear it, he only knew what Inez or what he remembered Inez repeated to him, but it is clear from Solis's testimony that there was some kind of threat made over that telephone regardless of who it was. Solis' testimony continued to confirm and corroborate the testimony that came from Inez Garcia later that this tip was actually an additional threat on her life and on the life of Freddie Medrano; that these guys had not been satisfied to rape her and show her what hometown boys were, but they had to go brag to their buddies that we did it, we beat up Freddie and raped Inez and have their buddy call Inez to ridicule her further about it and tell her how she wasn't any better than any of the rest of them now because they had gotten to her and how they better not call the police and that they were going to come back and take care of her. Now, I told you that I was going to try to speak directly from the facts and at this point I am not quoting testimony because I know it was conflicting, and I am not positive what it was, but as I recall, Inez said that they threatened to kill her, that they were going to come back and kill her. Solis was a little bit different, he didn't know exactly what the content of the threat was but only that they were coming back and it is at that point, if you believe Solis's testimony, that these two people got the gun or the guns and loaded them to defend themselves.

Now, I submit to you, ladies and gentlemen, that Inez had every right to load the gun and get out of that apartment if she reasonably believed that those guys were going to come back and give her worse than they had already given her because they had already given her plenty.

. . .

David and Dima, that means David Ferrel and Dima Gallardo, you remember those two people, they were the young couple that was standing on the porch something like a hundred feet away from the scene of this shooting and they both seemed to testify that they saw Inez get out of the passenger side of the car and then start firing and you people were able to listen to them and watch them very closely and I know you did. Now, you have to judge their credibility because at least in the prosecution theory, that is an important fact in this case whether or not she actually was in that car before the shooting. So, the question is, can you believe everything David and Dima said or can you only believe part of it or do you have to disbelieve some of it. Now, I have stated quite candidly a lot of witnesses that the prosecution put on seem to just plain be lying. They admitted they were lying. I want you to know that I make no such allegations about David and Dima. David Ferrel and Dima Gallardo, they seem to be making the best effort they could as seventeen-year olds who saw a very shocking event to report to you as accurately as they could what they saw, but what are the problems with their testimony, why is there a reasonable doubt as to whether or not the things they think they saw occur actually occurred? Well, let me point out a few things, Number 1, both of those witnesses admitted they were talking to each other and that they were not paying any attention to traffic passing on the street. David testified that he could only remember one other car going by other than Freddie's car which he testified only went by once. I think if I recall correctly, Dima's testimony was even more uncertain on that as to whether she could remember any other cars going by. Well, is that credible testimony, or are they telling an accurate story? There is other testimony that Freddie went by that particular spot at least three times, so the very least they would have seen his car go by more than one occasion if in fact they were watching. The fact of the matter is they weren't watching and they said they weren't, and they said they weren't interested in it and they both said that there was nothing unusual about that car that drew their attention to it, it was not speeding, it was not spinning its wheels, it was not doing anything unusual and they just happened to say they remember it, now because now that they have reconstructed the whole thing they realize that it is Freddie's car and at the time that they didn't really know who Freddie was but they had a vague connection between the car and the guy who drove it, even though they didn't know exactly who he was. So the first problem about the testimony is their inattentiveness and the second problem is as to their ability to see, physical ability to see. They both testified that after Mike and Louie passed, they were unable to see Mike and Louie any more. The testimony was they passed Dima's house and then they passed the other house and they got past that camper in the driveway and after that, the camper blocked the view of Mike and Louie. Well, if it blocked the view of Mike and Louie, I am sure that it similarly blocked the view of Freddie, if in fact Freddie were out on the street getting into any scuffle with Mike and Louie behind that camper, that could very well be the case, and those witnesses didn't try to say they saw everything and try to intentionally lie to you ladies and gentlemen, but they admitted quite candidly that they could not see exactly what was happening so it could be very possible that Freddie could have gotten out of the car and been back there talking to Mike and Louie and not have been seen by David and Dima. They testified they were both shocked, both of them testified they hadn't seen an event like this before and it was an exciting in the sense that it was upsetting and disturbing . . . Well, we don't need an expert to testify about people's ability to do that under traumatic conditions like that and the excitement of the event like that, you could not expect two seventeen-year-olds to accurately remember the sequence of events and to accurately remember exactly how much time there was between event A and event B and event C, to exactly remember who moved where and to exactly remember who got out of what car. You can't expect people to do that and they were candid enough to admit to you that they couldn't remember exactly, but they did testify that they thought Inez got out of the right-hand side of the car. I submit to you, ladies and gentlemen, if they said that the car went by and after that, they didn't pay any attention to it and they couldn't see Louie and Mike any more and they went back to their conversation or just kind of stood around, they could very easily have missed Inez walking down the other side of the street. Do you think that is impossible that they could have missed her? Well, let me tell you about a bit of some other evidence and remind you of some other evidence that there was. There was evidence that Louie and Mike walked from Freddie's apartment down to Joe Mendoza's house just a few minutes before that. There was evidence from both David and Dima that they were on the porch for at least forty-five minutes or perhaps more like an hour and fifteen minutes, and Louie and Mike would have had to walk right up to Joe's house which is only right across the street from them, within the time that they were out on the porch and yet neither of them saw Louie and Mike walk to Joe Mendoza's house. Now, if they missed Louie and Mike, Mike would be pretty hard for one to miss, isn't it plausible that they also might miss Inez walking on the other side of the street in the dark? I submit to you that that is a possibility. I don't know, ladies and gentlemen, I don't claim to know, I only say that there is a reasonable doubt about these things.

What is the next problem with their testimony, the next problem is that they testified that Louie came running up after the police came and started spilling out everything that he thought had happened, telling the police all about who did it and exactly what they did, and they heard that. Now, so did several other people. The policeman testified by the time he arrived there, there were six people standing around. Moran testified that David Ferrel and his brother, Val, were there and Connie Mendoza was there. I can't say about Joe, but I think there was testimony from one of the witnesses that he was on the scene also. In other words, there was a group of people and then Louie comes rushing up and just tells all about what happened. Now, Louie is hardly a disinterested party, and Louie's ability to perceive and report accurately are subject to some serious doubt, but the problem that it causes is all this rumor that was going around, these comments in particular by Louie that were made to the policeman in the presence of the other witnesses makes it impossible for the witnesses to be able to distinguish between what they actually saw and what they think they saw because somebody else said they saw it. So, that makes or also throws some doubt upon their testimony, and I think the most serious problem about their testimony is that although they were both standing or sitting in approximately the same place on the porch and although they both apparently had an average hearing and eyesight, they do not testify to the same set of facts and that, ladies and gentlemen, is proof of the pudding that even those two seventeen-year olds were doing their best to tell the truth and they didn't really know what happened because if they really knew what happened, they both saw the same thing and they would have testified to the same thing. Did they testify to the same thing? I am going to pick apart every little piece of it because I want to illustrate to you and I hope you don't get the impression that I am picking on these two, but I have to show why the credibility of their testimony is in doubt.

The very first thing David testified, Dima was sitting on that porch and Dima testified she was standing, and she was sure. I realize that is not material in the sense that it goes to the material question here, but it shows that people don't remember and that those two people don't really remember. David testified that he first saw Mike and Louie coming from Joe's house, Joe Mendoza's house, and Dima testified that she first saw Mike and Louie in front of their own house. Again, they were both standing in the same place, why didn't she see them earlier if David was able to see them earlier? They probably did both see the same thing, but they have forgotten, they have been unable to reconstruct accurately what happened.

The next thing David didn't see Freddie's car turn around, he did not see the U-turn and he was quite clear about that. Dima did see the car make a U-turn. Again, it shows you when exciting events happen you kind of duck out of the way or you get excited and you just don't know what happened. David was very frank about that, wasn't he? Well, it must have made a U-turn because the next time I saw it, it was turned around. Honestly, he couldn't testify that he saw it turn around. David testified that a girl got out of the right-hand side of the car while the car was still moving. Dima testified that from the time that she and David said hello to Mike and Louie until the time the car passed Dima and David was two seconds that had elapsed and that was her testimony and I am quoting it. She further testified that between the time that they said hello to Mike and Louie and the time the shooting started was a full minute that elapsed. Now, there is a big difference between two seconds and a minute, fifty-eight seconds as a matter of fact and that is ample time for Freddie to have gotten out of the car and gotten in a very brief scuffle with Louie and Mike before Inez arrived on the scene and started shooting. . . .

David testified that he thought there were three people in the car. Dima testified that she didn't know how many people were in the car. The physical evidence seems to show—I'm sorry, strike that. The other evidence of the other witnesses seems to show that there was either one or two people in the car, but surely not three. Now, the idea that David could see three people in there and Dima couldn't see any just doesn't jibe. There is something amiss there that one of them is mistaken and that is what is amiss. David testified that he heard the girl say the words, give me the shotgun. Dima who testified that she had perfectly good hearing and who was standing in the same place heard nothing. David testified that the guy in the car said one of two things, either no, let's go or he said, no, get in. Dima heard nothing. This points out two additional problems, one a conflict between what they heard. If he could hear it, why couldn't she hear it? Secondly, the second problem that it points out is that even David isn't positive of what he heard. One time he said he heard the words, no, let's go, and the other time he said he heard the words, no, get in.

. . .

Now, I would like to turn to what I have called up there Carbajal, etal, Carbajal is one of our dear friends from Texas and the etal is the other people who testified about what happened after Inez and Freddie showed up at Rosa's place. I hardly know what to say about that. The testimony given by those three people can be described only as bizarre. The idea that a guy who had only met his aunt on two prior occasions would bash a woman in the face because his aunt said to bash her in the face, the idea of that is so preposterous that it has to be—there has to be some reasonable doubt as to whether it ever happened. I don't think that we can be sold that kind of an idea that there are human beings around that can do that kind of thing. I just can't believe it and that guy who sat on the witness stand didn't think I was the kind of guy that really would do that and I doubt that it ever happened. I say to you, ladies and gentlemen, that there are some severe and serious questions about the credibility of all three of those people. It is like most of the other witnesses that the prosecution called here, they told a lot of lies and they admitted they told lies and they didn't think there was a thing wrong with it. Rosa told me two days before she testified and she admitted it that she didn't remember a thing and then she said that I really do remember a lot, and I said, did you remember that on Saturday when you talked to me, and she said, oh, yeah, I just wanted to get rid of you.

. . .

The point I am making is, they all talked it over, Alicia, Juan, Rosa and none of them really knew what happened, and they concocted what sounded like a pretty bizarre story as far as I am concerned and I think as far as you ladies and gentlemen are concerned.

. . .

There are some comments of the District Attorney made about the evidence that I feel I should bring your attention to, to see if you think that perhaps they were not accurate and perhaps you should look at the evidence a little bit more closely; for one thing, Counsel commented that the knife at the scene was found right near and next to the body of Mike Jimenez. The evidence was that it was four feet ten inches away, which indicates and corroborates the story told by the defendants that Mike was either in the process of throwing that knife or had actually gotten it off.

. . .

The first problem the prosecution has, if he wants to prove anything against either defendant is to show intent, murder, manslaughter, these are called specific intent crimes. The defendant has to have the intent to kill in either case. With regard to Freddie we know he didn't kill anyone but the only way he could be involved would be if he were an aider and abettor, aiding and abetting which also requires specific intent and criminal, general criminal intent and knowledge of what the other person is going to do, so that is why I mention the first two words there, intent and knowledge. If you have a reasonable doubt that the specific intent has been proven as to Freddie, you have no choice but to acquit him. If you have a reasonable doubt as to whether or not he had knowledge of what Inez was going to do before she did it, you have no choice but to acquit him, even if you thought that he had knowledge of what she was going to do at some time, but you believe that he did everything he could to stop her as some interpretations of the facts would have it, you still would have to acquit him because the Judge will give you another instruction that says even if a person aids and abets, if before the crime occurs he tries and does everything he can in his power to stop it from happening, then he is not responsible in any way and that is only if he had formed the state of mind beforehand. I don't have a word up there about malice, about premeditation and deliberation, and there is a reason for that, because this is not a murder case. The District Attorney can charge anything he wants. The Judge's instructions on the subject are going to be so clear that there is no possible way a murder verdict could be returned against either defendant. Murder requires malice and that is the reason it can't be done, and when you hear his instructions—I am not going into all that detail, but when you hear those instructions, I am so confident that you will agree there is no use in me wasting my time talking about malice and premeditation and all of that.

. . .

(RTA 1468-1521)

Argument of Mr. Garry to the Jury

BY MR. GARRY:

Ladies and gentlemen of the jury, Mr. Braudrick, Sergeant Perez, Mr. Medrano, Mr. Worthington, Mrs. Garcia, Mrs. Richards, I know it has been a long time since we first met but I recall asking each and every one of you about the presumption of innocence, asking each and every one of you as you look at Inez Garcia now, is she guilty or innocent? We have come a long way since then. We have gone through a tremendous amount of evidence, and you know our appellate courts have said—our Federal appellate courts, our supreme courts have said you, the jury, are the conscience of the community and you bring to this courtroom the aura of being able to ascertain the truth. Remember in my opening statement to you which was only about twelve or fifteen minutes, I said the only important thing in this trial is going to be the ascertainment of the truth, and I said certain things to you and I said I want you to hold me responsible for what I say, and in reading or rereading the statements to you, my opening statements to you, I find that I have more than fulfilled that responsibility to you. I am not interested in anything else except the ascertainment of truth, although this is called a closing argument of counsel, I do not wish to call it that, I wish to call it thinking out loud with you about the evidence that has been presented to you. It has been a pleasure to be in this case with Mr. Worthington, a young man who belongs to this County and this community and you have seen the excellent presentation and his conduct in the highest tradition of the bar. Mr. Braudrick who is a young man who is part of the District Attorney's staff has done his job as best he can with what he has had to work with. He is a sincere young man and it has been a pleasure to be in the same courtroom with him. His Honor has been——

THE COURT: —Please, Mr. Garry, let's get on with the argument.

MR. GARRY: I say those things to you so that I do not want to be in a position where I am going to talk to you in a biased manner. I represent Inez Garcia and I have a tremendous love and respect for Inez Garcia, and in her regard, I am full of bias and prejudice, and on her behalf, I am prejudiced. I am prejudiced because I believe in her innocence. I believe that what she did on the 19th day of March was something that was inevitable to happen and would have happened without going into any of these aspects of it, I don't intend to spend too much time in argument to you because Mr. Worthington has spent a good deal of time analyzing the evidence, I just want to talk to you about some highlights in this case before I talk about Inez Garcia to you.

One of the jobs a defense lawyer has to do when he is engaged and hired to represent a client is to be able to present in vivid recollection as to what actually happened on the day in question. Now, you have to present it the best way you can and one of the things you have to do is present the person that you are representing. Many of you have read the book of What Makes Sammy Run and what makes Inez Garcia run. That was the first question that I had to ask myself when I first met her in the County Jail in Salinas. I had to find out who she was and why she was there, and the circumstances and what made her or put her there, and those are the kinds of questions that you are going to have to ask when you are determining guilt or innocence of Mrs. Garcia, and in order to do that, I have presented to you and I have tried to present to you Inez Garcia as she is, without flowering her up, without buttering her up, I brought her to you in the unvarnished human person that she is so that you could see her as she is, so that you could understand her as she is. I brought to you psychiatrist to testify in this case. I brought to you an outstanding psychiatrist from San Francisco, Dr. Jane Oldden to tell you about Inez Garcia. I brought a woman psychiatrist so that she could relate to a women where she does not relate to men. She does not trust men and for a good reason and good causes, and we will go into that in a little more detail as I present the picture to you.

I first met Inez Garcia and I could not communicate with her because I am a man and she relates to me in a suspicious manner. I have asked my associate, Pat Richards, to help me in this case. I wish that I was a woman so that I could properly represent her so that she could have trust and confidence that she is entitled to for a serious charge of murder that she is charged with in this case. I would like to say a few things about the witnesses that we have had that you have been confronted with. Louie Castillo, I am just going to highlight, I have analyzed every bit of the evidence and I have written down all the evidence and highlighted it. I think it is important if we got some time sequences in this case because I think time always has a relevant meaning, and if you recall that I started when I was cross-examining the different witnesses, I started putting things on the board here. His Honor was kind enough to make arrangements so that I could use this paper to put down some of the things we have. At six o'clock, Freddie arrived at home and he said Solis arrived at Freddie's place at six o'clock at night, and from six o'clock to eight o'clock, Solis said he smoked pot. I don't know what effect pot has on different individuals, I personally have never indulged in it, I prefer the liquid type of refreshment myself, because I belong to the old school and from—and he said he sat there in this bedroom while Mr. Medrano was on the telephone for one hour talking to his girl-friend in Texas, not in Florida as was stated by the District Attorney this morning. While they were going on in these two hours, they are smoking pot. Now then, from eight to eight-thirty, they went to Gonzales. Now, I want you to bear in mind one particular aspect of this case and this is the part that I would like to make a few comments on before I pass on to something else. It was not until the 23rd or the 24th day of August after we started picking you ladies and gentlemen in picking the jury in this case that Mr. Braudrick heard for the first time from Louie Castillo that he had that argument and the argument was over drugs or the subject matter of drugs was involved in that argument and from then on, according to the prosecution's theory, the reason that we have had all of this evidence with regard to drugs is because to show the motive of Freddie Medrano for what happened, for the homicide and the death of Mike Jimenez, pray tell, from March 19 until August 23, what was the theory of the prosecution's case and even holding or even indicting Freddie Medrano? Would you ask that question to yourself and see if you can find an answer? In all these weeks that we have been on trial here, I have not been able to find an answer to that question. Until the 23rd or 24th day of August, what did Mr. Braudrick have to work with in this case, ask that question. And here we have wasted about six or seven weeks on this figment of imagination that was created out of the mouth of a man by the name of Louie

Castillo who the police officers or one of the witnesses who testified here said no one can trust him. No one can trust this man and yet the law enforcement arm of this County, the executive branch of the law enforcement part of this County has brought this man here as a credible witness for the first time on the 23rd or 24th day of August to say that this man, this defendant was involved in drugs, just think about that a little bit and we will go on to something else. Here is this man, Freddie Medrano, who was supposed to be a big dealer, a BTO as we used to say in the Service, a big time operator, he is supposed to be according to this since the 23rd or 24th of August, Freddie Medrano is supposed to be a big time operator and he can't so much as find a lid of marijuana, can't find a lid of marijuana in an area where it is allegedly infested with all kinds of drugs in the Soledad area. Now, these are the kinds of things that I want you to think about, just think about it because what kind of a case did they have before they got the Messiah to say that on the 23rd that the argument on March 19 was over drugs. Mike and Louie according to Solis left at 9:20 and I said, could it have been 9:30 and they said, well, it probably could have been 9:25. Why is it so important to find out when Mike and Louie left the house and where Freddie and Inez were, because we are talking about time. We know from at least two witnesses or at least one witness that the shooting took place at 9:37. Nine-thirty-seven is when the shooting took place according to the evidence. Nine-thirty-seven, that was the gentleman who lived across the street from where the shooting took place, remember he came home at 9:30 at night and he went into his wife's bedroom and he was getting ready to go to bed and he heard the shooting some seven minutes later after he got home, which was at 9:30, so that if we take the testimony of 9:20, ten minutes before it gets to be 9:30 and another seven minutes, we are talking about in the area of seventeen minutes from the time that Mike and Louie left the premises where Freddie and Inez lived, seventeen minutes and in that seventeen minutes, or before that seventeen minutes, immediately before that seventeen minutes, Inez Garcia was raped, and I will come to a little bit more about Inez Garcia being raped because I believe that this is the important point. Seventeen minutes, we won't have had any argument about this case if Inez was raped and she went immediately into the bedroom and got her rifle and shot that man, we wouldn't be here or we should not be here. Is there a difference between that time and the seventeen minutes that followed when you consider the events that followed thereafter and when you take into consideration the entire subject matter and the entire picture and what is this entire picture? The entire picture is that according to Mr. Louis—Louie Castillo, he said the argument started at 9:15 and it lasted for, according to him, a few minutes. Chofo, or Solis said they left at 9:20. Did the argument last five minutes or ten minutes, who knows? Who knows how much of this time element is believable, but we do know when the shooting took place by a person who is independent about this matter and he came home and at seven minutes after he got home from 9:30 to 9:37, the shooting started out.

Now, one other thing that I want you to bear in mind when you are analyzing the evidence is Louie Castillo said on cross-examination and I asked him these questions very deliberately and very much to the point, I said, after the beating that was administered to Freddie Medrano, after that beating, what did Inez Garcia do, and I said in addition to that, were there any threats, any threats made to either one of you by either one, Mr. Medrano or by Mrs. Garcia, and his answer, his answer and this is important . . . he said no threats by anyone, and he also said that Inez Garcia said outside of these premises don't worry about a thing, things will be fine and told Mike to forget about everything. She had no animosity either. I asked him did she have any animosity and Louie Castillo said no. Inez Garcia said to Mike, don't worry about things, things will work themselves out and that is the testimony immediately after the beating, the type of beating that had been described to you and in the type of beating that has been described by Mr. Castillo in referring to the type of beating that Freddie Medrano received. Louis Castillo said he was banging him all over the place and kicking him and I wrote it down just exactly the way it was said. After that, no animosity, no animosity by my client, Inez Garcia, according to Louie Castillo.

Two weeks before this trial commenced, Tom Worthington sent his investigator to talk to Louis and he said nothing whatsoever about drugs, he said absolutely nothing about drugs; as a matter of fact, we first heard about the drugs in the opening statement made by Mr. Braudrick to you when the trial commenced after you were picked as jurors and it was after that the Judge granted us a recess that afternoon so that we could talk to Louis and Solis, which we did, and you have heard about the interplay and the exchange that has gone on during the course of the cross-examination. In all the years that I have been at this bench trying cases before men and women like yourselves, very seldom have I ever heard a witness who sat on that witness box and admitted time and time and time again that he lied not only to me, which is insignificant but to lie in court within the space of ten minutes, to lie several times and admit lying to the jury and admit thinking it is funny that he would lie to the jury? Ladies and gentlemen of the jury, we know that this is not a funny case. I represent a very serious defendant whose honor was squelched and destroyed and who has had the humiliation having to stand trial before her peer group and it is not funny and I don't think it is funny under any circumstances, and yet some of these witnesses have sat up there thinking it is a laughable matter and to think it is funny, and when I asked Louie Castillo if he raped Inez

Garcia, he laughed and thought it was funny. I don't know whether it is his youth or his misguided direction in drugs or is it part of our handicap that we are going through because of our mismanagement of our economic setup that we have been living under, I don't know what the cause is, but at this particular moment, I am not interested in the cause, I am interested in representing Inez Garcia.

Freddie Medrano, as I told you in the beginning of this case, has no business in this courtroom unless he came here as a spectator, and he has no business here and it is an insult to Inez Garcia to say that this man instigated or aided and abetted her in any way, it is an insult to Inez Garcia. Inez Garcia is a proud person and is a person who has an identity of her own and she does not have to be aided and abetted by a man whom she hardly knew who was just sharing rent because of the economic conditions and all of the other things that go on in areas where we have poor housing conditions. We don't need that kind of help. Inez Garcia does not need to be aided and abetted in any way by Freddie Medrano. I am not going to spend much time on Mr. Solis. Solis is a very pathetic person. I find them all very pathetic. I find this as disharmonizing as the conduct of some of these witnesses who have been brought here, I find it very sad, I find it very sad when I see a seventeen-year-older say to me that for two years he has been using heroin. I find it very sad for a fifteen year older to be in that category and selling dope in order to make their way. I find it very, very sad but sad as it may be, I am not going to let the sadness of one person crucify the dignity and freedom of a beautiful human being like Inez Garcia, I am not going to permit that to happen. We are not going to permit it because the evidence will show that what the true is and the ascertainment of the truth is going to be our job and your job and it is my responsibility to present it to you and it is your responsibility to analyze it and do what you may with it. We know that Inez was not happy that Mike and Louie was in the house that day. I could read portions of the transcript which I am not going to take the time because I hope fully to be able to finish this case today so that the Judge can instruct you tomorrow so that we can get this case behind us but I want you to remember this much in passing, and may I say this: Mr. Solis told you that Freddie took out the .22 and Inez the shotgun, now listen to this, wrapped in a white sheet and put it inside his coat, a white sheet and put it inside his coat. The rifle was taken out in a case at almost ten o'clock and that was the testimony of Mr. Solis. We know that Mr. Medrano was arrested soon after the events when Alicia and Freddie went out to get cigarettes for Inez who is a chain smoker, and when he was arrested, they came and found the automobile that was involved in this matter and Officer or Sergeant Perez testified that he searched that automobile and I am sure they searched it very carefully and there is not one piece of evidence of ever finding a white sheet, not one piece of evidence of ever finding a case in the automobile, as a matter of fact, the case in question was found right here. This is from the prosecution's evidence, it was not in the automobile and it speaks for itself.

I want to go to some other evidence. You know, in this entire trial, the most interesting and startling piece of evidence was the tape recording that you heard, unvarnished, uncoached of Freddie Medrano. I heard it for the first time like you did. I had seen the written transcription of it but I heard the tape just like you did, and if that doesn't show a confused state of mind of Mr. Medrano, then I don't know what a confused state of mind is, but confused or not, on the morning of March 20, after he had been arrested for murder, he gave the statement exactly as had been testified to by Mr. Medrano here in court and by Inez Garcia. I am not responsible for how other people see different aspects of it, but I was—familiar with the testimony of Dima and David before we came—before this trial ever started because under our discovery procedures, we are entitled to get these things. I do know that Inez Garcia has testified under oath that she immediately walked down —she walked down and got this gun and walked down and these are the shoes that she walked down with, these are no outside shoes, those of you who are familiar, these are shoes that you wear inside the house, look at these, these have been walked on on the outside. This is what she walked down with. I want you to also bear in mind that the evidence is replete and abundant that until such time as the telephone call came in after Mike and Louie had left, either at 9:20 or 9:25 or 9:30, until that time happened, no one proceeded to get a gun and that is clear and we don't have to argue about that. It is very, very clear that that did not—the gun event did not come on. What caused Inez Garcia who had been raped by them but was in a confused state where she said she was thinking over what had happened to her, and what she could have done to have prevented it, and all of these things going on in her mind, but not thinking about getting a gun or doing anything about it, what happened in the next two or three minutes to cause Inez Garcia, a devout Catholic, a very religious person who had just been raped, what caused her to go into her bedroom, come into the closet and come out with a rifle and load it, and the case was left in that picture that I just showed you, and to take off in her slippers out on the street, what caused her to do that? Will you ask that question to yourself and see if you can come up with an answer, I had to do it and I think you have to do it. What caused her to do that? What caused Fred Medrano after he had been severely beaten to see Inez Garcia walk in through the front door and she was all messed up and in kind of a trance to take off immediately and get into his car and go and look for Mike and Louis?

. . .

What caused her–what caused Freddie to do that, he had just been severely beaten, and what caused him to take off, ask that question to yourself. What caused Inez Garcia to load that gun, was there a plan afoot, or is the insinuation that Inez Garcia and Freddie Medrano planned this thing ahead of time, what would be the reason for it? We know what the reason for it was, I brought a man all the way from Miami, Florida to tell you what happened. She told you what happened. She told you yesterday morning what happened. She got that telephone call immediately after these people left and said you are no good and we are going to get rid of you. We are going to kill you and all kinds of other things, laughing all the time they are doing this, and in panic, she gets her gun and calls her family. Remember because the psychiatrist, Dr. Oldden, don't sell her short, don't be misled by the extensive examination by Mr. Braudrick. Well, did you do that, well, didn't you think this was important, did you think that was important, don't be misled by that. Dr. Oldden gave you the inside, the inner person of Inez Garcia. Why did she call her family? Did she call her family in a hysterical condition, yes, and she said I have been raped and I think my life is being threatened and before they kill me, I am going to kill them. What would any other reasonable human being do under those same circumstances in the same atmosphere and under the same environment? What would any other person do? I am not going to ask you what you would do, I am not going to tell you what I would have done because I don't know. I don't know whether you would know what you would do, but these are the facts, I didn't manufactcture them, I didn't create them, I brought them to you as they exist. The psychiatrist testified, both psychiatrists testified as to the state of mind of Mrs. Garcia when she went there and saw Freddie being beaten, with a knife up in the air, and she fired, the state of mind of self-defense, self-defense. In many, many areas in this case, this case cries with self-defense. If a person cannot defend themselves under these circumstances, then self-defense doesn't mean anything at all. I personally do not like to see death, I have been in the Army and I know what death is. I know what human destruction is. I do not like to see it but if there ever was a case that had any justification for one human being in order to protect their own integrity and their own self and their own freedom, this is it, this is it. This cries out, this spells itself out, it just weeps itself and you can't escape that. We have three defenses to this case, ladies and gentlemen of the jury, three defenses. May I tell you what they are?

Number 1, the state of mind was such of Inez Garcia's emotionally impaired consciousness, she was unconscious as to being able to make that kind of a determination that you and I could make in the jury room or in this courtroom in the cold light of day with a bailiff and a judge and an audience and everybody else to make that cold decision.

Inez Garcia was in that state of mind where she was in basically and she was hysterical and neurotic, or hysterical neurosis, and that is what the psychiatrist said. Dr. Clausen who came here yesterday was not familiar with one aspect of her case, and the reason he wasn't familiar with it was because Inez Garcia doesn't want to talk about it, and I want to talk about it because I have a duty to perform even though it embarrasses her. At the age of fourteen, psychiatric reports show, the medical reports show that she was bed-wetting, not because she didn't know any better but because of the emotional instability caused her to be in this kind of situation, the hysterical aspects of her life caused her to have this bed-wetting condition and Dr. Clausen said to you that was very significant, and I said, you didn't know about that, did you, and he said no, I did not. Then during the recess I showed him part of the medical reports where it is in there. Secondly, I said, what is the significance after this event on March 19 where she had long periods of constant bed-wetting where she had to take tranquilizers, thorazine, twenty-five milligrams of thorazine and other types of tranquilizers, what is the significance of that, and he said it is regressing. What does regressing mean, and he said, going backwards that this creates the hysterical situation, and he said if it wasn't for the fact that she had clearly admitted what she had done, she would say that it was hysterical neurosis, because he said people with hysterical neurosis do not admit, they try to cover up their acts. He said if it wasn't for that, he would say she was hysterical neuroses. Dr. Oldden says hysterical neurosis. She spent three hours with her. She spent an awful lot of time evaluating this thing and testified at length. This is the background that I have presented to you, first, the emotional instability where she could not make that kind of judgment that you would make in the cold hour of the day or the analysis between—in the District Attorney's office or in a lawyer's office. These were under impulsive situations where one man had almost been killed by the kind of beating that he received and immediately thereafter, when she tries to console and be the arbiter with Mike and Louie, and says she thinks this will cool and everything will work themselves out, and what happens, she gets raped. Now, the question is, do we have to talk about some other things at 11:30 at night on March 19 when Inez Garcia was in the custody of the police department and Chief Jimenez arrested her and had taken a statement from her? You did not hear the tape, you did not hear the statement but you heard portions of it being referred to time and time again by the very psychiatrist that testified here.

One other significant factor that I would like to call your attention to so that you will have it and that is, Sergeant Moranda, Yvonne Moranda, not Sergeant, just a police officer, I'm sorry, from Soledad Police Department who has known Inez Garcia for approximately two years and their children were together in scout work, and Inez was going to be a den mother and she testified that she took her undergarments but did not take the panties. She also testified yesterday that she examined the upper part of her body and found no bruises in her breast area, that is her extremities except the one on the right side of her cheek or face where it was red, but specifically she said she did not look at the lower extremities, and you heard Inez Garcia testify about the black and blue marks that she found the next day. Even if she had been examined that night, we know what human experience is, that the black and blue marks take a little time to develop, and it takes some hours before they do develop. That testimony is uncontroverted. I don't think anyone should be mimicking that. Now, what is the important factor of Yvonne's testimony that I brought here this witness, Number 1, she is a police officer and has been a police officer for some time. She testified that the reputation of Inez Garcia for truth and honesty and integrity is good and excellent, that means that she is believable. Now, this isn't some narcotic user, this isn't somebody who is a stumble-bum coming into the community who said, yes, I would vouch for her, and I believe Inez Garcia. This is a police officer in Soledad, part of the law enforcement body who can speak and knowing her for two years said that she is a truthful and honest person, and you know how truthful and honest she is because she doesn't hesitate one bit by telling you she killed that man when the events were relived and relived and when she got emotionally upset she said she is sorry she did not kill Louis. That was when you get her into that state in her emotional life, it goes back to that hour, the moment of truth, that hour that she relives. Every time we sit in this courtroom and every time these events come up, she relives that life. She relives that moment. She relives those events as vividly as if they happened immediately right now. Who said that, is that Garry talking, no, Dr. Clausen, the prosecution's psychiatrist who testified here yesterday. He said as a matter of fact in his office when she started talking about those events, her emotions started rising and she was very emotionally, almost going to the verge of hysteria, and that is what you have witnessed in this courtroom time and time and time again. I am sorry that you have had to witness this but you have seen her as the person that she is, the person that Louis Castillo and Mike Jimenez violated on that night. Now, what does this woman say in addition to that, what did Yvonne Moranda say in addition to that? She said she was there at the interrogation at 11:30 and she was there with Sergeant Perez at 1:30 that morning, and I said throughout this entire period of time, was Inez Garcia in a state of shock and what was her answer, yes, she was in a state of shock from 11:30 until 1:30, in a state of shock. Inez Garcia was in a state of shock and you can't take that away, even though on cross and on redirect or cross-examination, Mr. Braudrick said, are you a medical doctor, and of course, she isn't and yet he brought her for the examination for the physical features. A state of shock for a long time thereafter and believe me, from what happened to her and her background, a state of shock existed a long time after two hours or three hours that followed, the state of shock I don't think is even over with at the present time because every time she relives the violation to her body, that sacred body that she has been taught since she was in her birth that cannot be violated by anyone except one person and that one person is her husband, you can't get around that, I'm sorry, there is no way of getting around that. There is no way to make Inez Garcia any person except what she is and she will be herself no matter what the consequences may be, whether we want to make her a different person or not doesn't make any difference. She cannot read or write. Dr. Stephens–Mr. Stephens said that she is now beginning to be able to tell time, and I don't know whether she can or not. Inez Garcia, we find her as she is and not someone else.

I want to say a few things to you, ladies and gentlemen, I am talking about this case again, assuming you are the police chief of this investigation and you are the police officer investigating this case and you are going to be the jury that is going to be making these decisions, at 11:30 at night Inez Garcia said she killed a man, why did you kill him, she tells the police, she said they tried to rape me and they got fresh with me. Inez Garcia at 11:30 at night told the police chief of the County of Soledad that they tried to rape her and they got fresh with her and a lot of other things. What would you have done if you were the police chief, wouldn't you have asked her more questions about it? Wouldn't you have investigated to see what she's talking about and ask what do you mean by they tried to rape me? What do you mean they got fresh with me? Don't you think that was in order? Don't you think that she was entitled to that type of investigation immediately or didn't it make any difference or does it happen so often that women get raped in Soledad and other parts of our country that the police do not consider it to be significant, I don't know. People are beginning to understand what rape is and the significance of rape and that is why I brought Father Boyle here to testify to you as to what it means to be raped, if you are a Catholic woman. You heard Father Boyle, Father Eugene Boyle, talk about the sacredness and the chasteness that is being developed and dug in from the day of birth until you are here. I don't happen to be a woman Catholic but I am a person who respects religions of all faiths. I wanted to find out what the story is being Catholic and I what does rape and Catholicism mean, and Father Boyle told you. Father Boyle's story about rape and how it affects and what you are supposed to be doing in that regard to the culture and background of that is the story of Inez Garcia. I don't know what else I can tell you. Mr. Braudrick says to you he doesn't believe that she was raped. I brought in a person who has specialized in the field of rape, a young lady, a young woman who came here from Santa Cruz and goes to the University of California at Santa Cruz, and she has interviewed some 300 women, most of them who have been either raped or sexually assaulted in order to be able to understand why Inez Garcia was reticent about telling the police or telling anybody why she was raped or that she was raped. I said, what has been your experience in your studies and your evaluation as an expert in this field when it comes to women who say they have been raped, and she said her experience, her studies and her expert opinion is that only two out of ten ever report it to the law enforcement body, that means 80 percent of the women who get raped never report it to the law enforcement bodies, why? Why don't they, because most of the law enforcement bodies are men, men like myself, men like you gentlemen on the jury, men like the officers in this courtroom, and most of the Judges are men, and our attitudes over the period of years has been such that we make fun of women who have been raped, we make jokes about it, we laugh about it. I have heard it time and time again and you have heard it. Did you enjoy it? When rape is inevitable, relax and enjoy it. You have heard these remarks by men time and time again. Shakespeare in one of his plays talks about Rape Le Raper Lecrece, and I am probably not even pronouncing it correctly. It tells the story in one of the battles, the various husbands are together and they are talking about their wives, and this one man talks about his wife who is absolutely chaste and that she would not look at another man under any circumstances, another man who was in earshot goes that night and rapes this woman and ravishes her, and she calls upon her husband and the lords of the period in the area and she says that she has been raped and her honor must be avenged, and immediately thereafter she commits suicide and kills herself. Thereafter the husband and his family destroy the entire family, the entire clan that has raped her. I am doing an injustice to William Shakespeare because I don't happen to be a Shakespearean student. I cannot use the language and words and the verbage that a Shakespearean does, but it tells you the story that it goes way back and what it means to a woman like Inez Garcia not to be violated. The Judge is going to give you an instruction that says that when Inez Garcia saw someone being ravaged and their lives being endangered, does she had the right to use reasonable force to see that that did not happen. The evidence in this case from the psychiatrist, both of them, is that she thought that not only her life was in danger but the life of Freddie Medrano was in danger with the knife hanging over him and repeating the same battles and the same threats. I don't know what else I can tell you, ladies and gentlemen of the jury, you have been very patient and I just want to tell you this: That Inez Garcia is an exceptional person. Inez Garcia has brought for the first time in our courts the story of rape in such a manner and in such a dignified manner that shows that a person, a woman has the right to be able to defend her honor and to say women should not be violated and assaulted or threatened in any way. I thank you very much.

. . .

1523-1545

CLOSING REBUTTAL

MR. BRAUDRICK: Ladies and gentlemen: You have heard a very powerful argument by a very experienced attorney, Mr. Garry. I want you to note one thing about his argument and that is it almost totally went to your emotions and your sympathies for the defendant, and if you decide this case based on emotions and sympathies for these people, you haven't done your job, that is not what you took the oath for. You are here to decide on the facts and the law, and when you find out you are sitting there and a man gets up and starts to argue to you and you feel he is starting to affect you and he is not talking about the facts, then you just better wait one second and sit back and think for a second because that is not your job, your job is to decide this case on the facts, the facts and the law, and if you decide it because you are sympathetic, because you are emotional, because you react emotionally, because a woman comes in and says she was raped, then we just might as well forget about the whole judicial system because that is not what we are here talking about, what we are interested in is the facts and the law and your common sense and experience, and that is your job. You have got to go into that jury room tomorrow and you are going to be deliberating a long time about this case because there has been seven weeks of trial and you are going to discuss all the facts because it is not an easy case.

. . .

I will tell you something, and that is, be very careful about it and that is when somebody waltzes up here and they say,well, out of all this testimony, this guy is lying because I cross-examined him and he said I am lying, but then he turns around and said well, he testified as to this and this and I want you to believe that and forget everything else. He is just trying to hoodwink you when you do that. You have got to look at everybody's testimony and compare their testimony to everybody else's.

. . .

(1546-1547)

QUESTIONS FOR STUDY AND ANALYSIS

PROSECUTION'S CLOSING ARGUMENT (pp. 300-310)

1. What is the strategy of the prosecutor's "right to live" argument?

2. How does Mr. Braudrick interpret the evidence at the scene of the shooting to argue that the shooting could not be in self-defense?

3. Why does Mr. Braudrick term the alleged rape as a "preposterous" theory?

MR. WORTHINGTON'S CLOSING ARGUMENT (pp. 310-319)

1. Why does Mr. Worthington spend so much time dealing with the testimony of David Ferrel and Dima Gallardo? Does he manage to raise serious doubts about their ability to observe and remember events accurately?

MR. GARRY'S CLOSING ARGUMENT (pp. 319-331)

1. What is the strategy of Mr. Garry's closing argument? Does he attempt to appeal "totally . . . to your emotions and your sympathies for the defendant" as claimed by Mr. Braudrick in his closing rebuttal?

2. Does Mr. Garry succeed in painting a picture of the real Inez Garcia as he claims?

3. Does Mr. Garry develop a theory to show why Ms. Garcia's outbursts and sarcastic replies on cross-examination support his view of emotional instability and trauma due to the alleged rape?

4. What are the three defenses to the charge of homicide which Mr. Garry claims for Ms. Garcia?

JUDGE LAWSON'S INSTRUCTIONS TO THE JURY

THE COURT: All right, ladies and gentlemen of the jury:

It is my duty to instruct you in the law that applies to this case and you must follow the law as I state it to you.

As jurors, it is your exclusive duty to decide all questions of fact submitted to you and for that purpose to determine the effect and value of the evidence. . . .

You must not be governed by mere sentiment, conjecture, sympathy, passion, prejudice, public opinion or public feeling. Both the People and the defendants* have a right to expect that you will conscientiously consider and weigh the evidence and apply the law of the case, and that you will reach a just verdict regardless what the consequences of such verdict may be.

DEFINITIONS OF EVIDENCE

Direct evidence means evidence that directly proves a fact, without an inference, and which in itself, if true, conclusively establishes that fact.

Circumstantial evidence means evidence that proves a fact from which an inference of the existence of another fact may be drawn.

An inference is a deduction of fact that may logically and reasonably be drawn from another fact or group of facts established by the evidence.

For example, if a witness testified, "I saw that man break the window with his fist," this is direct evidence; but if the witness testified that he saw the man standing near the broken window, his hand bleed-

* The instructions relating solely to the charges against Freddie Medrano have been omitted.

ing, and pieces of broken glass embedded in his knuckles, this is circumstantial evidence from which you could draw the inference that he had put his fist through the window.

It is not necessary that facts be proved by direct evidence. They may be proved also by circumstantial evidence or by a combination of direct evidence and circumstantial evidence. Both direct evidence and circumstantial evidence are acceptable as a means of proof. Neither is entitled to any greater weight than the other.

You are not permitted to find the defendant guilty of the crime charged against him* based on circumstantial evidence unless the proved circumstances are not only consistent with the theory that the defendant is guilty of the crime, but cannot be reconciled with any other rational conclusion and each fact which is essential to complete a set of circumstances necessary to establish the defendant's guilt has been proved beyond a reasonable doubt.

Also, if the evidence is susceptible of two reasonable interpretations, one of which points to the defendant's guilt, and the other to his innocence, it is your duty to adopt that interpretation which points to the defendant's innocence and reject the other which points to his guilt.

Every person who testifies under oath is a witness. You are the sole and exclusive judges of the credibility of the witnesses who have testified in this case.

In determining the credibility of a witness, you may consider any matter that has a tendency in reason to prove or disprove the truthfulness of his testimony, including but not limited to the following:

His demeanor while testifying and the manner in which he testifies;

The character of his testimony;

The extent of his capacity to perceive, to recollect, or to communicate any matter about which he testifies;

The extent of his opportunity to perceive any matter about which he testifies;

His character for honesty or veracity or their opposites;

The existence or nonexistence of a bias, interest or other motive;

A statement previously made by him that is consistent with his testimony;

A statement made by him that is inconsistent with any part of his testimony;

The existence or nonexistence of any fact testified to by him;

His attitude toward the action in which he testifies or toward the giving of testimony;

His admission of untruthfulness.

---

* While the instructions that Judge Lawson reads are written in the masculine gender, they apply to Inez Garcia.

A witness willfully false in one material part of his testimony is to be distrusted in others. You may reject the whole testimony of a witness who willfully has testified falsely as to a material point, unless, from all the evidence, you shall believe the probability of truth favors his testimony in other particulars.

However, discrepancies in a witness's testimony or between his testimony and that of others, if there were any, do not necessarily mean that the witness should be discredited. Failure of recollection is a common experience; and innocent misrecollection is not uncommon. It is a fact, also, that two persons witnessing an incident or a transaction often will see or hear it differently. Whether a discrepancy pertains to a fact of importance or only to a trivial detail should be considered in weighing its significance.

. . .

Motive is not an element of the crime charged and need not be shown. However, you may consider motive or lack of motive as a circumstance in this case. Presence of motive may tend to establish guilt. Absence of motive may tend to establish innocence. You will therefore give its presence or absence, as the case may be, the weight to which you find it to be entitled.

There has been admitted in evidence the testimony of a medical expert of statements made to him by the defendant in the course of an examination of the defendant which was made for the purpose of diagnosis. The testimony of such statements may be considered by you only for the limited purpose of showing the information upon which the medical expert based his opinion. Such testimony is not to be considered by you as evidence of the truth of the facts disclosed by defendant's statements.

PRESUMPTION OF INNOCENCE AND BURDEN OF PROOF

A defendant in a criminal action is presumed to be innocent until the contrary is proved, and in case of a reasonable doubt whether his guilt is satisfactorily shown, he is entitled to an acquittal. This presumption places upon the State the burden of proving him guilty beyond a reasonable doubt. Reasonable doubt is defined as follows: It is not a mere possible doubt; because everything relating to human affairs, and depending on moral evidence, is open to some possible or imaginary doubt. It is that state of the case which, after the entire comparison and consideration of all the evidence, leaves the minds of the jurors in that condition that they cannot say they feel an abiding conviction, to a moral certainty, of the truth of the charge.

You are not permitted to find the defendant guilty of the crime charged against him except upon proof beyond a reasonable doubt of every fact necessary to constitute the crime with which he is charged.

In other words, reasonable doubt means just what the term implies, doubt based upon reason, doubt that presents itself in the minds of reasonable people who are weighing the evidence in the scales, one side against the other, in a logical manner in an effort to determine wherein lies the truth.

DEFINITIONS OF HOMICIDE

The word homocide means the killing of one human being by another, either lawfully or unlawfully. As used in these instructions, the word homicide includes murder and manslaughter, which are unlawful and the acts of excusable and justifiable homocide, which are *unlawful.*

Murder is the unlawful killing of a human being with malice aforethought.

"Malice" may be either express or implied. Malice is express when there is manifested an intention unlawfully to kill a human being.

All murder which is perpetrated by any kind of willful, deliberate and premeditated killing with malice aforethought is murder of the first degree.

The word "deliberate" means formed or arrived at or determined upon, as a result of careful thought and weighing of considerations for and against the proposed course of action. The word "premeditated" means considered beforehand.

If you find that the killing was preceded and accompanied by a clear, deliberate intent on the part of the defendant to kill, which was the result of deliberation and premeditation, so that it must have been formed upon preexisting reflection and not under a sudden heat of passion or other condition precluding the idea of deliberation, it is murder of the first degree.

The law does not undertake to measure in units of time the length of the period during which the thought must be pondered before it can ripen into an intent to kill which is truly deliberate and premeditated. The time will vary with different individuals and under varying circumstances. The true test is not the duration of time, but rather the extent of the reflection. A cold, calculated judgment and decision may be arrived at in a short period of time, but a mere unconsidered and rash impulse, even though it include an intent to kill, is not such deliberation and premeditation as will fix an unlawful killing as murder of the first degree. To constitute a deliberate and premeditated killing, the slayer must weigh and consider the question of killing and the reasons for and against such a choice and, having in mind the consequences, he decides to and does kill.

Murder of the second degree is the unlawful killing of a human being with malice aforethought when there is manifested an intention unlawfully to kill a human being but the evidence is insufficient to establish deliberation and premeditation.

Manslaughter is the unlawful killing of a human being without malice aforethought. It is not divided into degrees but is of two kinds, mainly voluntary manslaughter and involuntary manslaughter.

Voluntary manslaughter is the intentional and unlawful killing of a human being without malice aforethought.

There is no malice aforethought if the killing occurred upon a sudden quarrel or heat of passion or if the evidence shows that due to diminished capacity caused by mental illness, mental defect, or intoxication, the defendant did not have the capacity to attain the mental state constituting malice aforethought, even though the killing be intentional, voluntary, deliberate, premeditated, and unprovoked.

To reduce an intentional felonious homicide from the offense of murder to manslaughter upon the ground of sudden quarrel of heat of passion, the provocation must be of such character and degree as naturally would excite and arouse such passion, and the assailant must act under the smart of that sudden quarrel or heat of passion.

"Heat of passion," as the term is used in our law, means such passion as naturally would be aroused in the mind of an ordinarily reasonable person of average disposition in the same or similar circumstances as those in question, and such as would cause him to act rashly, without reflection and deliberation, and from passion rather than from judgment. Hence, the defendant may not set up his own standard of conduct and be permitted to justify or excuse himself merely because his passions were aroused. To apply the proper standard by which to judge the conduct of the defendant, you will ask and answer whether or not the ordinarily reasonable person, if placed in the same position in which the defendant found himself and if knowing what the defendant then knew, would have been thrown into a heat of passion.

If there was provocation, but of a nature not calculated to naturally arouse passion, or if sufficient time elapsed between the provocation and the fatal blow for passion to subside and reason to return, and if an unlawful killing of a human being followed such provocation and had all the elements of murder, as I have defined it, the mere fact of slight or remote provocation will not reduce the offense to manslaughter.

There is no malice aforethought and intent to kill if by reason of diminished capacity caused by mental illness, mental defect, or unconsciousness resulting from voluntary intoxication, the defendant did not have the mental capacity to harbor malice aforethought and to form an intent to kill.

The distinction between murder and manslaughter is that murder requires malice while manslaughter does not.

When the act causing the death, though unlawful, is done in the heat of passion or is excited by a sudden quarrel such as amounts to adequate provocation, the offense is manslaughter. In such a case, even if an intent to kill exists, the law is that malice, which is an essential element of murder, is absent.

To reduce a killing upon a sudden quarrel or heat of passion from murder to manslaughter the killing must have occurred while the slayer was acting under the direct and immediate influence of such quarrel or heat of passion. Where the influence of the sudden quarrel or heat of passion has ceased to obscure the mind of the accused and sufficient time has elapsed for angry passion to end and for reason to control his conduct, it will no longer reduce an intentional killing to manslaughter. The question as to whether a cooling period has elapsed and reason has returned is not measured by the standard of the accused, but the duration of the cooling period is the time it would take the average or ordinarily reasonable person to have cooled his heat of passion and for his reason to have returned.

DIMINISHED CAPACITY

If you find from the evidence that at the time the alleged crime was committed, the defendant had substantially reduced mental capacity, whether caused by mental illness, mental defect, intoxication, or any other cause, you must consider what effects, if any, this diminished capacity had on the defendant's ability to form any of the specific mental states that are essential elements of murder and voluntary manslaughter. Thus, if you find that the defendant's mental capacity was diminished to the extent that you are of reasonable doubt whether he did, maturely and meaningfully, premeditate, deliberate, and reflect upon the gravity of his contemplated acts, or form an intent to kill, you cannot find him guilty of a willful, deliberate and premeditated murder of the first degree.

Also, if you find that the defendant's mental capacity was diminished to the extent that you have a reasonable doubt whether he was able to form the mental state constituting either express or implied malice aforethought, you cannot find him guilty of murder of either the first or second degree. If you have a reasonable doubt whether he was able to form an intention, unlawfully to kill a human being, you cannot find that he harbored express malice. Further, if you have a reasonable doubt, one, whether his acts were done for a base, anti-social purpose, or two, whether he was aware of the duty imposed on him not to commit acts which involved the risk of grave injury or death, or three, whether he did act despite that awareness, you cannot find that he harbored malice.

Furthermore, if you find that as a result of mental illness, mental defect, or unconsciousness caused by voluntary intoxication, his mental capacity was diminished to the extent that he neither harbored malice aforethought nor had an intent to kill at the time the alleged crime was committed, you cannot find him guilty of either murder or voluntary manslaughter.

. . .

In the crime of murder there must exist in the mind of the perpetrator the specific intent to kill a human being and unless such intent so exists, that crime is not committed.

. . .

The intent with which an act is done is shown by the circumstances attending the act, the manner in which it is done, the means used, and the soundness of mind and discretion of the person committing the act.

JUSTIFIABLE HOMICIDE
ACTION UNDER THREATS OR MENACE

A person is not guilty of crime when he commits an act or engages in conduct, otherwise criminal, when acting under threats and menaces under the following circumstances: One, where the threats and menaces are such that they would create in the mind of a reasonable person the fear that his life would be in imminent danger and immediate danger or if he did not commit the act or engage in the conduct charged, and two, if such person then believed that his life would be so endangered.

This rule does not apply to threats, menaces, and fear of future danger to his life.

SELF-DEFENSE

Homocide is justifiable and not unlawful when committed by a person in the lawful defense of himself, when he has reasonable grounds to apprehend that he is in danger of death or great bodily injury and that there is imminent danger of such a design being accomplished.

In order to justify the taking of human life in self-defense, the slayer as a reasonable man must have reason to believe and must believe that he is in danger of death or great bodily injury; and, further, the circumstances must be such that an ordinarily reasonable person, under similar circumstances, would believe that it was necessary for him to use, in his defense and to avoid death or great bodily injury to himself, such force or means as might cause the death of his adversary.

A bare fear of death or great bodily injury is not sufficient to justify a homicide. To justify taking a life of another in self-defense, the circumstances must be such as to excite the fears of a reasonable man placed in a similar position, and the party killing must act under the influence of such fears alone. The danger must be apparent and must be present and imminent, or must so appear at the time to the slayer as a reasonable man, and the killing must be done under a well-founded belief that it is necessary to save one's self from death or great bodily harm.

Upon a trial of a charge of murder, it is a defense that the homocide was justifiable. To establish this defense, the burden is on the defendant to raise a reasonable doubt as to his guilt of the charge of murder.

It is unlawful for a person who, as a reasonable person, has grounds for believing and does believe that bodily injury is about to be inflicted upon another to protect him from attack.

In doing so, he may use all force and means which he believes to be reasonably necessary and which would appear to a reasonable person, in the same or similar circumstances, to be necessary to prevent the injury which appears to be imminent.

A person who is threatened with an attack that justifies the exercise of the right of self-defense, need not retreat. In the exercise of his right of self-defense, he may stand his ground and defend himself by the use of all force and means which would appear to be necessary to a reasonable person in a similar situation and with similar knowledge; and he may pursue his assailant until he has secured himself from danger if that course likewise appears reasonably necessary. This law applies even though the assailed person might more easily have gained safety by flight or by withdrawing from the scene.

Actual danger is not necessary to justify self-defense. If one is confronted by the appearance of danger which arouses in his mind, as a reasonable person, an honest conviction and fear that he is about to suffer death or great bodily harm, and if a reasonable man in a like situation, seeing and knowing the same facts, would be justified in believing himself in like danger, and if the person so confronted acts in self-defense upon such appearances and from such fear and honest conviction, his right of self-defense is the same whether such danger is real or merely apparent.

. . .

The right of self-defense ceases to exist when there is no longer any apparent danger of further violence on the part of the assailant. Thus, where a person is attacked under circumstances which justify his exercise of the right of self-defense, and thereafter he uses such force upon his attacker as to render the attacker incapable of inflicting further injuries, the law of self-defense then ceases to work in favor of thy person attacked.

. . .

THE EFFECT OF RAPE

The question of rape is important only insofar as it bears upon the mental state of Inez Garcia at the time she shot Miguel Jimenez.

Rape is an act of sexual intercourse with a female person who is not the wife of the perpetrator, where she resists, but her resistance is overcome by force or violence.

The conduct of the female person need only be such as to make the absence of consent and the actual resistance reasonably apparent. The resistance must be proportioned to the outrage and the amount of resistance required depends upon the surrounding circumstances, such as the relative strength and ability of the parties, the age and the condition of the female, the uselessness of resistance as it would appear to hear, and the degree of force shown by the perpetrator. She is not required to resist until either her strength or consciousness is gone; her resistance need continue only until it becomes so apparently useless as to justify its cessation.

Rape is an act of sexual intercourse with a female person without her consent and who is not the wife of the perpetrator, where she is prevented from resisting by threats of great and immediate bodily harm, accompanied by the apparent power of the perpetrator to carry out such threats.

When a woman reasonably determines that she cannot resist without peril to her life or safety, no resistance is required and if she submits to an act of sexual intercourse, induced by fear that it is necessary to save her from violence or death, her conduct under such circumstances does not constitute consent to the act.

. . .

You have been instructed as to all the rules of law that may be necessary for you to reach a verdict. Whether some of the instructions will apply will depend upon your determination of the facts. You will disregard any instruction which applies to a state of facts which you determine does not exist. You must not conclude from the fact that an instruction has been given that the court is expressing any opinion as to the facts.

. . .

In your deliberations the subject of penalty or punishment is not to be discussed or considered by you. That is a matter which must not in any way affect your verdict.

You shall now retire and select one of your number to act as foreman who will preside over your deliberations. In order to reach a verdict, all twelve jurors must agree to the decision. As soon as all of you have agreed upon a verdict, you shall have it dated and signed by your foreman and then shall return with it to this room.

The Aftermath

Inez Garcia was convicted of second degree murder by her predominantly middle aged, middle class jury of seven women and five men after three days of deliberation. Inez Garcia's most ardent supporters were shocked at the verdict. The worst they had expected was conviction for manslaughter. Protests were staged in various cities and the judge's home was picketed.

No charges were ever brought against the alleged rapist, Louie Castillo. The jury could not agree whether Freddie Medrano was guilty of murder and a mistrial was declared. He subsequently pleaded guilty to being an accessory after the fact and was granted probation.

Inez Garcia took the verdict calmly. She gave the defiant power fist to the sisters as the police drove her away from the court. Her eleven-year-old son cried. Inez Garcia stated in an interview: "[i] f I go to jail . . . it really doesn't matter. Because I have won. Because people believe in me and they believe in what I say, they identify with me. . . . Now, maybe men will think twice before they do a thing like that. . . ."

Inez Garcia was sentenced to the prescribed term by law in California for second degree murder: 5 years to life in prison. Despite a passionate plea by Mr. Garry for a reduction from second degree murder to manslaughter and probation, she was denied probation and bail on appeal by Judge Lawson. After refusing to set aside the verdict Judge Lawson said to the court, "I think she's guilty of first degree murder, so I'm not about to reduce the verdict from second to manslaughter as you ask. . . . I cannot allow bail pending appeal. I think this woman is dangerous."

Inez Garcia is currently serving her sentence in the women's prison at Frontera, California. Her conviction is on appeal. Inez Garcia has hired a new attorney, Susan Jordan, a San Francisco criminal attorney to handle the appeal.

The original Inez Garcia Defense Committee and other committees in support of Inez Garcia's trial disbanded after the conviction. Since the change in attorneys, other women have become involved in the case and a new organization called Viva Inez has been formed. They are working for her release and vindication and to inform others around the country about her case.

The appellate court reversed the conviction by finding an error in Judge Lawson's jury instructions and ordered a new trial. The retrial shoud occur sometime in 1976.

WRITING ASSIGNMENTS

1. Prepare an outline or abstract of the case for the prosecution and defense based on the opening statements and the testimony for each side.

2. Research the law of rape in your state. Determine under what circumstances, if any, use of force against the assailant is warranted.

3. Use the definitions of homicide, diminished capacity, justifiable homicide, self-defense and the effect of rape in the Judge's Instructions to outline the prosecution's case that it had to prove. Did the prosecution successfully prove all the necessary elements for homicide?

4. Summarize the evidence that argues for the conviction of Inez Garcia on the charge of homicide. Summarize the evidence that argues for acquittal. Write your recommendations as to which side's evidence is more compelling and indicate why.

BIBLIOGRAPHY

BOOKS

Amir, M., *Patterns in Forcible Rape,* 1971.

Brownmiller, Susan, *Against Our Will: Men, Women and Rape,* Simon and Schuster, 1975.

MacKellar, Jean, *Rape: The Bait and the Trap.* Crown Publishers, 1975.

Medea, A. and K. Thompson, *Against Rape,* 1974.

ARTICLES

Blitman, Nan and Robin Green, "Inez Garcia on Trial," *Ms.,* May 1975.

Brussell, "Comment," *Sexual Behavior,* November 1971, p. 30.

Burgess and Holmstrom, "The Rape Victim in the Emergency Ward," 73 *Am. J. Nursing* 1741 (1973).

Cohen, Garofalo, Boucher, and Seghorn, "The Psychology of Rapists," 3 *Seminars in Psychiatry* 307.

Comment, "Rape and Rape Laws: Sexism in Society and Law," 61 *Cal. L. Rev.* 919 (1973).

Del Drago, Maria., "The Pride of Inez Garcia," *Ms.,* May 1975.

Hayman, Lanza, and Fuentes, "Sexual Assault on Women and Girls in the District of Columbia," 62 *S. Med. J.* 1227 (1969).

LeGrand, "Rape and Rape Laws: Sexism in Society and Law," 61 *Cal. L. Rev.* 919.

Mermey, "Rape: Who's on Trial," *Juris Doctor,* December 1974, p. 23.

Schwendinger and Schwendinger, "Rape Myths: In Legal, Theoretical and Everyday Practice," 1 *Crime and Social Justice* 18 (1974).

Selkin, "Rape," *Psychology Today,* January 1975, p. 71.

Steinem, Gloria, "But What Do We Do With Our Rage," *Ms.,* May 1975.

Tappan, "Some Myths About the Sex Offender," 19 *Fed. Probation,* June 1955, p. 7.

STUDIES

Rape and Its Victims: A Report for Citizens, Health Facilities and Criminal Justice Agencies, by Center for Women Policy Studies et al. Available at no charge from National Criminal Justice Reference Service, P.O. Box 24036 SW Post Office, Washington, D.C. 20024.

Nat'l Comm'n on the Causes and Prevention of Violence, 11 *Staff Reports (Crime of Violence)* (1969).

Queen's Bench Foundation, *Rape: Victimization Study* (1975) San Francisco Bar Association, San Francisco, California.

Rape Corroboration Requirement: "Repeal Not Reform," 81 *Yale L. J.* 165.